THE ANNUAL DIRECTORY OF
Midwestern Bed & Breakfasts

1999 Edition

THE ANNUAL DIRECTORY OF
Midwestern Bed & Breakfasts

1999 Edition

Tracey Menges, *Compiler*

RUTLEDGE HILL PRESS®
NASHVILLE, TENNESSEE

Copyright © 1989, 1990, 1991, 1992, 1993, 1994, 1995, 1996, 1997, 1998 by Barbour & Company, Inc.

All rights reserved. Written permission must be secured from the publisher to use or reproduce any part of this book, except for brief quotations in critical reviews or articles.

Published in Nashville, Tennessee, by Rutledge Hill Press®, Inc., 211 Seventh Avenue North, Nashville, Tennessee 37219. Distributed in Canada by H. B. Fenn and Company, Ltd., 34 Nixon Road, Bolton, Ontario L7E 1W2. Distributed in Australia by The Five Mile Press Pty. Ltd., 22 Summit Road, Noble Park, Victoria, 3174. Distributed in New Zeland by Tandem Press, 2 Rugby Road, Birkenhead, Auckland 10. Distributed in the United Kingdom by Verulam Publishing, Ltd., 152a Park Street Lane, Park Street, St. Albans, Hertfordshire AL2 2AU.

Cover design and book design by Harriette Bateman
Page composition by Roger A. DeLiso, Nashville, Tennessee

Printed in the United States of America.

1 2 3 4 5 6—02 01 00 99 98

Contents

Introduction vii
Illinois 2
Indiana 24
Iowa 42
Kansas 53
Michigan 58
Minnesota 84
Missouri 98
Nebraska 112
North Dakota 116
Ohio 119
Oklahoma 140
South Dakota 145
Wisconsin 152
Manitoba 172
Ontario 182

Introduction

The 1999 edition of *The Annual Directory of Midwestern Bed & Breakfasts* is one of the most comprehensive directories available today. Whether planning your honeymoon, a family vacation or reunion, or a business trip (many bed and breakfasts provide conference facilities), you will find what you are looking for at a bed and breakfast. They are all here just waiting to be discovered.

Once you know your destination, look for it, or one close by, to see what accommodations are available. Each state has a general map with city locations to help you plan your trip efficiently. There are listings for all 50 states, Canada, Puerto Rico, and the Virgin Islands. Don't be surprised to find a listing in the remote spot you thought only you knew about. Even if your favorite hideaway isn't listed, you're sure to discover a new one.

How to Use This Guide

The sample listing below is typical of the entries in this directory. Each bed and breakfast is listed alphabetically by city and establishment name. The description provides an overview of the bed and breakfast and may include nearby activities and attractions. *Please note that the descriptions have been provided by the hosts. The publisher has not visited these bed and breakfasts and is not responsible for inaccuracies.*

Following the description are notes that have been designed for easy reference. Looking at the sample, a quick glance tells you that this bed and breakfast has four guest rooms, two with private baths (PB) and two that share a bath (SB). The rates are for two people sharing one room. Tax may or may not be included. The specifics of "Credit Cards" and "Notes" are listed at the bottom of each page.

GREAT TOWN

Favorite Bed and Breakfast
123 Main Street, 12345
(800) 555-1234

This quaint bed and breakfast is surrounded by five acres of award-winning landscaping and gardens. There are four guest rooms, each individually decorated with antiques. It is close to antique shops, restaurants, and outdoor activities. Breakfast includes homemade specialties and is served in the formal dining room at guests' leisure. Minimum stay of two nights.

Hosts: Sue and Jim Smith
Rooms: 4 (2 PB; 2 SB) $65-80
Full Breakfast
Credit Cards: A, B
Notes: 2, 5, 8, 10, 11, 12, 13

For example, the letter A means that MasterCard is accepted. The number 10 means that tennis is available on the premises or within 10 to 15 miles.

In many cases, a bed and breakfast is listed with a reservation service that represents several houses in one area. This service is responsible for bookings and can answer other questions you may have. They also inspect each listing and can help you choose the best place for your needs.

Before You Arrive

Now that you have chosen the bed and breakfast that interests you, there are some things you need to find out. You should always make reservations in advance, and while you are doing so you should ask about the local taxes. City taxes can be an unwelcome surprise. Make sure there are accommodations for your children. If you have dietary needs or prefer nonsmoking rooms, find out if these requirements can be met. Ask about check-in times and cancellation policies. Get specific directions. Most bed and breakfasts are readily accessible, but many are a little out of the way.

When You Arrive

In many instances you are visiting someone's home. Be respectful of their property, their schedules, and their requests. Don't smoke if they ask you not to, and don't show up with pets without prior arrangement. Be tidy in shared bathrooms, and be prompt. Most places have small staffs or may be run single-handedly and cannot easily adjust to surprises.

With a little effort and a sense of adventure you will learn firsthand the advantages of bed and breakfast travel. You will rediscover hospitality in a time when kindness seems to have been pushed aside. With the help of this directory, you will find accommodations that are just as exciting as your traveling plans.

We would like to hear from you about any experiences you have had or any inns you wish to recommend. Please write us at the following address:

>The Annual Directory of
>Midwestern Bed & Breakfasts
>211 Seventh Avenue North
>Nashville, Tennessee 37219

THE ANNUAL DIRECTORY OF
Midwestern Bed & Breakfasts

1999 Edition

Illinois

Illinois

Victorian Rose Garden

ALGONQUIN

Victorian Rose Garden Bed and Breakfast

314 Washington Street, 60102
(847) 854-9667; (888) 854-9667
FAX (847) 854-3236
www.7comm.com/rosegarden

Built in 1886, the Victorian Rose Garden invites guests to come and relax on its wraparound porch and enjoy the garden. Rooms are decorated with a mix of antiques and much loved-furniture. Play the baby grand piano or Baldwin organ, or just relax by the fireplace. The area provides golfing, antiquing, bike trail, acclaimed restaurants, and is only one hour from Chicago. "Let us pamper you!" Packages are available.

Hosts: Don and Sherry Brewer
Rooms: 4 (PB) $65-139
Full Breakfast
Credit Cards: A, B, C
Notes: 2, 5, 7, 10, 12, 14

BELLEVILLE

Victory Inn Bed and Breakfast

712 South Jackson Street, 62220
(618) 277-1538; (888) 277-8586
FAX (618) 277-1576
www.victoryinn.com

The stately home, built in 1877, offers an inviting picture from first sight. Guests often feel transformed back in time while sipping tea in the dining room or sharing experiences in the parlor. Modern conveniences are also present, including two whirlpool tubs, private telephones, fax, computer, electronic entry, and modem access.

Hosts: Tom and Jo Brannan
Rooms: 4 (2 PB; 2 SB) $50-85
Continental Breakfast
Credit Cards: A, B, C
Notes: 2, 5, 7, 9, 10, 12, 14

Victory Inn

NOTES: Credit cards accepted: A MasterCard; B Visa; C American Express; D Discover; E Diner's Club; F Other; 2 Personal checks accepted; 3 Lunch available; 4 Dinner available; 5 Open all year; 6 Pets welcome; 7 No smoking; 8 Children welcome; 9 Social drinking allowed; 10 Tennis nearby; 11 Swimming nearby; 12 Golf nearby; 13 Skiing nearby; 14 May be booked through a travel agent; 15 Handicapped accessible.

CHAMPAIGN

Golds Bed and Breakfast
2065 County Road 525 East, 61821
(217) 586-4345

Restored 1874 farmhouse with antique furnishings, just off I-74 west of Champaign, surrounded by farm fields. Antique shopping, golf, university, and parks nearby. Continental breakfast includes homemade coffee cake, muffins, jam, fresh fruit, and juice. Enjoy a cool beverage on the deck. The hosts will strive to make the stay an enjoyable bed and breakfast experience. Call or write for a descriptive brochure.

Hosts: Rita and Bob Gold
Rooms: 3 (P1/2B; SB) $50
Continental Breakfast
Credit Cards: None
Notes: 2, 5, 7, 8, 9, 12, 14

The Golds

CHICAGO

Amber Creek's Chicago Connection
122 South Bench, Galena, 61036 (mailing)
10 West Elm, 60610 (location)
(815) 777-8400; FAX (815) 777-8446

Charming apartment in quiet secure building on Chicago's Gold Coast in the heart of the restaurant and entertainment district. Walk to Michigan Avenue shopping, Water Tower Place, and Lake Michigan. Spacious living room with lake and city views, antique décor, fully equipped kitchen, bath with tub and shower. Romantic, master bedroom with king-size bed, second bedroom with double bed, TV, telephone, answering machine, air conditioned. One block to airport limousine and public transportation. Parking garage across the street. Ideal for one or two couples or a small family.

Hosts: Doug and Kate Freeman
Apartment: 1 (PB) $109-169
Continental Breakfast
Credit Cards: A, B, C, D, E
Notes: 2, 3, 4, 5, 7, 8, 9, 11, 12

Bed and Breakfast/ Chicago, Inc.
P.O. Box 14088, 60614-0088
(773) 248-0005; (800) 375-7084
FAX (773) 248-7090; e-mail: bnbchicago@aol.com
www.bnbchicago.com

2. This historic Kenwood home was recently restored by the architect/owner and her co-host who is a public TV producer. Its Prairie-style architecture is wonderfully harmonized with antique furniture for an Old World European charm. $85-100.

3. This self-contained, one-bedroom garden apartment is in a charming brick building of a single family home. Attractively decorated, it is furnished with a queen-size bed, a futon couch in the living room, offers a kitchen and private bath, and includes a quaint patio. $115-135.

4. This spacious, self-contained two-bedroom apartment is in a vintage high-rise building in the north part of the Gold Coast. It has a king-size bed, a double bed, one full bath, a living room, and a kitchen. The Magnificent Mile is a short walk from this great location. $145-175.

5. This historic townhouse has a separate entrance to a very sophisticated guest suite,

---
NOTES: Credit cards accepted: A MasterCard; B Visa; C American Express; D Discover; E Diner's Club; F Other; 2 Personal checks accepted; 3 Lunch available; 4 Dinner available; 5 Open all year; 6 Pets welcome;

which is private from the rest of the home. Included are a living room, queen-size bed, and a bright bathroom. The hosts, who live upstairs, are both involved in the visual arts and their offering reflect their good taste and experience. $125-145.

9. This self-contained one-bedroom garden apartment has been recently decorated and offers a queen-size bed, bath, full kitchen, and a living room. Air conditioning and TV. Just a short walk to the metro and many fine restaurants. No smoking. $95-125.

33. This is a warm, one-bedroom apartment featuring wood floors, a working fireplace, interesting artwork, and pleasant outdoor space for guest use. Full kitchen, queen-size bed, and a sleeper-sofa in the living room. Four blocks to the elevated train. The hosts, who live upstairs, are an architect and a graphic designer. $105-135.

40. This exquisite two-bedroom, one-bath apartment in a small Victorian building has a wood-burning fireplace in the living room. The unit has a queen-size bed in each bedroom and a trundle in the living room. The style is "Ralph Laurenish" with period antiques. The unit has a new kitchen and bath. $115-195.

64. This Victorian mansion in prime Lincoln Park has been rehabbed to maintain the original feeling but has been opened up to make the space feel more contemporary. The lovely home is furnished with antiques, wicker furniture, etc. It offers two guest rooms with private baths. One room has a private entrance. $75-105.

71. This beautifully rehabbed Victorian Queen Anne, built in the late 1800s, offers charm, original woodwork, hardwood floors, two fireplaces, and at the same time provides the best in modern comforts. The guest room offers a double bed, private hall bath, and sitting area. Air conditioning and TV. No smoking. $85.

78. This magnificent property is one guests cannot pass up. The guest suite within this two-story loft has its own entrance, a queen-size bed in the bedroom, two private bathrooms, access to a private kitchen, as well as a lovely living room with a fireplace. The view is of the lake and the city. $185.

Annie's. This comfortable, completely furnished studio apartment has a fully equipped kitchen, queen-size bed, private bath, and private entrance. Close to some of Chicago's best restaurants, live theater, and fine shopping. Air conditioned. TV. $105-125.

City View Inn. This lovely 22-room property was originally a private club. On the 40th floor of a building in the financial district, all rooms have king-size beds, marble baths, and gorgeous views. Included in the rate is use of the first-class health club in the building. Parking and Continental breakfast. $135-185.

Gold Coast Guest House. The hostess welcomes guests to this charming, newly rehabbed four-room guest house just blocks west of Michigan Avenue. Each guest room has an attached bath. Three rooms have queen-size beds and the other has twin-size beds. There is a lovely garden where the Continental breakfast will be served, weather permitting. There are spiral staircases between levels. $85-135.

Maud Travels. This single-family home has just been redone. The host, who has traveled extensively and loves staying in bed and breakfasts, lives in a coach house behind this accommodation. Three guest rooms with private baths offered. Breakfast is self-serve from the kitchen. This is an ideal arrangement for groups traveling together or visitors in Chicago for an

---

7 No smoking; 8 Children welcome; 9 Social drinking allowed; 10 Tennis nearby; 11 Swimming nearby; 12 Golf nearby; 13 Skiing nearby; 14 May be booked through a travel agent; 15 Handicapped accessible.

extended time who want to settle in and feel they have found a home away from home. Air conditioning and TV. Weekly and monthly rates are available. $75-95.

Windy City Inn. This lovely Victorian inn is in the Lincoln Park neighborhood, just four blocks west of the lake. The more elegant main house offers six guest rooms, each with queen-size or twin beds and private luxury baths. The cottage-like coach house has four guest rooms, all with queen-size beds and private luxury baths and fireplaces. The two buildings are separated by a lovely garden, where breakfast is served, weather permitting. $135-185.

City Scene Bed and Breakfast

2101 North Clifton Avenue, 60614
(773) 549-1743; FAX (773) 529-4711
e-mail: cityscene@aol.com

A cozy, private suite with one or two bedrooms, sitting room, kitchen, and bath in a Victorian four-flat. The furnishings are an interesting mix of antiques and collectibles. Each bedroom has one double bed and the well-stocked kitchen allows guests to prepare breakfast at their leisure. On a quiet residential street in a historic Lincoln Park neighborhood, three miles from downtown Chicago. Nearby are a variety of restaurants, unusual shops, beautiful homes, gardens, and parks.

Host: Mary A. Newman
Suite: $95-175
Continental Breakfast
Credit Cards: None
Notes: 2, 7

The Heritage Bed and Breakfast Registry

75 East Wacker Drive, Suite 3600, 60601
(312) 857-0800; (800) 431-5546
FAX (312) 857-0805

H605-606. This charming, cottage-like hosted home has two guest rooms available, each offering different types of bed and breakfast arrangements. One guest room has a private entrance, private bath, refrigerator, and microwave. The other guest room also has a private bath. $85.

H614. This accommodation is in the Belmont Harbor area of Lakeview. There is one guest room. Close to public transportation to and from downtown. Parking available at an additional charge. $95.

H615. This hosted accommodation is in a condominium that has just been beautifully renovated. The guest room has its own bathroom across the hall that offers an oversize bathtub with Jacuzzi jets. This location is only one or two blocks away from public transportation lines to and from downtown. $75.

H616-617. There are also two additional guest rooms available in the same condominium. The larger of the two can accommodate two people and the smaller one can accommodate one person. $85.

H650. This accommodation offers guests a quintessential stay in Chicago. It is on the top floor of a 34-story high rise of the international modernist style on Lakeshore Drive. $115.

H652. A passion for the arts and travel is evident in this accommodation. The guest room is on the first floor and includes a bathroom with a Jacuzzi tub and an adjacent sitting room with cable TV/VCR. The sitting room has a sleeper-sofa that can be used to accommodate two extra people at an additional charge. $115.

H657-658. The home is delightfully decorated in a Victorian motif throughout. There are two guest rooms on the second floor. The

---

NOTES: Credit cards accepted: A MasterCard; B Visa; C American Express; D Discover; E Diner's Club; F Other; 2 Personal checks accepted; 3 Lunch available; 4 Dinner available; 5 Open all year; 6 Pets welcome;

bathroom is shared with the hosts. Parking is available at an additional fee. $85.

DANVILLE

B & B MidWest Reservations

2223 Crump Lane, Columbus, IN 47203-2009
(812) 378-5855; (800) B AND B (342-2632)
FAX (812) 378-5822
e-mail: swanent@hsonline.net
www.BandBmidwest.hsonline.com/

11036. This classic Tudor Revival-style home features gabled dormers, side porches, antiques galore, and two and one-half acres of wooded surroundings. Within an easy drive to University of Illinois, Indianapolis activities, Chicago, and Rockville's Covered Bridge Festival, this home has four guest rooms with private or shared baths. Full breakfast. Ten dollars per additional person. $65-95.

The Bookwalter House Bed and Breakfast

1701 North Logan Avenue, 61832
(217) 443-5511; (800) 397-7039
FAX (217) 431-4966

A quiet retreat with unbeatable hospitality. Escape to this vintage restored 1922 English Tudor Revival listed in the local historic register. Enjoy the fireplace in winter or the second-floor screened porch in summer. Breakfast by candlelight in the formal dining room. Antiques and vintage autos complete the setting. Great parks,

Bookwalter House

canoeing, hiking, tennis, golf, biking all nearby. Smoking permitted in designated areas only. Children over 12 welcome.

Hosts: Nanette and Gary Koerner
Rooms: 4 (3 PB; 2 SB) $75-105
Full Breakfast
Credit Cards: A, B, C
Notes: 2, 7, 9, 10, 11, 12, 13, 14

ELDRED

Bluffdale Vacation Farm

Rural Route 1, 62027
(217) 983-2854

Hosts' new hideaway cottage in the woods and log cabin are secluded and luxurious. Soak in the whirlpool while watching the sun set or gazing at the stars, then pop on a robe and enter the guest room where the fireplace is blazing. At the side of the bluff, guests have 200 acres of woodlands to explore.

Hosts: Bill and Lindy Hobson
Rooms: 8 (PB) $85
Full Breakfast
Credit Cards: None
Notes: 2, 5, 7, 8, 9, 12, 14

EVANSTON

B & B MidWest Reservations

2223 Crump Lane, Columbus, IN 47203-2009
(812) 378-5855; (800) B AND B (342-2632)
FAX (812) 378-5822
e-mail: swanent@hsonline.net
www.BandBmidwest.hsonline.com/

02055. Attractively appointed cozy garden apartment includes bedroom with double bed, bath, living room with TV, telephone, and single Hide-a-Bed sofa, fully equipped kitchen, and dining area. Conveniently near Northwestern University, Lake Michigan, and public transportation. Twenty minutes to the Loop. Self-serve breakfast items are provided. $125.

04125. Just two blocks from Northwestern University's campus, the immaculate home

---

7 No smoking; 8 Children welcome; 9 Social drinking allowed; 10 Tennis nearby; 11 Swimming nearby; 12 Golf nearby; 13 Skiing nearby; 14 May be booked through a travel agent; 15 Handicapped accessible.

is the upper level of a two-flat home. A very comfortable day porch and living room are available for guest use. The owner excitedly shares his extensive music library for guests' enjoyment. The accommodations include a king-size bed (side-by-side twins on king headboard) and shared bath with the owner. Very convenient for Evanston or downtown Chicago activities. Continental plus breakfast is served. $75.

16115. In the Evanston Lakeshore Historic District, this grand old Victorian-style home offers antiques, a beautiful wrap-around veranda, and a short walk to Lake Michigan. Accommodations include a queen-size bed with brass headboard, wood-burning fireplace in the room, circular bay window, window air conditioner, and private bath. An extended breakfast is served in the morning. $95.

GALENA

Accommodations and Reservations In and Around Galena

122 South Bench Street, 61036
(815) 777-8400; FAX (815) 777-8446
www.lodgings@galenareservations.com

Anna's Suite. Vintage townhouse in the heart of Galena's historic district with one-bedroom apartment available for overnight guests. Fireplace, antique decor, queen-size bed, full bath, TV/VCR, telephone, stereo/CD/tape player, fully equipped kitchen. Walk to most of Galena. No smoking. Sleeps two. $89-129.

The Blue Heron. A very private, one-bedroom cottage with a great view of the Mississippi River at Savanna. Five minutes from the Mississippi Palisades State Park and 30 minutes on the Great River Road to Galena. Fireplace, two-person whirlpool, loft with king-size bed, bath with shower, fully equipped kitchen, deck, charcoal grill, spacious yard with outdoor campfire circle. TV/VCR, stereo/CD/tape player, telephone. Walk to downtown for fishing, boating, terrific antique shopping, restaurants, and the movies. Pets permitted by request. No smoking. Sleeps two. $99-149.

Cottage at Amber Creek. This one-bedroom guest cottage on a 300-acre horse ranch was once the summer kitchen for the main house. Secluded in the hills, 20 minutes from Galena, it offers hiking, bird watching, stargazing and wildlife for nature lovers. Fireplace, two-person whirlpool, queen-size bed, fully equipped kitchen. Telephone, stereo/CD/tape player, deck, charcoal grill, small private garden with fountain, campfire circle. Pets permitted by request. No smoking. Sleeps two. $99-139.

Council Hill Guest House. One-room school house tucked into the hills 10 miles east of Galena; nicely restored and furnished in antique-country decor. Fireplace, TV/VCR, stereo/CD/tape player, telephone, fully equipped kitchen, bath with shower and two-person whirlpool. Spiral staircase leads to sleeping loft with queen-size bed. Deck with picnic table and charcoal grill overlooking a beautiful valley. No smoking or pets. Sleeps two. $109-149.

Cross Country. Escape to the country for total privacy and seclusion. One-bedroom A frame deep in the woods with hot tub on the deck, gas grill. Access to small lake with private beach. Fully equipped kitchen, bath with shower, TV/VCR, king-size bed in the loft. Fifteen minutes from the historic town of Mount Carroll, 30 minutes from the river town of Savanna, and 45 minutes from Galena. Rustic, but comfortable. Pets permitted by request. Not for city slickers. Sleeps two. $99-149.

NOTES: Credit cards accepted: A MasterCard; B Visa; C American Express; D Discover; E Diner's Club; F Other; 2 Personal checks accepted; 3 Lunch available; 4 Dinner available; 5 Open all year; 6 Pets welcome;

The Eagle's Nest. A delightful 1842 brick cottage tucked into a private wooded hillside in Galena's historic district. Faithfully restored and decorated with period antiques. Master bedroom with queen-size four-poster bed, second bedroom with full bed. Fireplace, TV/VCR, telephone, stereo, full bath with two-person tub, totally equipped kitchen, patio, charcoal grill, landscaped yard with small garden and fountain. Walk to most of Galena. Perfect for antique and history buffs. Children welcome. Pets permitted by request. No smoking. Note: Steep, narrow stairs and walkways in house and on property. Sleeps two to four. $99-169.

Hanover House. Luxurious one-bedroom apartment, over a gift shop, in the small town of Hanover just 15 minutes from Galena on the Great River Road. Spacious living room with fireplace, lots of windows, fully equipped kitchen, bedroom with queen-size bed and double whirlpool bath with two-person shower. TV/VCR, stereo/CD/tape player. Children welcome. No smoking. Sleeps two to four. $129-189.

Harvest Lane. Get back to nature in this casual home surrounded by woods and meadows. Stone fireplace, loft with window seat, and two-person whirlpool, TV/VCR, stereo/CD/tape player, telephone, fully equipped kitchen, washer/dryer. Master bedroom has king-size bed, second bedroom with queen-size bed, two bathrooms. Deck, charcoal grill, spacious yard, excellent hiking, and cross-country skiing. Access to Galena Territory Resort amenities. Children welcome. Pets permitted by request. No smoking. Sleeps two to four. $119-189.

Hazelwood Farm. Beautifully restored and furnished 1860s farmhouse set on a country acre, with lovely gardens just west of Galena. Three bedrooms, two baths, large country kitchen, formal dining room, living room, den with TV/VCR, stereo/CD/tape player, wood-burning fireplace, washer/dryer. Master bedroom has sleigh bed, private staircase, and balcony. Perfect for a family or group of friends. Children welcome. No smoking or pets. Sleeps eight. $200-225.

Logan House Inn. Comfortable suites and rooms at reasonable prices, discounts at the popular restaurant/bar on the main level and the downtown location make the Logan House a good value. All suites and rooms have a queen-size bed, private bath, and TV. Suites also have sleeper-sofas. Continental breakfast is served in the lounge area which has a refrigerator and microwave available for guests' use. Children welcome. Smoking permitted in designated areas only. $75-90.

O'Rourke's Garden Apartment. Contemporary home with one-bedroom garden apartment. Twin beds, antiques, fully equipped kitchen, bath with shower, den with TV/VCR, walking distance to downtown, and most of Galena. Sleeps two. By the week only. $349.

Pine Hollow Inn. The peace and quiet of this beautiful wooded valley just outside of Galena give Pine Hollow a special appeal. Hike along wildflower-lined streams. Enjoy the deer, wild turkeys, blue herons, and other wildlife that share the gorgeous surroundings with human visitors. The large guest rooms decorated in warm, country style, have queen-size four-poster beds, fireplaces, and private baths, several have whirlpool. Hearty, fresh-baked Continental breakfast. No smoking, children, or pets. $85-125.

Rosebud. This 1842 stone house with two suites is just steps away from Galena's downtown shops and restaurants. Each suite has a queen-size bed, gas fireplace,

---

7 No smoking; 8 Children welcome; 9 Social drinking allowed; 10 Tennis nearby; 11 Swimming nearby; 12 Golf nearby; 13 Skiing nearby; 14 May be booked through a travel agent; 15 Handicapped accessible.

two-person whirlpool, and private bath. Full breakfast is served in the parlor which is furnished with eclectic antiques from the owner's family. No children, pets, or smoking. $109-149.

Tuk-A-Way Center. A spacious, comfortable lodge nestled on 80 acres of rolling meadows and woodland between Stockton and Mount Carroll. Five bedrooms, two and one-half baths. Fireplace, fully equipped kitchen, washer/dryer, TV/VCR, telephone, fax, copier, stereo/CD/tape player. Large deck area and spacious lawn for outdoor activities. Great for meetings, retreats, family reunions, or a group of friends. Children welcome. No smoking. Sleeps up to 15. $195-245.

The Victorian Mansion. An elegant three-story Victorian home on Quality Hill surrounded by spacious lawns and tree-lined gardens. Antique furnishings, library, formal dining room, double parlor, porches with rocking chairs, and a full gourmet breakfast make staying here a first-class bed and breakfast experience. Each of the eight guest rooms has a private bath, antique marble-top dressers; one bedroom has a fireplace. No children, smoking, or pets. $115-149.

Avery Guest House

606 South Prospect Street, 61036
(815) 777-3883

This pre-Civil War home, within Galena's historic district, is a short walk from antique shops and historic buildings. Enjoy the scenic view from the porch swing. Breakfast is served in the sunny dining room with a bay window overlooking the Galena River valley. Two-night minimum stay required for weekends and holidays.

Hosts: Gerry and Armon Lamparelli
Rooms: 3 (1 PB; 2 SB) $65-90

Avery Guest House

Full Breakfast
Credit Cards: A, B, D
Notes: 2, 5, 7, 9, 12, 13

B & B MidWest Reservations

2223 Crump Lane, Columbus, IN 47203-2009
(812) 378-5855; (800) B AND B (342-2632)
FAX (812) 378-5822
e-mail: swanent@hsonline.net
www.BandBmidwest.hsonline.com/

06059. A restored cottage secluded in the hills near Galena. This accommodation has air conditioning and beautiful views of the countryside. The Early American flavor is carried throughout the suite. Suite consists of queen-size bed, living room with fireplace, Jacuzzi, loft, and private porch. Two-night minimum required on weekends. $125.

Belle Aire Mansion Guest House

11410 Route 20 West, 61036
(815) 777-0893; e-mail: belleair@galenalink.com
www.galena-bnb.com/belleaire

Belle Aire Mansion is a pre-Civil War home set on 11 beautiful acres just minutes from Galena. Three of the rooms feature

NOTES: Credit cards accepted: A MasterCard; B Visa; C American Express; D Discover; E Diner's Club; F Other; 2 Personal checks accepted; 3 Lunch available; 4 Dinner available; 5 Open all year; 6 Pets welcome;

Galena, IL 11

Belle Aire Mansion

gas fireplaces, and the two suites each have a double whirlpool. Two-night minimum stay for weekends is required. Closed Christmas. Guests say, "It's just like visiting friends." The hosts say, "Welcome home—to our home."

Hosts: Jan and Lorraine Svec
Rooms: 5 (PB) $70.85-168.95
Full Breakfast
Credit Cards: A, B, D
Notes: 2, 7, 8, 9, 11, 12, 13, 14

Brierwreath Manor Bed and Breakfast

216 North Bench Street, 61036
(815) 777-0608

Circa 1884 Queen Anne house with wrap-around porch only one short block from

Brierwreath Manor

historic Main Street. Cable TV, early morning coffee buffet, and full breakfast are only a few of the comforts guests will experience. The manor has three large suites with sitting rooms, gas log fireplaces, and private baths. Each room is furnished with antiques and modern comforts. Special packages available.

Hosts: Mike and Lyn Cook
Suites: 3 (PB) $85-105
Full Breakfast
Credit Cards: None
Notes: 2, 5, 7, 9, 11, 12, 13

Captain Harris Guest House

713 South Bench Street, 61036
(815) 777-4713; FAX (815) 777-4723
www.galena-bnb.com

Robert Scribe Harris, steamboat captain and lead mine owner, built this 1836 home that was enhanced with the addition of 50 leaded-glass windows in the 1920s. Within walking distance of downtown Galena, with three guest rooms and detached honeymoon cottage. Guest living room and library, color TV in every room.

Rooms: 4 (PB) $80-150
Full Breakfast
Credit Cards: A, B, D
Notes: 2, 5, 7, 11, 12, 13, 14

Farmers' Guest House

334 Spring Street, 61036
(815) 777-3456

A restored 1867 Farmers' hotel in Galena's historic district within walking distance to downtown. Seven queen-size rooms and two suites, all with private bath, central air conditioning, cable color TV. Hearty breakfast and use of outdoor hot tub. Offering packages and gift certificates.

Hosts: Tom and Pam Cummings
Rooms: 9 (PB) $69-130
Continental Breakfast
Creidt Cards: A, B, C, D
Notes: 5, 7, 9, 10, 11, 12, 13, 14

7 No smoking; 8 Children welcome; 9 Social drinking allowed; 10 Tennis nearby; 11 Swimming nearby; 12 Golf nearby; 13 Skiing nearby; 14 May be booked through a travel agent; 15 Handicapped accessible.

Grandview Guest Home

113 South Prospect Street, 61036
(815) 777-1387; (800) 373-0732

A 128-year-old brick traditional on Quality Hill, overlooking the city and countryside. Victorian furnishings. The full breakfast features home-baked goods and European coffees. Two blocks from Main Street shops, museums, and restaurants.

Hosts: Harry and Marjorie Dugan
Rooms: 3 (1 PB; 2 SB) $70-90
Full Breakfast
Credit Cards: A, B, C, D
Notes: 2, 5, 8, 9, 10, 11, 12, 13

Park Avenue

Park Avenue Guest House

208 Park Avenue, 61036
(815) 777-1075; (800) 359-0743

An 1893 Queen Anne "painted lady," with wraparound screened porch and shaded garden with gazebo. Original woodwork, queen-size beds, and antique furniture. Central air conditioning. In-room fireplaces and TV. Twelve full Christmas trees for viewing during November, December, and January. Walk to town; ample parking.

Host: Sharon Fallbacher
Rooms: 4 (PB) $75-115
Full Breakfast
Credit Cards: A, B, D
Notes: 2, 5, 7, 9, 10, 11, 12, 13

Pine Hollow Inn

4700 North Council Hill Road, 61036
(815) 777-1071

This cottage-style country home, on 120 acres, is secluded in a wooded valley two minutes north of Main Street Galena. The inn contains four suites and one guest room. All bedrooms have private bedside wood-burning fireplaces. Rooms are furnished in country decor and includes four-poster queen-size beds, private whirlpool and conventional baths, sky lights, stained-glass windows. This home includes a wraparound porch, giving guests a chance to put their feet up and enjoy the peace and quiet of this country setting. Pine Hollow also provides guests with access to cross-country skiing, wildlife, hiking, and streams to walk along.

Hosts: Sally and Larry Priske
Rooms: 5 (PB) $75-125
Continental Breakfast
Credit Cards: A, B, D
Notes: 2, 5, 7, 9, 10, 11, 12, 13

GALENA (ELIZABETH)

Forget-Me-Not Bed and Breakfast

1467 North Elizabeth Scales Mound Road, 61028
(815) 858-3744; e-mail: forget-me-not@juno.com
www.flinthills.com/~atway/il/forgtnot.html

Beautiful country ridge home with outstanding views, overlooking a forest valley, and far-viewing countryside. Three large guest rooms, each with private bath, private patio with entrance, queen-size bed, air conditioning, ceiling fan, and heat control. Hearty full breakfast. Wrap oneself in warmth by a rustic fireplace in a spacious

Forget-Me-Not

NOTES: Credit cards accepted: A MasterCard; B Visa; C American Express; D Discover; E Diner's Club; F Other; 2 Personal checks accepted; 3 Lunch available; 4 Dinner available; 5 Open all year; 6 Pets welcome;

great room with large TV and imported furnishings. Discover living nature by hiking the rolling forest trails or just unwind on the deck, screened porch, or private patio. In the midst of rolling hills and rugged cliffs, a wonderful wild bird haven.

Hosts: Christa and Richard Grunert
Rooms: 3 (PB) $70-95
Full Breakfast
Credit Cards: A, B, D
Notes: 2, 5, 7, 9, 10, 11, 12, 13, 15

GALESBURG

Seacord House Bed and Breakfast

624 North Cherry Street, 61401-2731
(309) 342-4107

This 1890s Eastlake Victorian is lovingly furnished in period decor with family antiques. Enjoy a landmark house filled with traditional comfort, hospitality, and charm. Guests may use the parlors for conversation or reading, or relax on the patio. Books and games are always on hand. The inn is close to Knox College, the Carl Sandburg birthplace, Bishop Hill, and Spoon River country. The Continental plus breakfast includes special-recipe muffins or waffles made from scratch daily. Inspected and approved by the Illinois Bed and Breakfast Association.

Seacord House

Hosts: Gwen and Lyle Johnson
Rooms: 3 (SB) $50
Continental Breakfast
Credit Cards: A, B, D
Notes: 2, 5, 7, 8, 9, 11, 12

GENEVA

B & B MidWest Reservations

2223 Crump Lane, Columbus, IN 47203-2009
(812) 378-5855; (800) B AND B (342-2632)
FAX (812) 378-5822
e-mail: swanent@hsonline.net
www.BandBmidwest.hsonline.com/

19068. Large, restored estate mansion in a country setting surrounded by seven acres of gardens and grounds. Outdoor swimming pool available (weather permitting). Seven master guest rooms offer a large range of accommodations with period furniture and some antiques. Large living room with fireplace available for guests. Some private baths and some rooms can accommodate up to four people. Nearby shopping at antique and craft shops. Lower rates Sunday through Thursday. Full country breakfast. $119-140.

Oscar Swan Country Inn

1800 West State Street, 60134
(630) 232-0173

A beautiful 1902 Colonial Williamsburg estate. The  inn and grounds are open for private parties. A large tent for 250 is on the eight-acre estate. The eight bedrooms are furnished with antiques, but also offer telephones and TVs. A hot, hearty breakfast is a highlight of guests' stay. The city of Geneva is a historical paradise with wonderful shops and restaurants. Continental breakfast served weekdays; full breakfast served weekends.

Rooms: 8 (6 PB; 2 SB) $99-139
Continental and Full Breakfast
Credit Cards: A, B, C
Notes: 2, 3, 5, 6, 8, 9, 10, 11, 12, 14

---

7 No smoking; 8 Children welcome; 9 Social drinking allowed; 10 Tennis nearby; 11 Swimming nearby; 12 Golf nearby; 13 Skiing nearby; 14 May be booked through a travel agent; 15 Handicapped accessible.

GURNEE

B & B MidWest Reservations
2223 Crump Lane, Columbus, IN 47203-2009
(812) 378-5855; (800) B AND B (342-2632)
FAX (812) 378-5822
e-mail: swanent@hsonline.net
www.BandBmidwest.hsonline.com/

10030. "Wonderful" describes this cozy country farmhouse, one-half mile from Six Flags Great America theme park. Handmade quilts, feather comforters, and antiques throughout make staying in one of the three guest rooms a special experience. Accommodations include two rooms with private baths; family two-room suite sleeping up to four; and separate cottage with kitchenette. Living room fireplace. Short drive to outlet mall, Lake Michigan, horseback riding, and other sports. Llama and sheep on premise. Full breakfast. Fifteen dollars per each additional person. $95-125.

JERSEYVILLE

The Homeridge Bed and Breakfast
1470 North State Street, 62052
(618) 498-3442

Beautiful brick Italianate Victorian private home, circa 1867, on 18 acres in comfortable country atmosphere. Drive through stately iron gates and pine-tree-lined driveway to the 14-room historic estate of Senator Theodore Chapman. Beautiful,

The Homeridge

expansive pillared front porch. Hand-carved stairway to spacious guest rooms and third floor. Large swimming pool. Central air conditioning. Between Springfield, Illinois, and St. Louis, Missouri.

Hosts: Sue and Howard Landon
Rooms: 4 (PB) $75-85
Full Breakfast
Credit Cards: A, B, C
Notes: 2, 5, 7, 10, 11, 12

METROPOLIS

Isle of View/Bed and Breakfast
205 Metropolis Street, 62960
(618) 524-5838; (800) 566-7491
e-mail: kimoff@worldnet.att.net
www.bbonline.com/il/isleofview

Elegant Victorian mansion one block from riverboat casino, offers five spacious guest rooms. Private baths feature antique clawfoot tubs and showers. Three rooms also have extra-large whirlpool tubs and two working fireplaces. A full gourmet breakfast is served at guests' convenience. Two hours north of Nashville, Tennessee, and two and one-half hours southeast of St. Louis, Missouri. Area offers hunting, fishing, antiquing, theater, and museums.

Hosts: Kim and Gerald Offenburger
Rooms: 5 (PB) $65-125
Full Breakfast
Credit Cards: A, B, C, D, E, F
Notes: 2, 5, 6, 9, 12, 14

MINONK

Victorian Oaks Bed and Breakfast
435 Locust Street, 61760
(309) 432-2771; FAX (309) 432-3309
e-mail: locust@davesworld.net

This 1895 Victorian home is nestled in a small midwestern town. Guests receive a full breakfast at the time they choose and choose their own menu. All meals are homemade on the premises. Guests dine on

NOTES: Credit cards accepted: A MasterCard; B Visa; C American Express; D Discover; E Diner's Club; F Other; 2 Personal checks accepted; 3 Lunch available; 4 Dinner available; 5 Open all year; 6 Pets welcome;

fine china with gold flatware. Tables covered with tablecloths, candles, and flowers. Guests use crisp linen napkins. Guests often dine in front of the roaring fire from the unique marble fireplace.

Host: Sharon Kimzey
Rooms: 5 (3 PB; 2 SB) $74.95-104.95
Full Breakfast
Credit Cards: A, B, D
Notes: 3, 4, 5, 6, 8, 9, 10, 11, 12, 14, 15

MORRISON

B & B MidWest Reservations

2223 Crump Lane, Columbus, IN 47203-2009
(812) 378-5855; (800) B AND B (342-2632)
FAX (812) 378-5822
e-mail: swanent@hsonline.net
www.BandBmidwest.hsonline.com/

23063. This 102-year-old bed and breakfast was built by E. A. Smith for his bride. Ten guest rooms with private baths, some with Jacuzzis. Separate cottage with gas-log fireplace, oversize spa for two, and deck. Breakfast, 7-9 A.M., includes a full range of home-cooked and baked items. Near the Quad Cities and riverboat gambling in Clinton, Iowa, there are many cultural and scenic activities available to guests. $55-160.

MOUNT CARMEL

B & B MidWest Reservations

2223 Crump Lane, Columbus, IN 47203-2009
(812) 378-5855; (800) B AND B (342-2632)
FAX (812) 378-5822
e-mail: swanent@hsonline.net
www.BandBmidwest.hsonline.com/

19056. This historic landmark home is along the Wabash River. Travelers enjoy a warm, friendly atmosphere found in earlier days. Browse through historic artifacts on display or sing around the antique player piano. Four guest accommodations include two two-bedroom suites, each with private bath. Each of the two other rooms has a double bed and private bath. Full breakfast served. Twenty-five-acre park with well-stocked lake adjacent to bed and breakfast, and lots more. $45-85.

MUNDELEIN

B & B MidWest Reservations

2223 Crump Lane, Columbus, IN 47203-2009
(812) 378-5855; (800) B AND B (342-2632)
FAX (812) 378-5822
e-mail: swanent@hsonline.net
www.BandBmidwest.hsonline.com/

12049. This grand old house, built in the early 1900s, features 44 windows throughout. Halfway between Chicago and Milwaukee, this location is convenient to Long Grove Village, Ravinia Park, Lamb's Farm, and more. Old-fashioned decor and a musical theme are woven together throughout this Victorian home. Three guest rooms share full bath. Two rooms have private baths. Two bedrooms with a bath booked as a suite. Another suite with one bedroom, a private bath, sitting area, and fireplace. Rates include Continental plus breakfast. $50-120.

NAPERVILLE

B & B MidWest Reservations

2223 Crump Lane, Columbus, IN 47203-2009
(812) 378-5855; (800) B AND B (342-2632)
FAX (812) 378-5822
e-mail: swanent@hsonline.net
www.BandBmidwest.hsonline.com/

08057. Nestled in historic Naperville, this circa 1904 home has been restored to reflect the elegance of the past. The home has unique antique furnishings and period fixtures and yet offers color TV and central air conditioning. Enjoy the luxury of monogrammed fluffy overside towels, fresh flowers, and complimentary refreshments and hearty full breakfast. Four guest rooms offer private baths. In addition, one suite also offers a Jacuzzi and shower. Antique quilts, feather beds, and lace curtains make this a bed and breakfast that guests never forget. $118-158.

---

7 No smoking; 8 Children welcome; 9 Social drinking allowed; 10 Tennis nearby; 11 Swimming nearby; 12 Golf nearby; 13 Skiing nearby; 14 May be booked through a travel agent; 15 Handicapped accessible.

NAUVOO

Mississippi Memories
1 Riverview Terrace, 62354
(217) 453-2771

Gracious lodging on the Mississippi riverbank. Elegantly served full homemade breakfasts; quiet wooded setting. Five minutes from restored Mormon city, "the Williamsburg of the Midwest." From two decks watch spectacular sunsets, abundant wildlife, and barges drifting by. Excellent geode hunting. Air conditioning, two fireplaces, two pianos, and fruit and flowers in rooms. AAA-rated three diamonds and Mobil-inspected.

Hosts: Marge and Dean Starr
Rooms: 4 (2 PB; 2 SB) $69-95
Full Breakfast
Credit Cards: A, B
Notes: 2, 5, 7, 12

OAK BROOK

B & B MidWest Reservations
2223 Crump Lane, Columbus, IN 47203-2009
(812) 378-5855; (800) B AND B (342-2632)
FAX (812) 378-5822
e-mail: swanent@hsonline.net
www.BandBmidwest.hsonline.com/

01043. Contemporary suburban home sits nestled in surprisingly quiet wooded acreage convenient to Drury Lane Theater, Oakbrook Shopping Center, many corporate centers, and thoroughfare highways. Three newly decorated guest accommodations offer queen-size beds and private baths. Guests have access to fully equipped kitchen to prepare other meals on their own and very large common great room with fireplace and lounge. Light Continental breakfast served. $65.

04044. Lovely sprawling home, conveniently near interstates and public transportation, offers four guest rooms with private baths. The master suite boasts a double Jacuzzi and queen-size bed. Two other rooms offer a queen-size bed with detached private bath. Fourth room has a single bed with detached private bath for one. A formal Continental plus breakfast served. $45-95.

OAKLAND

Inn on the Square
3 Montgomery, P.O. Box 945, 61943
(217) 346-2289

This 1878 restored Colonial inn offers a potpourri of the "village experience." Antiques, flowers, gifts, and ladies' apparel shops all pique guests' curiosity. The tea room offers simple but luxurious luncheons. Dinner is available Friday and Saturday, 5-8 P.M., and Sunday, 11 A.M.-2 P.M. Golf, swimming, conservation park, Amish settlement, and Lincoln historical sites nearby. Inquire about accommodations for children.

Hosts: Gary and Linda Miller
Rooms: 3 (PB) $50-55
Full Breakfast
Credit Cards: A, B
Notes: 2, 3, 4, 5, 7, 10, 11, 12, 13, 14

Inn on the Square

NOTES: Credit cards accepted: A MasterCard; B Visa; C American Express; D Discover; E Diner's Club; F Other; 2 Personal checks accepted; 3 Lunch available; 4 Dinner available; 5 Open all year; 6 Pets welcome;

OAK PARK

B & B MidWest Reservations

2223 Crump Lane, Columbus, IN 47203-2009
(812) 378-5855; (800) B AND B (342-2632)
FAX (812) 378-5822
e-mail: swanent@hsonline.net
www.BandBmidwest.hsonline.com/

02116. This newly refurbished Victorian-style home offers comfort, style, and hospitality galore. Two rooms sharing a bath on the main level are tastefully decorated with antiques. The hosts offer warmth and hospitality to each guest. The morning Continental breakfast during the week or the full breakfast on weekends is elegantly served in the dining room. $70.

13096. A 1909 English-style home furnished with Victorian antiques, oriental rugs, and Laura Ashley wallpapers. Two of the three guest rooms have entrance to a lovely second-floor screened porch with wicker furniture. The largest room has a queen-size bed with private bath, fireplace, and comfortable reading chaise lounge. The second room offers two beds, a reading chair, and shared bath. The third room has a four-poster bed, chair, and shared bath. A full breakfast is served in the paneled dining room with its restored mural border. $65-100.

15099. Queen Anne Victorian home in a prominent historic suburb one block from Frank Lloyd Wright's home and studio and 20 minutes from Chicago. The home, built in 1885, is air conditioned. One room has a large queen-size bed with private bath and Victorian-style antiques; two other rooms offer either twin beds with a desk work area and TV or a king-size bed with shared bath just steps from the room. Enjoy a family-style Continental breakfast or sit on the veranda when weather permits. Children an additional $10. $65-75.

19111. Truly for the followers and admirers of Frank Lloyd Wright, this home is one of Mr. Wright's architectural creations. Furnished entirely with his signatured pieces and in keeping with his choice of decor. Stay in one of two suites in the lower level of this remarkable home with private entrances. Each suite includes two bedrooms, dining area, bar sink, refrigerator, microwave, gas fireplace. Jacuzzis in large baths. Stocked refrigerator provides food for a light Continental self-serve breakfast. Two-night minimum stay most weekends. Additional $25 for second couple in same suite. $155.

OREGON

B & B MidWest Reservations

2223 Crump Lane, Columbus, IN 47203-2009
(812) 378-5855; (800) B AND B (342-2632)
FAX (812) 378-5822
e-mail: swanent@hsonline.net
www.BandBmidwest.hsonline.com/

16059. This 135-year-old Italianate country villa boasts 12 rooms and 7 marble fireplaces, 11-foot ceilings, arched doorways, and antique Parisian wallpaper, all adding to the charm. Accommodations include: one guest room with fireplace, private bath and Jacuzzi; two rooms with private baths and fireplaces; a three-room suite with two half-baths, shower, and sitting room. Two-night minimum stay on weekends. Special packages and baskets available. Chocolate Festival, winter sports, Christmas tree farm, and riverboat cruises available (in season). Full gourmet breakfast. $110-195.

PEKIN

Herget House: An Edwardian Inn

420 Washington Street, 61554
(309) 353-4025

Listed in the National Register of Historic Places, this Classical Revival home was

---

7 No smoking; 8 Children welcome; 9 Social drinking allowed; 10 Tennis nearby; 11 Swimming nearby; 12 Golf nearby; 13 Skiing nearby; 14 May be booked through a travel agent; 15 Handicapped accessible.

Herget House

built in 1912 during the Edwardian era. It has elegant architectural detail and provides deluxe accommodations for both business and vacation travelers. Each of the bedrooms is furnished to a standard of luxury not found since the turn of the century.

Host: Rick Walsh
Rooms: 5 (3 PB; 2 SB) $85-125
Full Breakfast
Credit Cards: None
Notes: 2, 5, 7, 10, 11, 12

PEORIA (MOSSVILLE)

Old Church House Inn Bed and Breakfast

1416 East Mossville Road, Mossville, 61552
(309) 579-2300
e-mail: church.house@MCIone.com

Come take sanctuary from the cares of life in this 1869 country church. Includes historic building, 18-foot ceilings, library loft, Victorian antiques, classical music, afternoon tea, crackling fire, pillow chocolates, featherbeds, flower gardens. Nearby are Rock Island Bike Trail, tearooms, antiquing, riverboat cruises, fine dining, scenic drives, and sweet memories. Continental plus breakfast. Inquire about accommodations for children.

Host: Dean and Holly Ramseyer
Rooms: 2 (1 PB; 2 SB) $75-109
Continental Breakfast
Credit Cards: A, B, D
Notes: 2, 3, 5, 7, 10, 11, 12, 13, 14

PINCKNEYVILLE

Oxbow Bed and Breakfast

Highways 13/127 South, 62274
(618) 357-9839; (800) 929-6888

The Oxbow Bed and Breakfast, a 16-room brick country home, has six lovely guest rooms with private baths and queen-size beds covered with pretty quilts. The honeymoon suite is in a 1915 restored barn. Guests can find the charm of the Old South and Civil War period on these 10 acres in a peaceful rural area. Enjoy antique furniture, Arabian horses, restored barns, a woodworking shop, windmills, and fountain. Delicious full country breakfast is served. Covered swimming pool. Children over six welcome.

Hosts: Al and Peggy Doughty
Rooms: 6 (PB) $50-65
Full Breakfast
Credit Cards: A, B
Notes: 2, 5, 7, 9, 10, 11, 12, 14

ROCHESTER

B & B MidWest Reservations

2223 Crump Lane, Columbus, IN 47203-2009
(812) 378-5855; (800) B AND B (342-2632)
FAX (812) 378-5822
e-mail: swanent@hsonline.net
www.BandBmidwest.hsonline.com/

13047. Newly constructed country getaway is just 10 miles from Springfield. Beautifully furnished with country antiques, the home offers a huge wraparound porch for guests to marvel over gorgeous sunsets and farm fields. Relax while star gazing in the late evening or sipping fresh coffee while smelling the fresh dew on the surrounding fields in the morning. Four guest rooms offer private baths, queen-size beds, and TVs. The romantic suite offers a gas fireplace and large double whirlpool tub also. Gracious hosts offer a hearty self-serve breakfast on weekdays; full breakfast on weekends. $75-125.

NOTES: Credit cards accepted: A MasterCard; B Visa; C American Express; D Discover; E Diner's Club; F Other; 2 Personal checks accepted; 3 Lunch available; 4 Dinner available; 5 Open all year; 6 Pets welcome;

Country Dreams Bed and Breakfast

3410 Park Lane, 62563
(217) 498-9210; FAX (217) 498-8178
e-mail: muhs1@fgi.net
www.softfoundry.com/countrydreams

Wide-open spaces and friendly faces. Country Dreams is a new bed and breakfast, built from ground up in 1997 to be a cozy, comfortable, country hideaway. Only 10 miles from downtown Springfield, Illinois. Country Dreams Bed and Breakfast is close enough to the city to be convenient and rural in all the best ways. On 16 acres of beautiful rural Illinois farmland, Country Dreams provides panoramic views of a small lake with swans, ducks, and geese and miles of fertile fields. View acres of green grass, flowers by the thousands, vegetable gardens, fruit orchards, and cattle. Continental breakfast is served Monday through Thursday.

Hosts: Ralph and Kay Muhs
Rooms: 4 (PB) $60-135
Continental and Full Breakfast
Credit Cards: A, B, C
Notes: 2, 5, 7, 9, 14, 15

ROCK ISLAND

Bed and Breakfasts of the Quad City Area Room Availability Cooperative

P.O. Box 3464, 61201
(319) 322-5055

Leisure Harbor Leisure Inn. (309) 654-2233. Pre-Victorian home. Four guest rooms with private baths plus library, sitting room, and sun porch, on the Mississippi River, will make guests' stay enjoyable. The river offers fantastic views of eagles in the winter as well as a peaceful summer resting spot. $69-79.

The Potter House. (800) 747-0339. Listed in the National Register of Historical Places, this home—a restored 1907 Colonial Revival—features stained glass, leather wallcoverings, six fireplaces, and more. It's near the Mississippi River in downtown. $75-95.

Top o' the Morning. (309) 786-3513. This 18-room brick mansion was originally built by Hiram S. Cable, president of Rock Island Railroad, in 1912. It sits in a central location overlooking the Mississippi River. $40-100.

Victorian Inn. (800) 728-7068. In the heart of old Rock Island. Antiques adorn six spacious guest rooms with private baths. Enjoy a formal breakfast on fine china and sterling silver. Step back in time to gracious living in this treasure, which is in the National Register of Historic Places. $65 and up.

Top o' the Morning

1505 19th Avenue, 61201
(309) 786-3513

Sam and Peggy welcome guests to this brick mansion on the bluffs overlooking the Mississippi River. Fantastic view day or night. Three-acre wooded estate with winding drive, orchard, and gardens. Air-conditioned bedrooms, whirlpool tub, and natural fireplaces in the dining area and parlor.

Hosts: Sam and Peggy Doak
Rooms: 3 (PB) $40-100
Full Breakfast
Credit Cards: A, B
Notes: 2, 5, 7, 8, 9, 10, 11, 12, 13

Victorian Inn Bed and Breakfast

702 20th Street, 61201
(309) 788-7068; (800) 728-7068
FAX (309) 788-7086

Light from the windows of the stained-glass tower welcomes guests to the Victorian Inn Bed and Breakfast. In the Broadway historic area near riverboat gambling and festival attractions. Antiques

---

7 No smoking; 8 Children welcome; 9 Social drinking allowed; 10 Tennis nearby; 11 Swimming nearby; 12 Golf nearby; 13 Skiing nearby; 14 May be booked through a travel agent; 15 Handicapped accessible.

St. Charles, IL

Victorian Inn

adorn the five spacious guest rooms with private baths. Close to Augustana College. Built with Old World charm in 1876. Step back in time to gracious living in this home listed in the National Register of Historic Places. Enjoy the black squirrels and birds in the sanctuary on the grounds. Inquire about accommodations for children. AAA three diamond-rated.

Hosts: David and Barbara Parker
Rooms: 5 (PB) $65-85
Full Breakfast
Credit Cards: A, B, C
Notes: 2, 5, 7, 9, 10, 11, 12, 13

ST. CHARLES

B & B MidWest Reservations

2223 Crump Lane, Columbus, IN 47203-2009
(812) 378-5855; (800) B AND B (342-2632)
FAX (812) 378-5822
e-mail: swanent@hsonline.net
www.BandBmidwest.hsonline.com/

07076. A very special hideaway near St. Charles offers a large grotto accommodation with a double bed, kitchenette, fireplace, private bath with oversize whirlpool, telephone, TV, and VCR. Nestled in a picturesque pine-covered courtyard with French doors leading to this quiet retreat. The property includes two acres and borders a forest preserve. Nearby entertainment includes canoeing, bike trails, and sports. Continental plus breakfast is served. $125.

SHEFFIELD

B & B MidWest Reservations

2223 Crump Lane, Columbus, IN 47203-2009
(812) 378-5855; (800) B AND B (342-2632)
FAX (812) 378-5822
e-mail: swanent@hsonline.net
www.BandBmidwest.hsonline.com/

02046. "The perfect bed and breakfast" is the comment often heard by satisfied guests after leaving this beautiful classic New England-style country inn built in 1845 in Sheffield just off I-80. The home offers gracious accommodations in the English tradition, a three-story floating spindle staircase, gleaming chandeliers, and magnificent French doors. Four guest rooms with private baths. Full breakfast and evening treats greet all the lucky guests. Weekend gourmet dinners are available for additional fee. $75-150.

SPRINGFIELD

B & B MidWest Reservations

2223 Crump Lane, Columbus, IN 47203-2009
(812) 378-5855; (800) B AND B (342-2632)
FAX (812) 378-5822
e-mail: swanent@hsonline.net
www.BandBmidwest.hsonline.com/

11037. Visit the hometown of the Abraham Lincoln family and enjoy this historic inn with four guest accommodations. Built in the 1860s, the Italianate-style national historic home offers three rooms with queen-size beds and one with twin beds. Each room has a private bath. The home has been professionally decorated in Traditional, Early 19th-Century, Art Deco, and

NOTES: Credit cards accepted: A MasterCard; B Visa; C American Express; D Discover; E Diner's Club; F Other; 2 Personal checks accepted; 3 Lunch available; 4 Dinner available; 5 Open all year; 6 Pets welcome;

Empire styles with antiques and historical artifacts of the capital's political influences. Continental breakfast is served. $65-75.

SPRINGFIELD

Inn at 835
835 South Second Street, 62704
(217) 523-4466; FAX (217) 523-4468

Experience Old World charm and attention to detail, while enjoying the conveniences of a modern hotel. Private verandas, cozy fireplaces, and Jacuzzis are just a few of the delights awaiting visitors. Guests are treated to delicious wines and cheeses upon arrival, as well as a sumptuous gourmet breakfast prepared by the chefs each morning. Built in 1909, this grand structure was placed in the National Register of Historic Places in 1995. Recently renovated, the building retains its significant period features and elegant character. Refined Arts and Crafts details highlight the elegant lobby and banquet rooms. Oak and cherry woodwork throughout reflect the craftsmanship of an era gone by. Restored wood floors are accented by lush Robert Morris-inspired rugs. Plump queen-size beds in each guest room inspire visitors to linger, while period antiques provide storage and add warmth to the professionally decorated rooms. The Inn at 835 also offers eight elegant and versatile meeting rooms, to accommodate groups from 10 to 150.

Hosts: Court and Karen Conn
Rooms: 7 (PB) $92.50-135
Continental Breakfast
Credit Cards: A, B, C, D, E
Notes: 2, 5, 7, 9, 10, 11, 12, 14, 15

SULLIVAN

The Little House on the Prairie
Rural Route 2, Patterson Road, P.O. Box 525, 61951
(217) 728-4727

A Victorian Queen Anne country homestead is surrounded by acres of woodlands, gardens, a swimming pool, and a pond. The little home was built in 1894 by Andrew Jackson Little, grandfather of the innkeeper. After 40 years of involvement in the theater world, the hosts has opened his home to the public. The home is filled with antiques and theatrical memorabilia. Some of the bedrooms open onto a large sunroom with a Jacuzzi, dining, and entertainment center.

Hosts: Guy S. Little Jr. and Kirk McNamer
Rooms: 5 (PB) $60-125
Full Breakfast
Credit Cards: None
Notes: 2, 9, 10, 11, 12, 14

TAYLORVILLE

B & B Midwest Reservations
2223 Crump Lane, Columbus, IN 47203-2009
(812) 378-5855; (800) B AND B (342-2632)
FAX (812) 378-5822
e-mail: swanent@hsonline.net
www.BandBmidwest.hsonline.com/

08015. Filled with antiques, this 1892 historic home was fully restored in 1994. The Victorian-style home offers seven guest

Inn at 835

---

7 No smoking; 8 Children welcome; 9 Social drinking allowed; 10 Tennis nearby; 11 Swimming nearby; 12 Golf nearby; 13 Skiing nearby; 14 May be booked through a travel agent; 15 Handicapped accessible.

rooms with private baths. Three rooms have double Jacuzzis; some have fireplaces. Taylorville is an easy 30-minute drive to Springfield and Decatur. Full gourmet breakfast is served. $75-95.

WEST DUNDEE

B & B MidWest Reservations
2223 Crump Lane, Columbus, IN 47203-2009
(812) 378-5855; (800) B AND B (342-2632)
FAX (812) 378-5822
e-mail: swanent@hsonline.net
www.BandBmidwest.hsonline.com/

08040. Guests step back into the early 1900s when visiting this newly renovated historical site. This mansion is filled with antiques and royal hospitality while convenient shopping malls, interstate highways, and business districts are within a few minutes' drive. The eight uniquely decorated rooms range from smaller country style to formal Colonial doubles to Victorian suites with Jacuzzis and private baths. Some rooms have shared baths with Jacuzzis for guests. Central air conditioning. Full breakfast is served. Small weddings and seminars are welcome. $49-179.

WHEATON

The Wheaton Inn
301 West Roosevelt Road, 60187
(630) 690-2600; (800) 447-4667
FAX (630) 690-2623

The Wheaton Inn was built in 1987 to reflect America's Colonial Williamsburg. Offering 16 individually decorated guest rooms, all with private baths, several with Jacuzzi tubs and gas fireplaces. A homemade full country breakfast wakes guests in the morning, complimentary wine buffet soothes the afternoon, and freshly baked cookies with milk are offered before

The Wheaton Inn

retiring. Biking, shopping, golf, and restaurants nearby. Only 25 miles west of Chicago. Romantic getaways available.

Host: Dennis Stevens
Rooms: 16 (PB) $99-215
Full Breakfast
Credit Cards: A, B, C, D, E
Notes: 2, 5, 8, 9, 10, 11, 12, 14, 15

WINNETKA

Chateau des Fleurs
552 Ridge Road, 60093
(847) 256-7272 (phone/FAX)

This authentic French country home, built in 1936, is filled with antiques and has been featured in two newspapers. It offers elegant respite from the world, welcoming guests with light, beauty, warmth, and lovely views from every window. Near a private road for walking and jogging. The inn is four blocks from the Northwestern

Chateau des Fleurs

NOTES: Credit cards accepted: A MasterCard; B Visa; C American Express; D Discover; E Diner's Club; F Other; 2 Personal checks accepted; 3 Lunch available; 4 Dinner available; 5 Open all year; 6 Pets welcome;

train commuting to the Chicago Loop. Antique shops and stores of all kinds are only blocks away. Lake Michigan is 10 blocks east and O'Hare Airport 30 minutes west. Two-night minimum stay on weekends. Children over 15 are welcome.

Host: Sally Ward
Rooms: 3 (PB) $125
Full Breakfast
Credit Cards: None
Notes: 2, 5, 7, 9, 10, 11, 12, 13

YORKVILLE

B & B MidWest Reservations

2223 Crump Lane, Columbus, IN 47203-2009
(812) 378-5855; (800) B AND B (342-2632)
FAX (812) 378-5822
e-mail: swanent@hsonline.net
www.BandBmidwest.hsonline.com/

12072. Spacious historic home built in 1901 offers two rooms, each with a sitting room and shared bath. The home has some antiques including a four-poster bed and a hand-carved six-foot-tall headboard. The rooms feature cable TV, hardwood floors, and oriental rugs. Home is close to 250 antique dealers, Joliet's riverboat gambling, and Starved Rock State Park, while only 55 minutes to downtown Chicago. Continental plus breakfast and complimentary afternoon snacks are provided. $60-109.

---

7 No smoking; 8 Children welcome; 9 Social drinking allowed; 10 Tennis nearby; 11 Swimming nearby; 12 Golf nearby; 13 Skiing nearby; 14 May be booked through a travel agent; 15 Handicapped accessible.

Indiana

Indiana

ANGOLA

Sycamore Hill Bed and Breakfast
1245 Golden Lake Road, 46703
(219) 665-2690

This two-story Colonial pillared home was built in 1963 by master craftsmen. Tucked away amid 26 acres of rolling hills and woods. Great for bird watching. Shady back yard with two picnic tables at guests' disposal. Sumptuous breakfast. Gas grill in the back yard. Six minutes from Pokagon State Park beaches, nature trails, canoeing, and golfing.

Host: Betsey Goranson
Rooms: 4 (1 PB; 3 SB) $40-60
Full Breakfast
Credit Cards: A, B
Notes: 2, 5, 7, 8, 10, 11, 12, 13, 14

BEVERLY SHORES

Dunes Shore Inn
33 Lake Shore County Road, Box 807, 46301-0807
(219) 879-9029

A casual bed and breakfast in secluded Beverly Shores, open since 1985. Surrounded by the Indiana Dunes State and National Lakeshore Parks. Miles of beaches and trails, spectacular sunrises and sunsets, and an ever-changing lake await guests. One block off Lake Michigan, one hour from Chicago, three hours from Indianapolis. Whether a party of one, a small group, or a family reunion, this is a great place to relax in a four-season oasis. Continental plus breakfast served. Open mid-April through mid-November.

Hosts: Rosemary and Fred Braun
Rooms: 12 (4 SB) $60-70
Continental Breakfast
Credit Cards: None
Notes: 2, 7, 8, 9, 10, 11, 12

BLUFFTON

The Washington Street Inn
220 East Washington Street, 46714
(219) 824-9070

The Washington Street Inn is an 1896 Queen Anne-style home. Charming guest rooms have TVs, telephones, and clock radios. (Three queen-size beds and one full-size bed.) The inn features a guest kitchen with a refrigerator and microwave. Common areas include living and dining room and a study. Sit by either of two cheery fireplaces and relax or admire the family heirlooms and antiques throughout the inn. Continental breakfast served Monday through Friday; full breakfast served weekends.

Rooms: 4 (4 SB)
Continental and Full Breakfast
Credit Cards: A, B
Notes: 2, 5, 7, 9, 12

The Washington Street Inn

NOTES: Credit cards accepted: A MasterCard; B Visa; C American Express; D Discover; E Diner's Club; F Other; 2 Personal checks accepted; 3 Lunch available; 4 Dinner available; 5 Open all year; 6 Pets welcome; 7 No smoking; 8 Children welcome; 9 Social drinking allowed; 10 Tennis nearby; 11 Swimming nearby; 12 Golf nearby; 13 Skiing nearby; 14 May be booked through a travel agent; 15 Handicapped accessible.

CHESTERTON

Gray Goose Inn
350 Indian Boundary Road, 46304
(219) 926-5781; (800) 521-5127

English-style country house on 100 wooded acres overlooks a private lake. Walking trails, paddleboat. Minutes from Indiana Dunes State and National Lakeshore Parks; 50 minutes from Chicago. Featured in *Country Inns*, 1994. Children over 12 welcome.

Hosts: Tim Wilk and Chuck Ramsey
Rooms: 8 (PB) $80-156
Full Breakfast
Credit Cards: A, B, C, D
Notes: 2, 5, 7, 9, 10, 11, 12, 13, 14

Gray Goose Inn

COVINGTON

Green Gables Bed and Breakfast
504 Fancy Street, 47932
(765) 793-7164

Covington's first bed and breakfast offers three guest rooms, each with private bath, including the spacious loft with two queen-size beds. Each room has a TV; the entire house is air conditioned. Home-cooked breakfasts are served by the private in-ground pool or by one of two fireplaces in this hilltop home near I-74 in western Indiana. Only five miles from Indiana's finest steak house. Art Fest in May; Apple Fest in October; both on the courthouse lawn.

Hosts: Bill and Marsha Wilkinson
Rooms: 3 (PB) $70
Full Breakfast
Credit Cards: A, B, C
Notes: 2, 5, 7, 10, 11, 12

CRAWFORDSVILLE

Sugar Creek Queen Anne Bed and Breakfast
901 West Market, P.O. Box 726, 47933
(765) 362-4095; (800) 392-6293

Surrounded by beautiful flowers and shrubs in the heart of Crawfordsville, this home, circa 1900, with Victorian decor, welcomes all who enjoy a cozy, warm atmosphere. Deluxe breakfast is served beside lace-curtained windows. An added feature is the Jacuzzi room. Honeymooners are offered a special package rate which includes flowers and non-alcoholic champagne in the room.

Hosts: Mary Alice and Hal Barbee
Rooms: 4 (PB) $65-75
Full Breakfast
Credit Cards: None
Notes: 2, 5, 7, 8

DARLINGTON

Our Country Home Bed and Breakfast, Stable, and Carriage Company
Rural Route Box 103 (CR 550 North), 47940
(765) 794-3139

Enjoy private candlelight dinner, country carriage or sleigh rides, hot tub under stars, horseback riding, swimming, or biking (there's a bicycle-built-for-two). All of this and more is waiting for guests at Our Country Home. Walk along the creek or relax on the porch and watch the Belgium draft horses graze. Romantic packages and gift certificates are available at Our Country Home. "Come as a guest and leave as a friend." Smoking permitted outside only.

NOTES: Credit cards accepted: A MasterCard; B Visa; C American Express; D Discover; E Diner's Club; F Other; 2 Personal checks accepted; 3 Lunch available; 4 Dinner available; 5 Open all year; 6 Pets welcome;

Hosts: The Smith Family
Rooms: 3 (3 SB) $75-130
Full Breakfast
Credit Cards: A, B, C, D
Notes: 3, 4, 5, 7, 8, 9, 10, 11, 12

DECATUR

Cragwood Inn Bed and Breakfast

303 North Second Street, 46733
(219) 728-2000

Enjoy the ambiance of the past with comforts of the present in this beautiful Queen Anne home, circa 1900. Magnificent woodwork and beveled leaded-glass windows reflect the craftmanship of a bygone era. The beautiful flower gardens may be enjoyed from three porches. Two guest rooms have their own fireplaces. Just 20 minutes south of Ft. Wayne on Highway 27. Chocolate lovers weekends are offered twice a year.

Rooms: 4 (2 PB; 2 SB) $55-65
Full Breakfast
Credit Cards: A, B
Notes: 2, 5, 7, 9, 10, 11, 12

FORT WAYNE

Carole Lombard House Bed and Breakfast

704 Rockhill Street, 46802
(888) 426-9896

Fort Wayne lodging in a comfortable home adjacent to downtown in the West Central neighborhood on the River Greenway. Convenient to the many good things Fort Wayne has to offer including great restaurants and quality cultural events. Easy access to all highways. To commemorate her fame, Carole Lombard's birthplace has been lovingly renovated to the elegance of its time and decorated reminiscent of the 1930s. Whether visiting Fort Wayne on business, for a getaway, to research genealogy, or to enjoy a special event, a stay in one of the Carole Lombard House's four guest rooms is very comfortable.

Hosts: Dave and Beverly Fiandt
Rooms: 4 (PB) $67-85
Full Breakfast
Credit Cards: A, B, D
Notes: 2, 5, 7, 9, 10, 12

GOSHEN

The Checkerberry Inn

62644 County Road 37, 46526
(219) 642-4445

At the Checkerberry Inn, in the heart of northern Indiana Amish country, guests will find a unique atmosphere, different from anywhere else in the Midwest. Each individually decorated room has a breathtaking view of the unspoiled countryside. Outdoor pool, tennis court, and croquet green. Cycling, jogging, and walking area. Shopping and golf within 10 to 15 minutes. Award-winning restaurant. Closed January.

Hosts: John and Susan Graff
Rooms: 14 (PB) $140-325
Continental Breakfast
Credit Cards: A, B, C
Notes: 2, 3, 4, 7, 8, 9, 10, 11, 12, 14

Indian Creek Bed and Breakfast

20300 C.R. 18, 46528-9513
(219) 875-6606; FAX (219) 875-3968
e-mail: 71224.1462@compuserve.com

Come visit Amish country and enjoy Hoosier hospitality in a new Victorian home, with gracious architecture and modern amenities. There are four tastefully decorated antique-filled bedrooms with private baths. Guests can enjoy the spacious 42-foot dining, kitchen, and great room combination where they can relax, visit, and watch TV. Watch deer and wildlife from a large deck while taking in the countryside, or guests can stroll back to the woods.

Rooms: 4 (PB) $79
Full Breakfast
Credit Cards: A, B, C, D
Notes: 2, 5, 7, 8, 11, 12, 14, 15

---

7 No smoking; 8 Children welcome; 9 Social drinking allowed; 10 Tennis nearby; 11 Swimming nearby; 12 Golf nearby; 13 Skiing nearby; 14 May be booked through a travel agent; 15 Handicapped accessible.

28 Goshen, IN

Prairie Manor

Prairie Manor
66398 US 33 South, 46526
(219) 642-4761; (800) 791-3952
FAX (219) 642-4762; e-mail: jeston@npcc.net
www.prairiemanor.com

This English country manor-style home, on 12 acres, was built in the 1920s by a Wall Street banker. The living room replicates his favorite painting of an English baronial hall featuring a fireplace big enough to walk into. Guests will enjoy the wood-paneled library with inviting window seats and fireplace. Interesting architectural details include arched doorways and hidden compartments! Refreshments. Prairie Manor is in the center of northern Indiana Amish country.

Hosts: Jean and Hesston Lauver
Rooms: 4 (PB) $65-95
Full Breakfast
Credit Cards: A, B
Notes: 2, 5, 7, 8, 10, 11, 12

Spring View Bed and Breakfast
63189 C.R. 31, 46528
(219) 642-3997; FAX (219) 642-2697

Specializing in country hospitality, this new bed and breakfast is in the heart of Amish country. Relax while strolling around the waterfront or rest in the gentle breeze of the screened lakeside sitting room. Walk the quiet trail on the spacious 48 acres. Enjoy a luxurious steam bath or whirlpool tub in the privacy of guests' own room. Two-bedroom suite available. Amish neighbors, Amish buggy rides available. Fishing and paddleboating.

Hosts: Phil and Rosalind Slabaugh
Rooms: 6 (5 PB; 1 SB) $59-79
Full Breakfast
Credit Cards: A, B, C, D
Notes: 2, 5, 7, 12, 15

Waterford Bed and Breakfast
3004 South Main Street, 46526
(219) 533-6044

In the heart of Amish country on State Route 15 at the south edge of Goshen, this northern Indiana home is surrounded by two acres that are landscaped with a pleasing variety of trees and gardens. All rooms, which are tastefully and completely furnished with antiques gathered from the Indiana area, include private baths and a full breakfast served with fresh breads and fruit.

Host: Judith Forbes
Rooms: 2 (PB) $60
Full Breakfast
Credit Cards: None
Notes: 2, 5, 9, 12

GRANDVIEW

The River Belle
P.O. Box 669, 47615
(812) 649-2500; (800) 877-5165

Come to the River Belle for a little bit of southern charm in southern Indiana on the Ohio River. Guests may choose from one of

The River Belle

NOTES: Credit cards accepted: A MasterCard; B Visa; C American Express; D Discover; E Diner's Club; F Other; 2 Personal checks accepted; 3 Lunch available; 4 Dinner available; 5 Open all year; 6 Pets welcome;

three accommodations: an 1866 white-painted brick Steamboat style, an 1890 red-brick Italianate, or the "little house under the pecan tree." Stroll along the river or relax under the trees. Within 20 miles of the Lincoln Boyhood National Memorial, Lincoln State Park, Lincoln drama, and Holiday World.

Hosts: Don and Pat Phillips
Rooms: 6 (2 PB; 4 SB) $45-65
Continental Breakfast
Credit Cards: A, B
Notes: 2, 5, 7, 8, 9

HARTFORD CITY

DéCoy's Bed and Breakfast

1546 West 100 North, 47348
(765) 348-2164

This charming country home offers its guests extraordinarily attractive accommodations with many extraspecial "Hoosier" touches. Visitors can relax in the quiet rural atmosphere of this old restored home, enriched with many amenities not customary to the typical motel or hotel setting. Each room demonstrates its own character with antique furnishings and comfortable arrangements.

Hosts: Chris and Tiann Coy
Rooms: 5 (3 PB; 2 SB) $52-75
Full Breakfast
Credit Cards: None
Notes: 2, 5, 7, 8, 10, 12, 14

HUNTINGTON

Purviance House

326 South Jefferson, 46750
(219) 356-9215; (219) 356-4218

This majestic Greek Revival-Italianate was built in 1859 and is listed in the National Register of Historic Places. Lovingly restored and decorated with period furnishings. Features include ornate plaster designs, solid cherry winding stairway, parquet floors, and four fireplaces with unique designs. In a safe, secure community near downtown. Off-street parking and air

Purviance House

conditioning are some amenities, along with complimentary snacks and beverages.

Hosts: Robert and Jean Gernand
Rooms: 5 (2 PB; 3 SB) $45-65
Full Breakfast
Credit Cards: A, B, D
Notes: 2, 5, 7, 9, 10, 11, 12, 14

INDIANAPOLIS

Boone Docks on the River

7159 Edgewater Place, 46240
(317) 257-3671

A 1920s English Tudor home on the White River, just north of Broad Ripple village, Boone Docks has a resortlike setting overlooking the river. Enjoy the comforts and charm of the River Room Suite, gracefully decorated in blue, white eyelet, and lace. A hearty breakfast is enjoyed seasonally in the sunroom or on the screen porch. Convenient to dining, entertainment, sporting events, shopping, museums, antiquing, and many downtown attractions.

Hosts: Lynne and Mike Boone
Room: 1 (PB) $55-75
Full Breakfast
Credit Cards: C
Notes: 2, 5, 7, 8, 10, 11, 12

JAMESTOWN

Oakwood Bed and Breakfast

9530 West U.S. Highway 136, 46147
(765) 676-5114; FAX (765) 676-5802

New antique-filled Victorian on nine acres. Peaceful, quiet rural setting. Relax on

7 No smoking; 8 Children welcome; 9 Social drinking allowed; 10 Tennis nearby; 11 Swimming nearby; 12 Golf nearby; 13 Skiing nearby; 14 May be booked through a travel agent; 15 Handicapped accessible.

30 Knightstown, IN

Oakwood

porches, deck, or gazebo. Flower gardens, lily pond, birds. Full breakfast and refreshments. Billiard room adjoins one guest room. Convenient to I-74, 25 miles northwest of Indianapolis, 15 miles east of Crawfordsville.

Hosts: Bob and Marilyn Kernodle
Rooms: 2 (PB) $60
Full Breakfast
Credit Cards: None
Notes: 2, 5, 7, 12

KNIGHTSTOWN

B & B MidWest Reservations

2223 Crump Lane, Columbus, IN 47203-2009
(812) 378-5855; (800) B AND B (342-2632)
FAX (812) 378-5822
e-mail: swanent@hsonline.net
www.BandBmidwest.hsonline.com/

12121. A historic country home midway between Indianapolis and Richmond provides four rooms for guests with easy access to I-70. Guest rooms include queen-size beds with fireplace, queen-size and twin beds, each with private bath. Overlook Hoosier farmland and a beautiful golf course available for guests' use, with a short drive to a quaint small town. Home in "Antique Alley." Golf packages available including room rates, breakfast, greens fees, and afternoon snack. Continental plus breakfast. $60-70.

LAFAYETTE

B & B MidWest Reservations

2223 Crump Lane, Columbus, IN 47203-2009
(812) 378-5855; (800) B AND B (342-2632)
FAX (812) 378-5822
e-mail: swanent@hsonline.net
www.BandBmidwest.hsonline.com/

14096. A grand Italianate home built in 1882 in the Centennial Historic District of Lafayette boasts of its original chandeliers and five guest accommodations with private baths with old-fashioned claw-foot tubs. Some rooms also offer whirlpools. Turndown service in the evening and a full formal breakfast in the morning is served by candlelight, making this a visit long to be remembered. Nearby enjoy Purdue University activities, historic Lafayette, the Wabash River, or historic battlefields. $70-175.

Historic Loeb House Inn

708 Cincinnati Street, 47901
(765) 420-7737

An elegant and comfortable luxury inn in Lafayette's Centennial Historic District features ornate plaster, walnut woodwork, and antique chandeliers. This 1996 decorator showhouse is restored and furnished to period. Spacious guest rooms have private baths, telephones, and cable TVs. Some rooms include whirlpool tubs and fireplaces. Guests are treated to many amenities. Turndown with apéritif at the bedside. Breakfast served in the formal dining room. Near Purdue University, downtown restaurants, museums, and antique shops. Exercise room and swimming pool available.

Historic Loeb House Inn

NOTES: Credit cards accepted: A MasterCard; B Visa; C American Express; D Discover; E Diner's Club; F Other; 2 Personal checks accepted; 3 Lunch available; 4 Dinner available; 5 Open all year; 6 Pets welcome;

Hosts: Janice Alford and Dick Nagel
Rooms: 5 (PB) $70-175
Full Breakfast
Credit Cards: A, B, C
Notes: 2, 5, 7, 8, 9, 10, 11, 12, 14

LAGRANGE

The 1886 Inn

212 Factory Street, 46761
(219) 463-4227

The 1866 Inn bed and breakfast is filled with historical charm and elegance and glows with old-fashioned beauty in every room. The finest lodging, but affordable, this inn is 10 minutes from the Shipshewana flea market. Continental plus breakfast served.

Hosts: Duane and Gloria Billman
Rooms: 3 (PB) $89-129
Continental Breakfast
Credit Cards: A, B
Notes: 2, 5, 7, 10, 12

LAPEL

Kati-Scarlett Bed and Breakfast

1037 North Main, P.O. Box 356, 46051
(765) 534-4937; e-mail: dopirak@inetdirect.net

The Kati-Scarlett is a lovely red brick 1928 American four-square-style house in the heart of Lapel. Guests can relax on the shaded front porch while enjoying the serenity of this quiet country community. The stress and strains are suspended the moment guests wander to the gazebo in the bricked, walled-in back yard, or rest in one of the three guest rooms reflecting the silver screen's greatest love story. Whether staying at the Kati-Scarlett in summer, savoring the garden, or in winter, while snuggling to that warmth of the wood-burning fireplace, guests' thoughts will wander back to a time of power, passion, and romance—a time that's *Gone With the Wind.*

Hosts: Charles and Sharon Wilson-Dopirak
Rooms: 3 (3 SB) $43-53
Continental Breakfast
Credit Cards: None
Rooms: 2, 5, 7, 8, 10, 11, 12

LAPORTE

Arbor Hill Inn

263 Johnson Road, 46350
(219) 362-9200; FAX (219) 326-1778

Historic 1910 Greek Revival structure. Four suites with fireplaces and whirlpool baths plus three well-appointed rooms with private baths. Dataport telephones and cable TV throughout. Pre-arranged dining available. Central air conditioning. LaPorte area noted for lakes, antique shopping, Lighthouse Outlet Center. Near Lake Michigan dunes. Business services available along with meetings and private parties. One and one-half hours from Chicago. Thirty minutes from Notre Dame. Continental breakfast served Monday through Saturday; full breakfast served on Sunday.

Hosts: Kris Demoret, Laura Kobat, Mark Wedow
Rooms: 7 (PB) $89-199
Full and Continental Breakfast
Credit Cards: A, B, C, D
Notes: 2, 3, 4, 5, 7, 8, 9, 11, 12, 14, 15

LEESBURG

Prairie House Bed and Breakfast

495 East 900 North, 46538
(219) 658-9211

Whether travelers have planned tranquil days or non-stop activities touring northern Indiana, the hosts invite them to experience the many delights of staying at the Prairie House where guests come as a stranger and leave as friends. On a working farm amid rolling

---

7 No smoking; 8 Children welcome; 9 Social drinking allowed; 10 Tennis nearby; 11 Swimming nearby; 12 Golf nearby; 13 Skiing nearby; 14 May be booked through a travel agent; 15 Handicapped accessible.

Prairie House

cornfields and wild flowers. Enjoy the gazebo in summer, or curl up by the fire in the winter. Full breakfast and bedtime snacks.

Hosts: Everet and Marie Tom
Rooms: 4 (2 PB; 2 SB) $45-65
Full Breakfast
Credit Cards: A, B
Notes: 2, 5, 7, 10, 11, 12

LIGONIER

Solomon Mier Manor
508 South Cavin Street, 46767
(219) 894-3668

This Italian/Queen Anne/Renaissance home was built in 1899. It has four guest rooms completely furnished in antique furniture of the period. Each room has its own private bath. This home is on the edge of Ligonier's business district, which is in an area that has been placed in the National Register of Historic Places. It contains some of the grandest architecture to be seen. It is minutes away

Solomon Mier Manor

from the Shipshewana flea market, Nappanee Amish Acres, Auburn-Cord-Duesenburg Museum, Das Essenhause at Middlebury, and much more. Air conditioning. Additional $25 per extra person in room.

Hosts: Ron and Doris Blue
Rooms: 4 (PB) $60
Full Breakfast
Credit Cards: A, B
Notes: 2, 5, 7, 10, 11, 12

MADISON

Cliffhouse Bed and Breakfast
122 Fairmount Drive, 47250
(812) 265-5272

Victorian mansion overlooking nearby antique shops and the beautiful Ohio River, in picturesque Madison. Canopied beds, silver, brass, and fine china all displayed the way it was. Available for tours and small receptions and parties.

Rooms: 6 (PB) $58-96
Continental Breakfast
Credit Cards: A, B, C, D
Notes: 2, 5, 8, 9, 10, 11, 12, 13, 14

Ghent House Bed and Breakfast
411 Main Street (US 42), P.O. Box 478,
  Ghent, KY 41045
(502) 347-5807
www.bbonline.com/ky/ghent/

Ghent House, in Ghent, Kentucky, is a gracious reminder of the antebellum days of the Old South. Federal style with a beautiful fantail window, two slave walls, rose and English gardens, gazebo, crystal chandeliers, fireplaces, outdoor hot tub, and whirlpool. Ghent House has a spectacular view of the Ohio River halfway between Cincinnati and Louisville, and one can almost visualize the steamboats. Go back in time and stay at the Ghent House. Come as a guest—leave as a friend.

Hosts: Wayne and Diane Young
Rooms: 3 (PB) $60-120

NOTES: Credit cards accepted: A MasterCard; B Visa; C American Express; D Discover; E Diner's Club; F Other; 2 Personal checks accepted; 3 Lunch available; 4 Dinner available; 5 Open all year; 6 Pets welcome;

Full Breakfast
Credit Cards: A, B, C, D
Notes: 2, 5, 7, 8, 9, 10, 11, 12, 14

Schussler House Bed and Breakfast

514 Jefferson Street, 47250
(812) 273-2068; (800) 392-1931

Experience the quiet elegance of a circa 1849 Federal Greek Revival home tastefully combined with today's modern amenities. Madison's historic district, antique shops, restaurants, historic sites, and the Ohio River are within a pleasant walk. This gracious home offers spacious rooms decorated with antiques and reproductions and carefully selected fabrics and wall coverings. A sumptuous breakfast in the sun-filled dining room is a relaxing beginning to the day.

Hosts: Judy and Bill Gilbert
Rooms: 3 (PB) $99
Full Breakfast
Credit Cards: A, B, D
Notes: 2, 5, 7, 9, 10, 11, 12, 14

MCCORDSVILLE

B & B MidWest Reservations

2223 Crump Lane, Columbus, IN 47203-2009
(812) 378-5855; (800) B AND B (342-2632)
FAX (812) 378-5822
e-mail: swanent@hsonline.net
www.BandBmidwest.hsonline.com/

09057. This renovated 1916 circular barn was recently transformed into a bed and breakfast. This historic site offers three guest rooms. One room has a king-size bed, queen-size sleeper sofa, TV, and private bath. The second room offers a queen-size bed with shared bath, and the third room offers two double beds with shared bath. A hearty buffet-style breakfast is served. The common areas offer a wide-screen TV and VCR, game room with pool table, picnic area, enclosed porch, and library/study area. Just 19 miles to downtown Indianapolis. $72-96.

METAMORA

Thorpe House Country Inn

19049 Clayborn Street, P.O. Box 36, 47030
(765) 647-5425

Circa 1840s, this peaceful, easy-feeling inn is only one block from the restored Whitewater Canal. Enjoy a hearty breakfast before exploring 100 plus shops, galleries, and museums in this quaint historic village. Transportation options include excursion train, horsedrawn carriage, and canal boat. Recreational diversions—canoeing, hiking, bicycling, fishing, water sports, golf, exploring Indian mounds—are nearby. "Although we are 150 years away, we're conveniently located between Indianapolis and Cincinnati."

Hosts: Mike and Jean Owens
Rooms: 5 (PB) $70-125
Full Breakfast
Credit Cards: A, B, C, D
Notes: 2, 3, 6, 8, 9, 10, 11, 12, 14

Thorpe House Country Inn

MIDDLEBURY

Bee Hive Bed and Breakfast

Box 1191, 46540
(219) 825-5023; FAX (219) 825-5023

Welcome to this cozy country bed and breakfast built with rough-sawn timber and

---

7 No smoking; 8 Children welcome; 9 Social drinking allowed; 10 Tennis nearby; 11 Swimming nearby; 12 Golf nearby; 13 Skiing nearby; 14 May be booked through a travel agent; 15 Handicapped accessible.

open beams. In the evenings, chat with Herb as he tells about the Amish community, gift shops, museums, parks, and flea markets, or enjoy an old-fashioned sing-along as Herb plays the accordion. Enjoy the old tractors and steam engine. Snuggle under handmade quilts, wake to the smell of a country breakfast being prepared. A great way to start the day. Guest cottage also available.

Hosts: Herb and Treva Swarm
Rooms: 4 (1 PB; 3 SB) $54-70
Full Breakfast
Credit Cards: A, B
Notes: 2, 5, 7, 8, 10, 11, 12, 13

Empty Nest Bed and Breakfast

13347 County Road. 12, 46540
(219) 825-1042

Four-level traditional home is on a hillside overlooking two ponds—home to swans, geese, and ducks—gentle hills, woods, and flowered fields. Antique and craft gift shops, Shipshewana's famous 1,000-stall flea market and popular antique auction, Amish country, museums, parks, rivers, lakes, Goshen College, and the University of Notre Dame are all nearby. Hosts will entertain guests with selections on the grand piano. A hearty breakfast is included. Guest rooms are newly furnished, including queen-size beds. Air conditioned.

Hosts: Sherry and Tim Bryant
Rooms: 3 (1 PB; 2 SB) $69-79
Full Breakfast
Credit Cards: A, B, D
Notes: 2, 5, 7, 9, 10, 12, 13

The Patchwork Quilt Country Inn

11748 County Road 2, 46540
(219) 825-2417; FAX (219) 825-5172

Relax and enjoy the simple grace and charm of this 100-year-old farmhouse. Sample the hosts' country cooking with homemade breads and desserts in the finest restaurant in the area. Let the hosts guide one on their backroads' tour and meet their Amish friends and buy their homemade articles, then return to the inn and rest in the quaint guest rooms. Lunch available April through December. Dinner available February through December. Cross-country skiing nearby.

Hosts: Ray and Rosetta Miller
Rooms: 15 (PB) $70-100
Full Breakfast
Credit Cards: A, B
Notes: 2, 7, 12, 13, 14, 15

Tiffany Powell's Bed and Breakfast

523 South Main Street, 46540
(219) 825-5951

Come enjoy the charm of Middlebury in this cozy bed and breakfast, just seven minutes from Shipshewana (large flea market and Amish community) and only 40 minutes from the University of Notre Dame. This bed and breakfast was featured on the *Oprah Winfrey* show's "Angel Network."

Host: Judy Powell
Rooms: 3 (PB) $50-75
Full Breakfast
Credit Cards: None
Notes: 2, 5, 7, 8, 9, 10, 11, 12, 14

Yoder's Zimmer mit Frühstück Haus

504 South Main Street, P.O. Box 1396, 46540
(219) 825-2378

Hosts enjoy sharing their Amish-Mennonite heritage in their spacious

---

NOTES: Credit cards accepted: A MasterCard; B Visa; C American Express; D Discover; E Diner's Club; F Other; 2 Personal checks accepted; 3 Lunch available; 4 Dinner available; 5 Open all year; 6 Pets welcome;

Nappanee, IN   35

Yoder's Zimmer mit Frühstück Haus

Crystal Valley home in northern Indiana's Amish country. Within walking distance of downtown, but secluded enough to give guests privacy. There is also a walking trail to the river. Many antiques and collectibles are seen throughout the house. Three rooms can accommodate small families. There are several common rooms available for relaxing, reading, TV, games, or socializing. Air condition, swimming pool, and children's playground available.

Hosts: Wilbur and Evelyn Yoder
Rooms: 5 (5 SB) $52.50
Full Breakfast
Credit Cards: A, B, D
Notes: 2, 5, 7, 8, 10, 11, 12, 14

MIDDLETOWN

B & B MidWest Reservations

2223 Crump Lane, Columbus, IN 47203-2009
(812) 378-5855; (800) B AND B (342-2632)
FAX (812) 378-5822
e-mail: swanent@hsonline.net
www.BandBmidwest.hsonline.com/

12034. In the country between Anderson and Muncie, this bed and breakfast offers two guest accommodations, including a cozy room within the main house with bed and shared bath. Larger accommodation includes small apartment with kitchenette, dining room, living room with TV and Hide-a-Bed, bath, bedroom , and patio. Twenty dollars per additional person. Five golf courses in surrounding area, Mounds State Park, and Basketball Hall of Fame all minutes from home. Handicapped accessible. Full breakfast. $55-75.

MILLERSBURG

The Big House in the Little Woods

4245 South 1000 West, 46543
(219) 593-9076

Recently built 3,500-square-foot Colonial-style home in a quiet country setting is in the heart of a large Amish community. Three spacious guest rooms have TVs, some antique furniture, handmade quilts, and air conditioning. Take a stroll down the quiet country road or relax in a guest room, living room, or in the quiet woods and watch for birds or woodland animals. Only nine miles to Shipshewana. King- and queen-size beds available.

Hosts: Sarah and Jacob Stoltzfus
Rooms: 4 (PB) $65-75
Full Breakfast
Credit Cards: A, B, D
Notes: 2, 5, 7, 10, 11, 12

NAPPANEE

Olde Buffalo Inn Bed and Breakfast

1061 Parkwood Drive, 46550
(888) 773-2223; FAX (219) 773-4275

As soon as guests arrive at the Olde Buffalo Inn, they can tell that their stay will be a relaxing and peaceful one. The property is picturesque with the huge lawn, windmill, and 23-room inn with brick sidewalk all on two and one-half acres. The history of the inn extends over 150 years. Built in 1840 by a pioneer farmer. Today the farmhouse still exists.

Hosts: The Lakins
Rooms: 6 (PB) $79-109
Full Breakfast
Credit Cards: A, B, D
Notes: 2, 5, 7, 8, 9, 10, 11, 12, 14

---

7 No smoking; 8 Children welcome; 9 Social drinking allowed; 10 Tennis nearby; 11 Swimming nearby; 12 Golf nearby; 13 Skiing nearby; 14 May be booked through a travel agent; 15 Handicapped accessible.

NASHVILLE

Allison House Inn
90 South Jefferson Street, P.O. Box 1625, 47448
(812) 988-0814

The Allison House is the perfect complement to the charm of Brown County in the rolling hills of southern Indiana. The mood and decor reflect the relaxed lifestyle of the region and the innkeeper. The emphasis is on cleanliness, comfort, and charm.

Host: Tammy Galm
Rooms: 5 (PB) $95
Full Breakfast
Credit Cards: None
Notes: 2, 7, 10, 11, 12, 13

Allison House Inn

NEW HARMONY

Raintree Inn Bed and Breakfast
503 West Street, P.O. Box 566, 47631
(812) 682-5625; (888) 656-0123
www.raintree-inn.com

Raintree Inn Bed and Breakfast is one of New Harmony's late Victorian architectural treasures. This stately Classic Revival home features magnificent interiors adorned with oak woodwork and ornate wallpapers. Each of the four well-appointed guest rooms has a private bath, and two feature private balconies. Guests may also make themselves at home in any of three parlors or relax on the spacious front porch. Raintree Inn is within walking distance of everything.

Hosts: Scott and Nancy McDonald
Rooms: 4 (PB) $95-115
Full Breakfast
Credit Cards: A, B, D
Notes: 2, 5, 7

OSGOOD

Victorian Garden Bed and Breakfast
243 North Walnut Street, 47037
(812) 689-4469

The Victorian Garden is a beautiful 1895 Victorian home. The bedrooms are all comfortably furnished, clean, cheerful, and air conditioned, and include private or shared baths, and TV. Guests are encouraged to feel at home on the wraparound porches and enjoy the garden gazebo, or sit and bird watch on the patio. A full breakfast is served in the dining room. Near Versailles State Park, river boat gambling, and antique shops.

Hosts: Paul and Linda Krinop
Rooms: 3 (2 PB; 2 SB) $50-85
Full Breakfast
Credit Cards: A, B
Notes: 5, 7, 8, 9, 11, 12

PAOLI

B & B MidWest Reservations
2223 Crump Lane, Columbus, IN 47203-2009
(812) 378-5855; (800) B AND B (342-2632)
FAX (812) 378-5822
e-mail: swanent@hsonline.net
www.BandBmidwest.hsonline.com/

23064. Bordering the beautiful Hoosier National Forest, the town of Paoli is nestled off the beaten trail in southern Indiana. The owners of this historic 1830 landmark tell how the home was moved

---

NOTES: Credit cards accepted: A MasterCard; B Visa; C American Express; D Discover; E Diner's Club; F Other; 2 Personal checks accepted; 3 Lunch available; 4 Dinner available; 5 Open all year; 6 Pets welcome;

and turned on the lot and incorporated into the lovely Queen Anne Victorian structure seen today. Six guest accommodations offered, all with private baths. Full breakfast is served. $60-65.

Hosts: Chip and Chartley Bondurant
Rooms: 4 (PB) $65-75
Full Breakfast
Credit Cards: A, B, C
Notes: 2, 5, 8, 10, 11, 12

RISING SUN

Mulberry Inn and Gardens Bed and Breakfast
118 South Mulberry Street, 47040
(812) 438-2206 (phone/FAX); (800) 235-3097

RICHMOND

Philip W. Smith Bed and Breakfast
2039 East Main Street, 47374
(765) 966-8972; (800) 966-8972

Elegant Queen Anne Victorian listed in National Register of Historic Places. It is in East Main-Glen Miller Park historic district, right on the Indiana/Ohio border off I-70. Home features stained-glass windows and ornate carved wood, furnished in antiques. Relax in the evening with homemade snacks, coffee, and tea. Awaken to a breakfast highlighting fresh, regional ingredients. Stroll through four historic districts, listen to outdoor concerts in the park, hike white-water river gorge, relax in the garden at the bed and breakfast, and shop the unique shops of Richmond and Antique Alley. AAA-rated three diamonds.

Explore a legacy of Old World charm and natural beauty in the heart of Rising Sun. Mulberry Inn and Gardens is set in a quiet residential area featuring charming gardens with a quiet and relaxed atmosphere. Each newly renovated guest room has its own remote control color TV, VCR, telephone, and pillow-top mattress. Mulberry Inn and Gardens caters to adults with no pets, no children, and smoking limited to the front and back porches allowing a quiet getaway while having the excitement of the Grand Victoria and other activities in the area. Fishing and antiquing nearby.

Innkeeper: Betty Harris
Owners: Janet and Jim Willis
Rooms: 5 (PB) $89-125
Full Breakfast
Credit Cards: A, B, C, D, E, F
Notes: 5, 7, 9, 10, 12, 13

ROCKPORT

The Rockport Inn
130 South Third, 47635
(812) 649-2664

Lovely Victorian inn, private baths, and antiques. One block from the Ohio River. Full breakfast included.

Hosts: John and Diana Headley
Rooms: 6 (PB) $55-68
Full Breakfast
Credit Cards: A, B, C
Notes: 2, 5, 7, 8, 9, 11, 12, 13, 14

Philip W. Smith

7 No smoking; 8 Children welcome; 9 Social drinking allowed; 10 Tennis nearby; 11 Swimming nearby; 12 Golf nearby; 13 Skiing nearby; 14 May be booked through a travel agent; 15 Handicapped accessible.

Trail's End

5931 Highway 56, Owensboro, KY 42301
(502) 771-5590; FAX (502) 771-4723
e-mail: jramey@mindspring.com
www.mindspring.com/~jramey

A condo cottage in Indiana, furnished with antiques and gas-log fireplace, has three bedrooms, fully equipped kitchen with stocked refrigerator of breakfast fixings, laundry facilities, patio, and stables for lessons or trail riding on the property. A second condo cottage in Kentucky has three bedrooms. Guests may enjoy indoor/outdoor tennis, Nautilus fitness, and a sauna. Country-style breakfast served at the tennis club on property. Pool and a fireplace. Cottages are air conditioned. Also available is a two-bedroom trailer with two baths. Weekly rates available. Ten dollars for additional persons over two.

Host: Joan G. Ramey
Condo: 2 (PB) $50-75
Trailer: 2 (PB) $35
Full Breakfast
Credit Cards: A, B, D
Notes: 2, 5, 6, 7, 8, 9, 10, 11, 12, 14, 15

ROCKVILLE

Knoll Inn Luxury Suites

317 West High Street, P.O. Box 56, 47872
(765) 569-6345; (888) 569-6345

Originally built in 1842, the Italianate/Greek Revival architecture of the home still retains all its flavor. In 1982, the Nolins purchased the home and, in 1996, added the inn. The inn, separate from the main house, offers privacy to its guests. The three-room suites, consisting of living room, bedroom, and private bath with large two-person whirlpool spa, are elegant yet very affordable. Each suite has vaulted ceiling, TV/VCR, and is beautifully decorated. In the historic district of the covered bridge capital of the world, the Knoll Inn is a new concept in affordable luxury accommodations.

Hosts: Mark and Sharon Nolin
Rooms: 3 (PB) $85 and up
Full Breakfast
Credit Cards: A, B
Notes: 2, 4, 5, 7, 8, 9, 10, 11, 12, 13

Owl Nest

303 Howard Avenue, 47872
(765) 569-1803

This 1889 Queen Anne home is nestled in Rockville's historic district. Covered bridge capital of the world. Original woodwork, pocket doors, and chandeliers are very evident. Beautiful carved staircase leading to guest rooms. All rooms named after well-known queens and decorated in same fashion. Yard is adorned with trees, flowers, and sitting areas where popcorn and beverages are served. A delicious hot country breakfast is enjoyed in the morning. Gift shop on wraparound porch welcomes browsers. Open year-round.

Hosts: Richard and Tulie Ann Jadzak
Rooms: 4 (2 SB) $65-85
Full Breakfast
Credit Cards: None
Notes: 2, 5, 7, 8, 10, 11, 12, 14

Suits Us Bed and Breakfast

514 North College Street, 47872
(765) 569-5660; (888) 4 SUITSUS

This classic plantation-style home, with its widow's walk and a generous front porch, dates to the early 1880s. In scenic Parke County with 32 covered bridges and just 10 minutes away from Turkey Run State Park. Spacious rooms include TVs and VCRs. All with private baths. Guests can sightsee or hike all day and relax later on the front porch with a book. Guests may even borrow a bike for a ride around the historic town.

Hosts: Marty and Bev Rose
Rooms: 4 (PB) $55-75
Full Breakfast
Credit Cards: None
Notes: 2, 5, 7, 8, 9, 10, 11, 12, 13, 14

NOTES: Credit cards accepted: A MasterCard; B Visa; C American Express; D Discover; E Diner's Club; F Other; 2 Personal checks accepted; 3 Lunch available; 4 Dinner available; 5 Open all year; 6 Pets welcome;

SHIPSHEWANA

Morton Street Bed and Breakfast
140 Morton Street, P.O. Box 775, 46565
(219) 768-4391; (800) 447-6475

In the heart of Amish country, guests will find themselves within walking distance of all kinds of shops and the famous Shipshewana flea market. Special winter and weekend rates available. Full breakfast Monday through Saturday, Continental breakfast on Sunday, and lunch and dinner are available at the restaurant next door. Inquire about arrangements for children.

Hostesses: Peggy Scherger and Kelly McConnell
  (mother and daughter)
Rooms: 10 (PB)
Full and Continental Breakfasts
Credit Cards: A, B, D
Notes: 2, 5, 7, 12, 13, 14

Morton Street

SHIRLEY

Sweet's Home Sweet Home
402 Center Street, 47384
(765) 737-6357

Large comfortable home specializing in small town hospitality. Large yard with rose garden and within walking distance of the historic district. Within an easy drive to several attractions. Each room is special. Have Christmas year-round in the Christmas Room, see all the treasures in PaPaw's Treasure Room, sleep in Greatma's antique feather bed, or lounge in bows and lace in the lovely Jo-lia-Reneé Room. Evening snacks are served.

Hosts: Jeanie and Ray Sweet
Rooms: 4 (4 SB) $45-75
Continental Breakfast
Credit Cards: None
Notes: 2, 4, 5, 8

SOUTH BEND

The Book Inn
508 West Washington Street, 46601
(219) 288-1990; e-mail: BookInn@aol.com
www.members.aol.com/bookinn/

Second Empire home in downtown South Bend. Designers' showcase—every room beautifully decorated. Fresh flowers, silver, fine china, and candlelight. The hosts emphasize service for the business person as well as leisured guests. The inn also houses a quality used bookstore, and guest rooms include the Louisa May Alcott, Jane Austen, and Charlotte Brontë Rooms. Corporate rates available. Full gourmet breakfast.

Hosts: Peggy and John Livingston
Rooms: 5 (PB) $75-120
Full Breakfast
Credit Cards: A, B, C
Notes: 2, 5, 7, 9, 10, 11, 12, 14

Queen Anne Inn
420 West Washington Street, 46601
(219) 234-5959; (800) 582-2379
www.business.michiana.org/queenann/

The Queen Anne Inn, an 1893 Victorian home listed on the historic register, is famous for the Frank Lloyd Wright bookcases and leaded glass. Antiques are used throughout the house. The inn is three blocks from downtown South Bend, near

---

7 No smoking; 8 Children welcome; 9 Social drinking allowed; 10 Tennis nearby; 11 Swimming nearby; 12 Golf nearby; 13 Skiing nearby; 14 May be booked through a travel agent; 15 Handicapped accessible.

40 Speedway, IN

Queen Anne Inn

Notre Dame and Oliver House Museum. Relax and step back into the past.

Hosts: Bob and Pauline Medhurst
Rooms: 6 (PB) $70-105
Full Breakfast
Credit Cards: A, B, C
Notes: 2, 5, 7, 8, 10, 11, 12, 13, 14

SPEEDWAY

Speedway Bed and Breakfast
1829 Cunningham Road, 46224
(317) 487-6531; (800) 975-3412

In the little town of Speedway, surrounded by the city of Indianapolis, guests will find a feeling of home at the Speedway. Through the doors walk race enthusiasts, wedding guests, convention and conference attendants. Easy access to the race tracks, museums, stadiums, shops, theaters, churches, and I-465. Honeymoon suite is available for special occasions.

Hosts: Pauline and Robert Grothe
Rooms: 5 (PB) $65-75
Full and Continental Breakfast
Credit Cards: A, B, D
Notes: 2, 5, 7, 10, 11, 12

VALPARAISO

The Inn at Aberdeen, Ltd.
3158 South State Road 2, 46383
(219) 465-3753; FAX (219) 465-9227
www.valpomall.com/theinn

Original home dates to the 1800s with a new addition in 1995 providing 11 guest suites, each with king-size or two queen-size beds, private bath, Jacuzzi, fireplace, ceiling fan, and balcony. Gourmet breakfast, evening snack and beverages included. Library, solarium, and parlor available. Executive Conference Center for business retreats, weddings, receptions, or family gatherings. Gazebo and gardens complement the peace and tranquility of the Inn at Aberdeen. Eighteen-hole championship golf, pool, tennis, and recreation fields adjacent.

Hosts: Gary Atherton (innkeeper); Linda and John Johnson (proprietors)
Rooms: 11 (PB) $90-150
Full Breakfast
Credit Cards: A, B, C, D, E
Notes: 5, 7, 8, 9, 10, 11, 12, 14, 15

VEVAY

Rosemont Inn
806 West Market Street, 47043
(812) 427-3050

This 1881 Victorian Italianate home, on the banks of the Ohio River, is on more than two acres. Eleven rooms, an open grand entrance stairway with stained glass, beautiful woodwork, and original chandeliers. Large front porch faces the river. Antiquing, casino, and scenic drives/hikes in the area. Grounds are planted in perennial and rose gardens. River-view and garden-view rooms are available. Queen-size beds (one room with twin/king-size beds), private baths, robes for guest use, complimentary refreshments.

Rooms: 5 (PB) $85-95
Full Breakfast

NOTES: Credit cards accepted: A MasterCard; B Visa; C American Express; D Discover; E Diner's Club; F Other; 2 Personal checks accepted; 3 Lunch available; 4 Dinner available; 5 Open all year; 6 Pets welcome;

West Baden Springs, IN 41

Credit Cards: None
Notes: 2, 5, 7, 9, 12

Credit Cards: A, B, C, D, E
Notes: 2, 3, 4, 5, 6, 7, 8, 9, 10, 11, 12, 13, 14, 15

WARSAW

WEST BADEN SPRINGS

Ramada White Hill Manor
2513 East Center Street, 46580
(219) 269-6933; FAX (219) 268-1936

The Ramada White Hill Manor is a restored English Tudor mansion with eight elegant bedrooms, private baths, telephones, desks, TVs, air conditioning, and conference room. Luxurious suite with double Jacuzzi bath. Full breakfast. Part of the newly renovated Ramada Plaza Hotel complex and adjacent to the Ramada Wagon Wheel Theater. Guests may enjoy many features of the main Ramada facility, including pools, sauna, whirlpool and exercise room. Lunch and dinner are available at restaurants of the complex. Historically renovated in 1988. Direct access to US 30. Nonsmoking facility. Rates are subject to change.

Host: Gladys Deloc
Rooms: 7 (PB) $80-101
Suite: 1 (PB) $129

E. B. Rhodes House Bed and Breakfast
Rhodes Avenue, Box 7, 47469
(812) 936-7378; (800) 786-5176

A spacious first-edition Victorian, built in 1901, with beautiful hand-carved wood and stained-glass windows. Two large porches complete with rockers for guests to enjoy southern Indiana vistas and just plain relaxing. Entertainment for all seasons and tastes includes gracious dining, historical tours, steam locomotive rides, antiquing, museums, and theater. For the more adventurous there are water or snow skiing, nearby state parks, and caving. A carriage house with full bath and fireplaces also available. Smoking permitted in designated areas only.

Hosts: Frank and Marlene Sipes
Rooms: 3 (PB) $45-85
Full Breakfast
Credit Cards: A, B, C, D
Notes: 2, 5, 8, 10, 11, 12, 13, 15

---

7 No smoking; 8 Children welcome; 9 Social drinking allowed; 10 Tennis nearby; 11 Swimming nearby; 12 Golf nearby; 13 Skiing nearby; 14 May be booked through a travel agent; 15 Handicapped accessible.

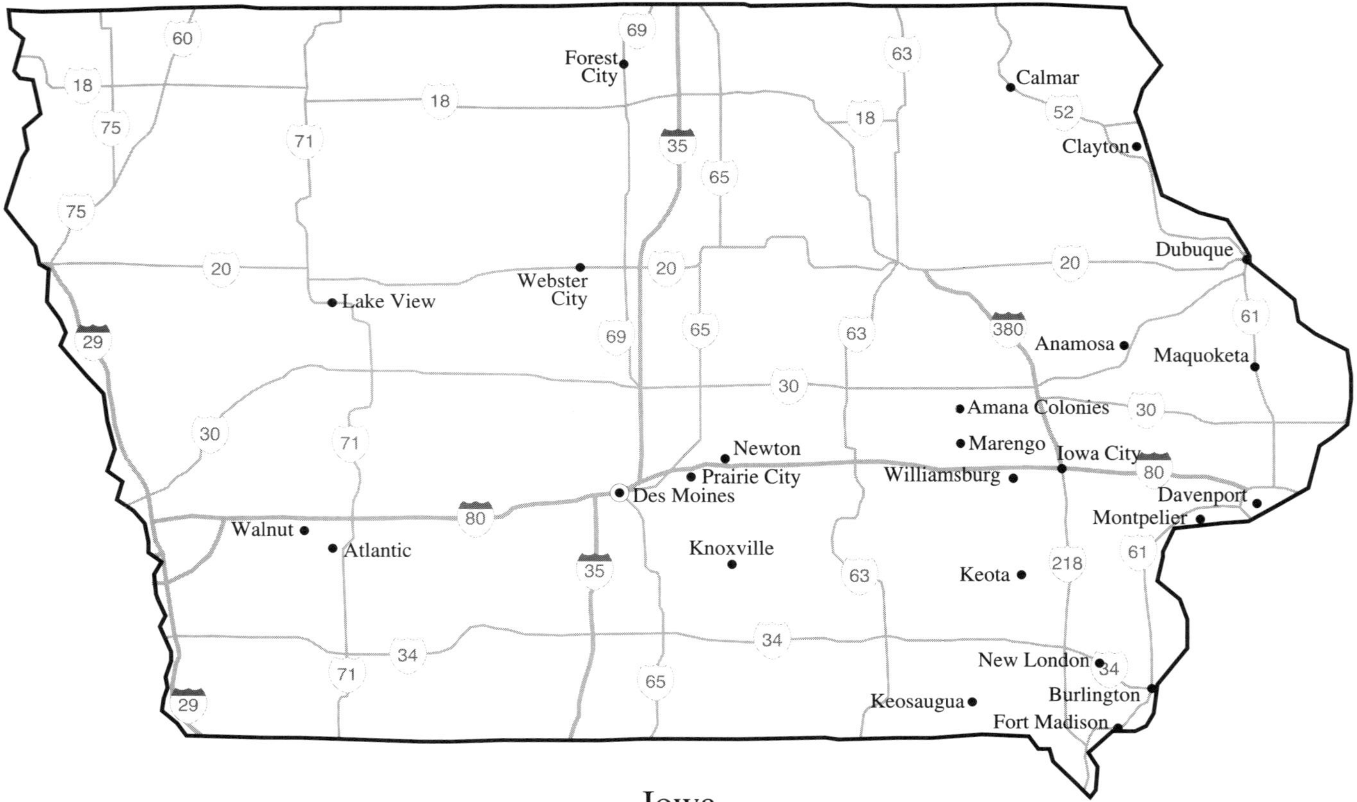
Forest City
Calmar
Clayton
Dubuque
Webster City
Lake View
Anamosa
Maquoketa
Amana Colonies
Marengo
Iowa City
Newton
Prairie City
Williamsburg
Des Moines
Davenport
Montpelier
Walnut
Atlantic
Knoxville
Keota
New London
Burlington
Keosaugua
Fort Madison

Iowa

Iowa

Die Heimat Country Inn

AMANA COLONIES

Die Heimat Country Inn
Amana Colonies, 1 Main Street, Homestead, 52236
(319) 622-3937

Choose the Amana Colonies' original bed and breakfast for quiet relaxation. A national register 1854 stage coach stop, now a 19-room restored inn with reasonable rates, Amana furniture, canopied beds, quilts, private baths, TV, air conditioning, and full hot breakfast. The hosts combine Australian charm and midwestern hospitality. Inquire about accommodations for pets.

Hosts: Warren and Jackie Lock
Rooms: 19 (PB) $48-70
Full Breakfast
Credit Cards: A, B, D
Notes: 2, 5, 7, 8, 9, 10, 11, 12

ANAMOSA

The Shaw House
509 South Oak, 52205
(319) 462-4485

Enjoy a relaxing step back in time in this three-story, 1866 Italianate mansion on a hilltop overlooking scenery immortalized in the paintings of native son Grant Wood. Special rooms include porch with panoramic countryside view, two-room tower suite, and ballroom. The mansion is on a 45-acre farm within easy walking distance of town. State park, antique shops, and canoeing are nearby.

Hosts: Connie and Andy McKean
Rooms: 4 (3 PB; 1 SB) $60-85
Full Breakfast
Credit Cards: None
Notes: 2, 3, 4, 5, 7, 8, 9, 10, 11, 12, 13, 14

ATLANTIC

Chestnut Charm Bed and Breakfast
1409 Chestnut Street, 50022
(712) 243-5652

This is one of Iowa's finest country inns. An enchanting 1898 Victorian mansion with carriage house suites. Private baths, Jacuzzis, in-room fireplaces, sauna, sunrooms, fountained patio, 12-foot gazebo, natural hardwood floors, and ornate woodwork. Full breakfast with gourmet coffee and fresh home-baking. Exquisite gourmet dinners. Air conditioned. Just a short drive to

NOTES: Credit cards accepted: A MasterCard; B Visa; C American Express; D Discover; E Diner's Club; F Other; 2 Personal checks accepted; 3 Lunch available; 4 Dinner available; 5 Open all year; 6 Pets welcome; 7 No smoking; 8 Children welcome; 9 Social drinking allowed; 10 Tennis nearby; 11 Swimming nearby; 12 Golf nearby; 13 Skiing nearby; 14 May be booked through a travel agent; 15 Handicapped accessible.

the famous bridges of Madison County, Walnut's Antique City, a Danish windmill with museum, championship golf courses, and many other Iowa treasures. Gift certificates.

Host: Barbara Stensvad
Rooms: 4 (PB) $65-100
Suites: 5 (PB) $100-250
Full Breakfast
Credit Cards: A, B
Notes: 2, 4, 5, 7, 10, 11, 12, 14

BURLINGTON

The Schramm House Bed and Breakfast

616 Columbia Street, 52601
(319) 754-0373; (800) 683-7117

Step into the past when entering this restored 1870s Victorian in the heart of the historic district. Unique architectural features and antique furnishings create the mood of an era past. Four guest rooms, all with private baths, offer queen-size or twin beds, quilts, and more. Experience Burlington hospitality while having lemonade on the porch or tea by the fire with the gracious hosts. Walk to the Mississippi River, antique shops, restaurants, and more.

Hosts: Sandy and Bruce Morrison
Rooms: 4 (PB) $65-85
Full Breakfast
Credit Cards: A, B, C, D
Notes: 2, 5, 7, 9, 10, 11, 12, 14

The Schramm House

CALMAR

Calmar Guesthouse

103 West North Street, 52132
(319) 562-3851

This Victorian home was lovingly restored in 1984. It continues to satisfy guests from all over the world. The area has beautiful corn fields, parks, bluffs, etc. Near Luther College, Vesterheim Norwegian-American Museum, Little Brown Church in the Vale, Niagara Cave, seed-saver farm, Laura Ingalls Wilder Park and Museum. Warm hospitality. Good food.

Host: Lucille Kruse
Rooms: 5 (1 PB; 4 SB) $45-50
Full Breakfast
Credit Cards: A, B
Notes: 2, 7, 8, 10, 11, 12, 13

CLAYTON

The Claytonian Bed and Breakfast Inn

100 South Front Street, 52049
(319) 964-2776

The Claytonian is a unique bed and breakfast inn, open year-round with large, charming rooms, each with its own distinct theme. Along the magnificent Mississippi River, one mile off the Great River Road, which affords one of the most scenic routes in the United States. The village of Clayton is surrounded by many historical sites, recreation areas, antique shops, and a rural warmth not found in other areas. The Claytonian provides a delicious breakfast, complimentary bicycles. Cable TV. A public boat ramp is available.

Hosts: Don and Eileen Christensen
Rooms: 5 (3 PB; 2 SB) $50-65
Full Breakfast
Credit Cards: A, B
Notes: 2, 5, 7, 8, 11, 12

NOTES: Credit cards accepted: A MasterCard; B Visa; C American Express; D Discover; E Diner's Club; F Other; 2 Personal checks accepted; 3 Lunch available; 4 Dinner available; 5 Open all year; 6 Pets welcome;

DAVENPORT

Bed and Breakfasts of the Quad City Area Room Availability Cooperative
P.O. Box 3464, Rock Island, IL 61201
(309) 786-3513

Fulton's Landing. (319) 322-4069. This large Italianate stone residence has a bird's-eye view of the Mississippi River. In the heart of downtown Davenport, it's only minutes from any Quad City activity. Five bedrooms and a full breakfast wait for visitors. $60-125.

Latimer Bed and Breakfast. (319) 289-5747. This 1905 house has been home to the Latimer family since 1949. There are four warm and cozy bedrooms, with one handicapped accessible. $40.

McCaffrey House. (319) 289-4254. Come relax at the captain's house. Enjoy the sights and sounds of an old river town, which sits on the outskirts of the Quad City area. This restored 1870 Italianate could become guests' "home away from home." From $51.

Varner's Caboose. (319) 381-3652. Stay in a real Rock Island Lines caboose. The caboose is self-contained with bath, shower, and complete kitchen. It sleeps four with a queen-size bed and two single beds in the cupola. A fully prepared country breakfast is left in the caboose for guests' pleasure. $55.

The Woodlands. (319) 289-3177. This is a secluded woodland escape that can be as private or social as visitors want. Nestled among 26 acres of forest and meadows on a private wildlife refuge. Guests delight in an elegant breakfast by a cozy fireplace. $75-115.

Fulton's Landing

Fulton's Landing Guest House
1206 East River Drive, 52803
(319) 322-4069

The old Fulton mansion is a large Italianate stone residence built in 1871 by Ambrose Fulton. Listed in the National Register of Historic Places, the home offers a majestic view of the Mississippi River and is only minutes away from all area attractions. Five bedrooms are available for guests. A full breakfast is served in the dining room. Two large porches overlook the river, one on the main floor and the other on the second floor with easy access from all the bedrooms. On Route 67 near downtown Davenport.

Hosts: Pat and Bill Schmidt
Rooms: 5 (PB) $60-125
Full Breakfast
Credit Cards: A, B, C
Notes: 2, 5, 7, 12

DES MOINES

Ellendale Scandinavian Bed and Breakfast
5340 Ashworth Road, West Des Moines, 50266
(515) 225-2219

Ellendale combines Old World Scandinavian decor and hospitality with established old farmstead setting and gardens. A short distance from I-80 and I-35, Ellendale is conveniently near Living History Farms,

---

7 No smoking; 8 Children welcome; 9 Social drinking allowed; 10 Tennis nearby; 11 Swimming nearby; 12 Golf nearby; 13 Skiing nearby; 14 May be booked through a travel agent; 15 Handicapped accessible.

creatively restored Historic Valley Junction (Iowa's antique capital), and a major mall. Des Moines offers many cultural events, beautiful parks and churches, botanical, art, and historical centers. Three-room suite plus fireplaced garden room.

Hosts: Ellen and Dale Jackson
Rooms: 2 (PB) $70-80
Full Breakfast
Credit Cards: None
Notes: 2, 5, 8, 10, 11, 12

DUBUQUE

The Mandolin Inn
199 Loras Boulevard, 52001
(319) 556-0069; (800) 524-7996
FAX (319) 556-0587

A 1908 Edwardian mansion where the comfort and pleasure of its guests is the primary focus. A gourmet breakfast is served in an oak dining room with an exquisite oil-painted mural while classical music plays softly in the background. For year-round comfort all rooms are provided with queen-size beds, down comforters, and air conditioning. During the summer the veranda is filled with wicker furniture for guests to relax in.

Host: Amy Boyntan
Rooms: 7 (5 PB; 2 SB) $75-135
Full Breakfast
Credit Cards: A, B, C, D
Notes: 2, 5, 7, 8, 9, 12, 13

The Mandolin Inn

The Richards House

The Richards House Bed and Breakfast
1492 Locust Street, 52001
(319) 557-1492

Relax in this 1883 Stick-style Victorian mansion with original interior, over 80 stained-glass windows, eight working fireplaces, embossed wall coverings, period furnishings, eight varieties of varnished woodwork, and more. Most rooms include working fireplaces, concealed TV/VCRs, and telephones. A full breakfast is served in the formal dining room. Easy access with plenty of parking.

Host: Michelle Delaney
Rooms: 5 (4 PB; 1 SB) $40-85
Full Breakfast
Credit Cards: A, B, C, D, E
Notes: 2, 5, 7, 8, 9, 10, 11, 12, 13, 14

FOREST CITY

1897 Victorian House Bed and Breakfast and Antiques
306 South Clark, 50436
(515) 582-3613

The 1897 house is in Queen Anne Victorian style, furnished in period furniture. The aroma of coffee and a large breakfast awakens guests each morning. House is available

NOTES: Credit cards accepted: A MasterCard; B Visa; C American Express; D Discover; E Diner's Club; F Other; 2 Personal checks accepted; 3 Lunch available; 4 Dinner available; 5 Open all year; 6 Pets welcome;

1897 Victorian House

for weddings, showers, dinners, teas, and weekend retreats. Antique shop and tea room within three blocks. Central air conditioning. "We specialize in cleanliness, comfort, and cheerfulness." One carriage house suite with whirlpool bath is also available.

Hosts: Richard and Doris Johnson
Rooms: 5 (PB)
Full Breakfast
Credit Cards: A, B
Notes: 2, 3, 5, 7, 11, 12

FORT MADISON

Kingsley Inn

707 Avenue H on Highway 61, 52627
(319) 372-7074; (800) 441-2327

Victorian inn on the Mississippi River. Enjoy lunch and dinner at Alpha's, the unique in-house theme restaurant and gift shop. Walk to the faithfully restored 1808 Old Fort Madison, train depot museum, the riverboat casino, and galleries. Guests are a 10-minute drive to historic Nauvoo, Illinois, with 40 restored 1840s shops and homes. Rooms have private baths; some have whirlpools. Cable TV, air conditioning, telephones, sprinklers, and alarms. Elevator and fax machine available. Also available is a suite with two bedrooms, two bath rooms, one of which has a whirlpool, living room, dining room, all major appliances, and laundry facility.

Host: Nannette Evans
Rooms: 14 (PB) $70-115
Continental Breakfast
Credit Cards: A, B, C, D, E
Notes: 2, 3, 4, 5, 7, 9, 10, 11, 12, 14, 15

IOWA CITY

Bella Vista Place Bed and Breakfast

2 Bella Vista Place, 52245
(319) 338-4129

Lovely air-conditioned 1920s home tastefully decorated with antiques and artifacts Daissy has acquired on her travels in Europe and Latin America. Two suites with in-room private baths, a suite with private bath and kitchen, two rooms with shared bath, all with comfortable beds. Guests can relax in the quietness of their room, share the company of other guests in the living room, or enjoy the view of the Iowa River from the deck. Guests will be very satisfied with Daissy's helpfulness, hearty breakfasts, and famous coffee. Short distance from downtown and the University of Iowa. One mile south of I-80 at exit 244. Special pricing for extended stays available. Fluent Spanish and some French spoken.

Hostess: Daissy P. Owen
Suites: 3 (PB) $85-95
Rooms: 2 (SB) $55-60
Full Breakfast
Credit Cards: None
Notes: 2, 5, 7, 9, 10, 11, 12

---

7 No smoking; 8 Children welcome; 9 Social drinking allowed; 10 Tennis nearby; 11 Swimming nearby; 12 Golf nearby; 13 Skiing nearby; 14 May be booked through a travel agent; 15 Handicapped accessible.

Iowa City, IA

The Golden Haug
517 East Washington Street, 52240
(319) 338-6452

Elegance and whimsy characterize this 1920 house. Guests can retreat to one of four accommodations with in-room private bath or enjoy camaraderie with other guests in the living room. A full breakfast is served family style. Ideal location in downtown Iowa City within a couple of blocks of the University of Iowa, eateries, and shopping. Smoking is permitted outside only.

Hosts: Nila Haug and Dennis Nowotny
Suites: 4 (PB) $68-100
Full Breakfast
Credit Cards: None
Notes: 2, 5, 7, 8, 9, 11, 12, 14

Haverkamps' Linn Street Homestay
619 North Linn Street, 52245
(319) 337-4363; FAX (319) 354-7057
e-mail: havb-b@soli.inav.net

A large and comfortable 1908 Edwardian-style home filled with antiques and collectibles. Wonderful front porch with old-fashioned swing. Walking distance to University of Iowa campus and the downtown area. Only a short drive to the Amana villages, Kalona, Hoover Museum in West Branch, and Cedar Rapids. One mile south of I-80 at exit 244.

Hosts: Clarence and Dorothy Haverkamp
Rooms: 3 (SB) $35-45
Full Breakfast
Credit Cards: None
Notes: 2, 5, 7, 8, 9, 10, 11, 12, 13

Haverkamps' Linn Street Homestay

KEOSAUQUA

Mason House Inn

Mason House Inn of Bentonsport
Route 2, Box 237, 52565
(800) 592-3133

The Mason House Inn was built in 1846, the year Iowa became a state, by Mormon craftsmen making their famous trek to Utah. It is the oldest steamboat river inn still serving overnight guests in the Midwest. The inn has the only fold-down copper bathtub in the state. Oral tradition has it that Abraham Lincoln and Mark Twain slept here. The entire village is listed in the National Register of Historic Places. Guests will find a full cookie jar in every room. AAA-approved.

Hosts: Sheral and William McDermet III
Rooms: 9 (5 PB; 4 SB) $54-74
Full Breakfast
Credit Cards: A, B
Notes: 2, 3, 4, 5, 7, 8, 9, 11, 12, 15

KEOTA

Elmhurst
1994 Keokuk Washington Road, 52248
(515) 636-3001

This 1905 Victorian mansion was built with no expense spared by Thomas

---

NOTES: Credit cards accepted: A MasterCard; B Visa; C American Express; D Discover; E Diner's Club; F Other; 2 Personal checks accepted; 3 Lunch available; 4 Dinner available; 5 Open all year; 6 Pets welcome;

Elmhurst

Singmaster. The family was the world's largest importer of draft horses. The mansion retains much of its original grandeur: prismed stained-glass and curved windows, circular solarium, parquet floors, beamed ceilings, Italian marble fireplace mantels, third-floor ballroom, beveled plate-glass windows, two grand stairways, leather wall coverings, and more. The house is filled with history and antiques. The house was designed and built by the famous Wetherells. The golf course, a swimming pool, and a nature trail are across the road.

Rooms: 7 (S21/2B) $45
Full Breakfast
Credit Cards: None
Notes: 2, 3, 4, 9, 10, 11, 12

KNOXVILLE-PELLA AREA

Heritage House Bed and Breakfast

1345 Highway 163, Leighton, 50143
(515) 626-3092

A 1918 home with great hospitality, air conditioning, TV, and VCR. Victorian Suite with antique pump organ, private bath. Blue Room with antiques, newly carpeted and decorated, private bath. Near Pella, a Dutch tourist town, and antique malls. Member of IBBIA. Gourmet full breakfast served with crystal and lace. Inquire about accommodations for pets.

Bike trails nearby. Near Knoxville National Sprint car races. Hunters with dogs welcome. Smoking is permitted in designated areas.

Hosts: Iola Vander Wilt and son, Mark
Rooms: 2 (PB) $55-60
Full Breakfast
Credit Cards: None
Notes: 2, 5, 8, 9, 10, 11, 12, 13, 14

LAKE VIEW

Armstrong House Bed and Breakfast

306 Fifth Street, 51450
(712) 657-2535

An elegantly restored Victorian (circa 1886) built by founding family of Lake View. Inside the eclectic decor displays a unique combination of Victorian, country, and international furnishings from owner's travels. Breakfast always includes freshly baked pastries and gourmet coffee. A new gift shop on the porch offers items from around the world. Three blocks from Black Hawk Lake and Sauk Rail Trail (for use by hikers, joggers, and bicyclists). Two bicycles are available for guests' use.

Host: Jeanet Henriquez
Rooms: 3 (PB) $57-63
Full or Continental Breakfast
Credit Cards: None
Notes: 2, 5, 7, 9, 10, 11, 12, 13, 14

MAQUOKETA

Squiers Manor Bed and Breakfast

418 West Pleasant Street, 52060
(319) 652-6961

Built in 1882, this restored brick Queen Anne mansion features rich, beautiful woodwork and period furnishings. Amidst this, three suites and five guest rooms provide a relaxing stay with expected modern

---

7 No smoking; 8 Children welcome; 9 Social drinking allowed; 10 Tennis nearby; 11 Swimming nearby; 12 Golf nearby; 13 Skiing nearby; 14 May be booked through a travel agent; 15 Handicapped accessible.

comforts, including in-room telephones, private baths, Jacuzzis, and TVs. In addition, candlelight evening dessert and gourmet breakfast are served.

Hosts: Virl and Kathy Banowetz
Rooms: 8 (PB) $75-185
Full Breakfast
Credit Cards: A, B, C
Notes: 2, 5, 7, 9, 10, 11, 12, 13

MARENGO

Loy's Farm Bed and Breakfast
2077 KK Avenue, 52301
(319) 642-7787

Beautiful modern country home on an active farm. Farm tours and hunting. Full gourmet breakfast with homemade products. Exercise and recreation equipment, available. Golf package available. Iowa agriculture ambassadors. The outlet mall, Amana Colonies, Iowa City, and Cedar Rapids are nearby. Close to I-80, exit 216. A rollaway is available at an additional $20.

Hosts: Loy and Robert Walker
Rooms: 3 (1 PB; 2 SB) $60
Full Breakfast
Credit Cards: None
Notes: 2, 4, 5, 7, 8, 9, 10, 11, 12

MONTPELIER

Varners' Caboose Bed and Breakfast
204 East 2nd, P.O. Box 10, 52759
(319) 381-3652

Stay in a real Rock Island Lines caboose. Set on its own track behind the hosts' house, the caboose is a self-contained unit, with bath, shower, and complete kitchen. It sleeps four, with a queen-size bed and two twins in the cupola. There are color TV, central air and heat, plus plenty of off-street parking. A fully prepared country breakfast is left in the caboose kitchen to be enjoyed by guests whenever they choose. On Route 22, halfway between Davenport and Muscatine.

Hosts: Bob and Nancy Varner
Room: 1 (PB) $60
Full Breakfast
Credit Cards: None
Notes: 2, 5, 6, 7, 8, 9

NEW LONDON

Old Brick Bed and Breakfast
2759 Old Highway 34, 52645
(319) 367-5403

This 1860s Italianate-style brick farmhouse, comfortably furnished with family pieces, beckons guests with electric candles in each window. The working grain farm offers an opportunity to view current farming techniques, equipment, and specialty crops. Enjoy peaceful surroundings, walk down a country road, visit area antique shops, or relax in spacious rooms with queen-size beds and private baths. Full breakfast and arrival refreshments are served daily.

Hosts: Jerry and Caroline Lehman
Rooms: 2 (PB) $50
Full Breakfast
Credit Cards: None
Notes: 2, 4, 5, 7, 8, 10, 11, 12

NEWTON

La Corsette Maison Inn
629 1st Avenue East, 50208
(515) 792-6833

This opulent, Mission-style mansion built in 1909 by Iowa state senator August Bergman maintains the charm of its original oak woodwork, Art Nouveau stained-glass windows, brass light fixtures, and even some original furnishings. Despite the addition of contemporary comforts, the bedchambers' original features have been

NOTES: Credit cards accepted: A MasterCard; B Visa; C American Express; D Discover; E Diner's Club; F Other; 2 Personal checks accepted; 3 Lunch available; 4 Dinner available; 5 Open all year; 6 Pets welcome;

La Corsette Maison Inn

retained. Down-filled pillows and comforters are available. Enjoy hot spiced wine in front of one of three fireplaces. Pets are welcome by pre-arrangement. Children are welcome with prior arrangements.

Host: Kay Owen
Rooms: 7 (PB) $70-185
Full Breakfast
Credit Cards: A, B, C
Notes: 2, 4, 5, 7, 9, 10, 11, 12, 14

PRAIRIE CITY

The Country Connection Bed and Breakfast
9737 West 93rd Street South, 50228-8306
(515) 994-2023

The Country Connection

Guests can experience the friendly atmosphere of a working farm community, surrounded by the tranquility of bountiful cropland...away from the hustle and bustle of everyday life. Turn-of-the-century farmhome, period furnishings, walnut woodwork, leaded glass, lace, all blended with privacy, charm, and hospitality; treasures lovingly preserved from six generations. Arise to the aroma of a hearty country breakfast. Complimentary bedtime snack and homemade ice cream are available. Open May through November. Near Walnut Creek Wildlife Refuge and Pella Tulip Time.

Hosts: Jim and Alice Foreman
Rooms: 2 (2 SB) $50-60
Full Breakfast
Credit Cards: A, B
Notes: 2, 7, 8, 11, 12

WALNUT

Antique City Inn Bed and Breakfast
400 Antique City Drive, P.O. Box 584, 51577
(712) 784-3722

This 1911 Victorian home has a wraparound porch, beautiful woodwork, French doors, butler's pantry, and dumbwaiter ice

---

7 No smoking; 8 Children welcome; 9 Social drinking allowed; 10 Tennis nearby; 11 Swimming nearby; 12 Golf nearby; 13 Skiing nearby; 14 May be booked through a travel agent; 15 Handicapped accessible.

box. One block from antique shops with 250 antique dealers, turn-of-the-century brick streets, storefronts, globed street lights, and historical museum. Children over 12 are welcome. One room is handicapped accessible.

Host: Sylvia Reddie
Rooms: 6 (2 PB; 4 SB) $45-55
Full Breakfast
Credit Cards: A, B, C, D
Notes: 2, 3, 4, 5, 7, 9, 12

WEBSTER CITY

Centennial Farm Bed and Breakfast

1091 220th Street, Rural Route 2, 50595-7571
(515) 832-3050

Parts of the original homestead and barns, built in 1869, have been incorporated into the air-conditioned farmhouse, which is among fields of corn and soybeans. The hosts are fourth-generation farmers here, and Tom was born in the downstairs bedroom. Guests can see the farm operation and Tom's 1929 Model A Ford pickup. Close to golf, tennis, swimming, antiques, parks, and fine dining. Just 22 miles west of I-35 at exit 142 or 144.

Hosts: Tom and Shirley Yungclas
Rooms: 2 (SB) $35
Full Breakfast
Credit Cards: None
Notes: 2, 5, 8, 9, 10, 11, 12

NOTES: Credit cards accepted: A MasterCard; B Visa; C American Express; D Discover; E Diner's Club; F Other; 2 Personal checks accepted; 3 Lunch available; 4 Dinner available; 5 Open all year; 6 Pets welcome;

Kansas

Balfours House

ABILENE

Balfours' House Bed and Breakfast
940-1900 Avenue, 67410
(785) 263-4262
www.BBHost.com/BalfoursHouseBnB

A relaxing contemporary country home. Landscaped into the hillside just outside of town with breathtaking views from horizon to horizon. Enjoy the flower beds and grapevine-covered patio. Private-entrance suites with private baths and patios, TV, VCR, stereo.

Hosts: Gil and Marie Balfour
Suites: 2 (PB) $75-100
Full Breakfast
Credit Cards: A, B, C
Notes: 2, 5, 7, 8, 9, 10, 11, 15

BASEHOR

Bedknobs and Biscuits
15202 Parallel, 66007
(913) 724-1540

A little bit of country close to Bonner Springs, Kansas City, Lawrence, and Leavenworth. The guest parlor is warm and inviting with cedar beams and walls covered in hand-painted vines. Stenciling, quilts, collectibles, bittersweet, and lace curtains decorate the three country Victorian bedrooms with two shared baths. Cookies in the evening and a huge country breakfast in the morning.

Host: Sandra (Soni) Mance
Rooms: 3 (3 S2B) $60-75
Full and Continental Breakfast
Credit Cards: A, B, C
Notes: 2, 5, 7, 10, 11, 12

BONNER SPRINGS

Back in Thyme
1100 South 130th Street, 66012
(913) 422-5207

A lovely guest home that has been featured in several national magazines and on local home tours. This "new-old" Queen Anne is nestled on 10 wooded acres with herb gardens and a fishing pond with arbor/swing and picnic area. Guests are welcome to enjoy the wraparound veranda or the front parlor with fireplace. Dining room and sunroom with 12-foot tin ceiling overlooking kitchen herb garden are common areas enjoyed by guests. Just minutes from Kansas City.

Hosts: Clinton and Judy Vickers
Rooms: 3 (PB) $75-125
Full Breakfast
Credit Cards: A, B, C
Notes: 5, 7, 8, 9, 12

NOTES: Credit cards accepted: A MasterCard; B Visa; C American Express; D Discover; E Diner's Club; F Other; 2 Personal checks accepted; 3 Lunch available; 4 Dinner available; 5 Open all year; 6 Pets welcome; 7 No smoking; 8 Children welcome; 9 Social drinking allowed; 10 Tennis nearby; 11 Swimming nearby; 12 Golf nearby; 13 Skiing nearby; 14 May be booked through a travel agent; 15 Handicapped accessible.

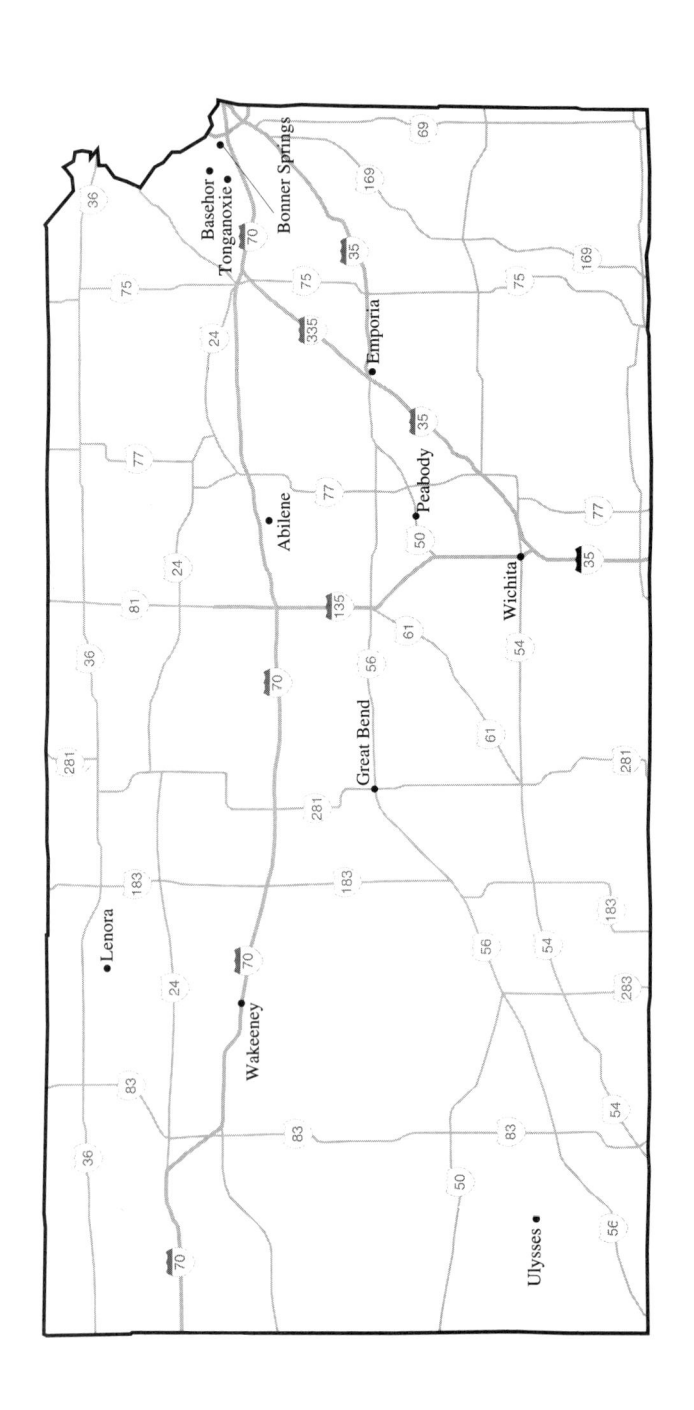

Kansas

EMPORIA

Plumb House Bed and Breakfast
628 Exchange, 66801
(316) 342-6881; (888) 445-4663 ext. 6881
www.fhtc.kansas.net/~plumb/

Step back in time for a restful stay in the restored Victorian home of early-day Emporians, George and Ellen Plumb. Experience the elegance of pocket doors, beveled glass windows, lace curtains, and antique furnishings, combined with 1990s convenience. Guests will awaken to the smell of fresh bread and home cooking. Morning coffee or afternoon tea may be taken on the balcony, front porch, or in the garden. Please inquire about accommodations for pets.

Host: Barbara Stoecklein
Rooms: 4 (PB) $50-80
Full Breakfast
Credit Cards: A, B, C, D
Notes: 2, 5, 7, 8, 9, 10, 11, 12, 14

GREAT BEND

Peaceful Acres Bed and Breakfast
Route 5, Box 153, 67530
(316) 793-7527

This sprawling farmhouse has a working windmill, small livestock, chickens, and guineas. Five miles from Great Bend and close to Cheyenne Bottoms and Quivira Wetlands, Fort Larned, Pawnee Rock, Wilson Lake, Lake Kanopolis, and Santa Fe Trail. Enjoy hospitality and the quiet of the country in this farmhouse furnished with some antiques. Homegrown and homemade foods. Full country breakfast is served. Kitchen available for guests' use.

Hosts: Dale and Doris Nitzel
Rooms: 2-3 (SB) $30
Full Breakfast
Credit Cards: None
Notes: 2, 5, 6, 7, 8, 10, 11, 12, 14

LENORA

Barbeau House
210 East Washington Avenue, 67645
(913) 567-4886

This Queen Anne Victorian, circa 1899, has been restored to a new reign as a "painted lady" of the Plains. Delightful features of the house are a massive handworked oak staircase, exquisite etched glass exterior doors, and elegant light fixtures. The fireplace and a working player piano reflect the elegance of the period. Hosts' collection of trains and pocket watches will also intrigue the guests. Full French breakfast is served. Open May through September.

Host: Lea Hall
Rooms: 4 (1 PB; 3 SB) $40-50
Full Breakfast
Credit Cards: F
Notes: 2, 3, 4, 7, 8, 9

PEABODY

Jones Sheep Farm Bed and Breakfast
Rural Route 2, Box 185, 66866
(316) 983-2815

Enjoy a turn-of-the-century home in a pastoral setting. On a working sheep farm "at the end of the road," the house is furnished

Jones Sheep Farm

---

7 No smoking; 8 Children welcome; 9 Social drinking allowed; 10 Tennis nearby; 11 Swimming nearby; 12 Golf nearby; 13 Skiing nearby; 14 May be booked through a travel agent; 15 Handicapped accessible.

in 1930s style (no telephone or TV). Quiet and private. A wonderful historic small town is nearby. The full country breakfast features fresh farm produce. Only one party is booked at a time. One room has a double bed and crib.

Hosts: Gary and Marilyn Jones
Rooms: 2 (SB) $45
Full Breakfast
Credit Cards: None
Notes: 2, 5, 6, 7, 8, 10, 11, 12

TONGANOXIE

Almeda's Bed and Breakfast Inn
220 South Main Street, 66086
(913) 845-2295

In a picturesque small town which was designated a historic site in 1983, the inn dates back to World War I. Sip a cup of coffee at the stone bar used as a bus stop in 1930. In fact, this room was the inspiration for the play *Bus Stop*. Close driving distance to Kansas City International Airport, Kansas City Country Club Plaza, the Renaissance Festival, Sandstone Theatre, Woodlands racetrack, the National Agriculture Hall of Fame, the University of Kansas, Weston and Snow Creek skiing, Topeka state capitol, and antique shops. Continental plus breakfast is served.

Hosts: Almeda and Richard Tinberg
Rooms: 7 (PB and SB) $40-65
Continental Breakfast
Credit Cards: None
Notes: 2, 5, 7, 9, 11, 12

ULYSSES

Fort's Cedar View, Inc.
1675 West Patterson, 67880-8423
(316) 356-2570

Fort's Cedar View is in the heart of the world's largest natural-gas field. It is on the Santa Fe Trail, eight miles north of famed Wagon Bed Springs, the first source of water after crossing the Cimarron River west of Dodge City, which is 80 miles northeast.

Host: Lynda Fort
Rooms: 5 (2 PB; 3 SB) $45-65
Full Breakfast
Credit Cards: None
Notes: 2, 5, 7, 8, 10, 11, 12

WAKEENEY

Thistle Hill Bed and Breakfast
Route 1, Box 93, 67672
(785) 743-2644
www.bbonline.com/ks/thistlehill

Halfway between Kansas City and Denver along I-70, Thistle Hill is described by guests as "an oasis on the prairie." Thistle Hill is surrounded by cottage-style herb and flower gardens. The indoor spa provides a view of the adjoining 60-acre prairie-wildflower restoration with hiking paths. Experience farm life and the natural beauty of western Kansas or visit Castle Rock, the Cottonwood Ranch, and Sternberg Museum. The hosts' special freshly ground whole-wheat pancakes are available on request. Gift shop on premises.

Hosts: Dave and Mary Hendricks
Rooms: 3 (3 PB) $55-75
Full Breakfast
Credit Cards: A, B
Notes: 2, 5, 7, 8, 9, 10, 11, 12, 14

WICHITA

The Castle Inn Riverside
1155 North River Boulevard, 67203
(316) 263-9300

The Castle Inn Riverside, the historic Campbell Castle, was built in 1888 by Colonel Burton Harvey Campbell. This small luxury inn features 14 uniquely appointed guest rooms. Amenities include Jacuzzi tubs for two (six rooms), fireplaces (12 rooms), complimentary wine and hors d'oeuvres, and an assortment of homemade desserts and gourmet coffees served each evening. Enjoy

---

NOTES: Credit cards accepted: A MasterCard; B Visa; C American Express; D Discover; E Diner's Club; F Other; 2 Personal checks accepted; 3 Lunch available; 4 Dinner available; 5 Open all year; 6 Pets welcome;

Castle Inn Riverside

features such as the 250-year-old English staircase, fretwork, six stained-glass windows, and eight antique European fireplaces. Children over 10 are welcome.

Hosts: Terry and Paula Lowry
Rooms: 14 (PB) $125-250
Full Breakfast
Credit Cards: A, B, D
Notes: 2, 5, 7, 9, 10, 12, 14, 15

Inn at the Park

3751 East Douglas, 67218
(316) 652-0500; (800) 258-1951

Elegant Old World charm and comfort in a completely renovated mansion. Twelve distinctive suites, 10 in the main house and 2 in the carriage house. Some of the amenities include fireplaces, whirlpool baths, a private courtyard, a hot tub, and many spacious three-room suites. A preferred hideaway among people looking for a romantic retreat or convenient base of operation for corporate guests. Named one of the top 10 outstanding new inns in the country by *Inn Review* newsletter in 1989, it has been rated "outstanding" by the ABBA for the last five years. Smoking is permitted in designated areas only.

Host: Michelle Hickman
Rooms: 12 (PB) $89-149
Continental Breakfast
Credit Cards: A, B, C, D
Notes: 2, 3, 4, 5, 8, 9, 10, 14

---

7 No smoking; 8 Children welcome; 9 Social drinking allowed; 10 Tennis nearby; 11 Swimming nearby; 12 Golf nearby; 13 Skiing nearby; 14 May be booked through a travel agent; 15 Handicapped accessible.

Michigan

Michigan

Saravilla

ALMA

Saravilla Bed and Breakfast

633 North State Street, 48801-1640
(517) 463-4078; FAX (517) 463-8624
e-mail: ljdarrow@saravilla.com

Enjoy the charm and original features of this 1894, 11,000-square-foot Dutch Colonial home. Guests may enjoy the pool table, the fireplace in the library, and the hot tub in the sunroom. The guest rooms are spacious and quiet; several have fireplaces, and one has a whirlpool tub. A full breakfast is served each morning in the elegant turret dining room. Soaring Eagle Casino is just 20 minutes away.

Hosts: Linda and Jon Darrow
Rooms: 7 (PB) $70-110
Full Breakfast
Credit Cards: A, B, D
Notes: 2, 5, 7, 8, 9, 10, 11, 12, 14

ANN ARBOR

Bed and Breakfast on Campus

921 East Huron, 48104
(734) 994-9100; (734) 741-7527
www.annarbor.org/pages/bbcampus.html

Bed and Breakfast on Campus is housed in a unique contemporary building across the street from the University of Michigan campus and five university theaters. It is within walking distance to the hospital and Ann Arbor's cosmopolitan downtown area with diverse restaurants and theaters. It has a spacious common area and six elegantly furnished guest rooms with private baths. A full gourmet breakfast is served. Covered parking is provided at the main entrance.

Host: Virginia Mikola
Rooms: 5 (PB) $60-90
Full Breakfast
Credit Cards: A, B, C
Notes: 5, 7, 10, 11, 12

Bed & Breakfast On Campus

The Urban Retreat Bed and Breakfast

2759 Canterbury Road, 48104
(734) 971-8110

This contemporary ranch homestay has provided quiet comfort to business and

---

NOTES: Credit cards accepted: A MasterCard; B Visa; C American Express; D Discover; E Diner's Club; F Other; 2 Personal checks accepted; 3 Lunch available; 4 Dinner available; 5 Open all year; 6 Pets welcome; 7 No smoking; 8 Children welcome; 9 Social drinking allowed; 10 Tennis nearby; 11 Swimming nearby; 12 Golf nearby; 13 Skiing nearby; 14 May be booked through a travel agent; 15 Handicapped accessible.

pleasure travelers since 1986. Minutes from downtown, the Urban Retreat is tucked away on a quiet, tree-lined street, with adjacent parkland offering walking trails. Guest rooms and common areas are lovingly furnished with antiques. Breakfast is served overlooking the gardens. Central air. Resident cats. Inspected and approved. The Urban Retreat welcomes guests from all cultures, races, and lifestyles. Smoking is permitted in designated areas only.

Hosts: Gloria Krys and André Rosalik
Rooms: 2 (1 PB; 1 SB) $55-65
Full Breakfast
Credit Cards: A, B
Notes: 2, 5, 9, 10, 11, 12, 13

Woods Inn

2887 Newport Road, 48103
(313) 665-8394

Built in 1859, this large, two-story stone and wood Early American home contains four commodious guest rooms as well as an ample kitchen, dining room, parlor, and a large screened porch filled with wicker furniture. Nestled on three acres of pine and hardwoods, the inn shares its scenic setting with abundant gardens, a barn, and one of the few remaining smokehouses in Michigan. Inside, the comfortable Early American furnishings and period collections of ironstone, colored art glass, and Staffordshire figurines all create a welcoming, hospitable ambiance that puts visitors at their ease and brings them back again and again.

Host: Barbara Inwood
Rooms: 4 (2 PB; 2 SB) $60-75
Full Breakfast
Credit Cards: D
Notes: 2, 5, 7, 8, 9, 10, 11, 12, 13, 15

BATTLE CREEK

Greencrest Manor

6174 Halbert Road, 49017
(616) 962-8633

To experience Greencrest is to step back in time to a way of life that is rare today. From the moment of entrance through iron gates, guests will be mesmerized. This French Normandy mansion on the highest elevation of St. Mary's Lake is constructed of sandstone, slate, and copper. Formal gardens, fountains, and garden architecture. Chosen by *Country Inns* as one of the "top twelve inns" in North America. Air conditioning, cable TV, and telephones are in all rooms. Continental plus breakfast is served.

Hosts: Kathy and Tom Van Daff
Rooms: 8 (6 PB; 2 SB) $75-200
Continental Breakfast
Credit Cards: A, B, C, E
Notes: 2, 5, 7, 8, 9, 10, 12, 13

BAY CITY

Clements Inn

1712 Center Avenue M-25, 48708
(800) 442-4605; www.laketolake.com/clements/

This 1886 Queen Anne Victorian home features six fireplaces, magnificent woodwork, an oak staircase, amber-colored glass windows, working gas lamps, organ pipes, two claw-foot tubs, and a third-floor ballroom. Each of the six bedrooms includes cable TV, VCR, telephone, a private bath, and air conditioning. Special features include in-room gas fireplaces, in-room whirlpool tubs, and the 1,200-square-foot, Alfred Lord Tennyson Ballroom Suite.

Woods Inn

NOTES: Credit cards accepted: A MasterCard; B Visa; C American Express; D Discover; E Diner's Club; F Other; 2 Personal checks accepted; 3 Lunch available; 4 Dinner available; 5 Open all year; 6 Pets welcome;

Hosts: Brian and Karen Hepp
Rooms: 6 (PB) $70-175
Continental Breakfast
Credit Cards: A, B, C, D, E
Notes: 2, 5, 7, 9, 10, 12, 14

BAY VIEW

Gingerbread House

1130 Bluff Street, P.O. Box 1273, 49770
(616) 347-3538
www.achildsview.com/mghouse.ibm

Pastel hues and white wicker furniture provide a romantic setting for this 1881 renovated Victorian cottage surrounded by flowers. All rooms have views of Little Traverse Bay. Deluxe home-baked Continental plus breakfast is served. No smoking or pets. On U.S. 31, one mile to Petoskey Gaslight Shopping District. Featured in *Country Home*, *Midwest Living*, *Michigan Living*, *Fodor's*.

Hosts: Mary Gruler and Margaret Perry
Rooms: 4 (PB) $90-130
Continental Breakfast
Credit Cards: A, B
Notes: 2, 7, 8, 9, 10, 11, 12

BELLAIRE

Bellaire Bed and Breakfast

212 Park Street, 49615
(616) 533-6077; (800) 545-0780
e-mail: belbed@aol.com

Stately 1879 home in the northern part of Michigan's Lower Peninsula. The home boasts a wraparound porch which overlooks expansive front grounds with maples that turn to brilliant colors for the Fall Color Tour. Golfers find "the Legend" at Shanty Creek to provide superior golfing enjoyment. During the ski season, Shanty is home to some of the finest skiing in Michigan. Water lovers have their pick of the many pristine lakes and rivers for weekend fun. Continental plus breakfast is served. Children over 12 are welcome.

Hosts: David Schulz and Jim Walker
Rooms: 4 (2 PB; 2 SB) $70-100

Continental Breakfast
Credit Cards: A, B, D
Notes: 2, 5, 7, 9, 10, 11, 12, 13

BLANEY PARK

Celibeth House Bed and Breakfast

Route 1, Box 58A, Blaney Park Road, 49836
(906) 283-3409

This lovely home is on 86 acres overlooking a small lake. The rooms are spacious and tastefully furnished with antiques. Guests may also use a large living room with fireplace, reading room, enclosed front porch, a large outside deck, and nature trails. Within an hour's drive of most of the scenic attractions in Michigan's Upper Peninsula.

Host: Elsa R. Strom
Rooms: 7 (PB) $50-78
Continental Breakfast
Credit Cards: A, B
Notes: 2, 7, 8, 9

BOYNE CITY

Deer Lake Bed and Breakfast

00631 East Deer Lake Road, 49712-9614
(616) 582-9039; FAX (616) 582-5385
e-mail: info@deerlakebb.com
www.deerlakebb.com

Waterfront bed and breakfast in a quiet country setting. Breakfast served by candlelight in the parlor at tables set with fine china and crystal. Guest rooms each have air conditioning and individual heat. Between the home and the lake is a small pond that's perfect for a quick swim or a place to sit in the morning with a cup of coffee and watch the countryside wake up. A jewelry class is available.

Hosts: Shirley and Glenn Piepenburg
Rooms: 5 (PB) $80-95
Full Breakfast
Credit Cards: A, B, D
Notes: 2, 5, 7, 8, 9, 10, 11, 12, 13, 14

---

7 No smoking; 8 Children welcome; 9 Social drinking allowed; 10 Tennis nearby; 11 Swimming nearby; 12 Golf nearby; 13 Skiing nearby; 14 May be booked through a travel agent; 15 Handicapped accessible.

BROOKLYN

The Buffalo Inn
10845 US 12, 49230
(517) 467-6521 (phone/FAX)

Comfortable, inviting...A uniquely different kind of home with a southwestern charm. Enjoy the full breakfast by the large stone fireplace. Play pinball in the game room where smoking is permitted. Five unique bedrooms with private and shared baths, one with fireplace. The inn is along the road known as Antique Alley. The area also offers 54 lakes, numerous golf courses, fine dining, and family attractions. The hostess, Carol Zarr, welcomes guests to the beautiful Irish hills.

Host: Carol Zarr
Rooms: 5 (1 PB; 4 SB) $45-85
Full Breakfast
Credit Cards: A, B
Notes: 2, 5, 8, 9, 11, 12

The Buffalo Inn

The Chicago Street Inn
219 Chicago Street, 49230
(517) 592-3888; www.getaway2smi.com/esi

An 1880s Queen Anne Victorian, in the heart of the Irish Hills. Furnished with family and area antiques. Antiquing, hiking, biking, swimming, shops, museums, and more are available. Area of quaint villages. Four Jacuzzi suites are available.

Hosts: Karen and Bill Kerr
Rooms: 6 (PB) $80-165
Full Breakfast
Credit Cards: A, B, D
Notes: 2, 5, 7, 9, 11, 12

Dewey Lake Manor

Dewey Lake Manor Bed and Breakfast
11811 Laird Road, 49230
(517) 467-7122; FAX (517) 467-2356
www.getaway2smi.com/dewey

Sitting atop a knoll on Dewey Lake, a country retreat awaits guests in the Irish Hills of southern Michigan. This century-old home, furnished with antiques and original kerosene chandeliers, has four fireplaces and central air conditioning. Enjoy the paddleboat, canoe, picnics, and bonfires. Great golf and antiquing nearby. Hearty buffet breakfast is served.

Hosts: Joe and Barb Phillips
Rooms: 5 (PB) $55-85
Full Breakfast
Credit Cards: A, B, C
Notes: 2, 5, 7, 9, 11, 12, 14

CANTON

Willow Brook Inn Bed and Breakfast
44255 Warren Road, 48187
(888) 454-1919

Childhood memories...pampering pleasures. Mallard ducks in a brook, pastel flower gardens, deck, and hot tub. Accom-

---

NOTES: Credit cards accepted: A MasterCard; B Visa; C American Express; D Discover; E Diner's Club; F Other; 2 Personal checks accepted; 3 Lunch available; 4 Dinner available; 5 Open all year; 6 Pets welcome;

Dimondale, MI 63

Willow Brook Inn

modations include suites with private baths, one with a whirlpool. Comfortable antiques, childhood keepsakes, snuggly feather beds, handmade quilts, garden flowers, fluffy robes, in-room TV/VCR, and CD system. Guests' elegant candle-light breakfast (featuring recipes appearing in several nationally known cookbooks) consists of fresh fruit, home-baked delecacies, and choice of entrée. Local attractions include Greenfield Village, the Detroit Zoo, Pheasant Run Golf Course, the Summit, and antique, craft, and gift shops. Packages available. Metro airport 10 miles; 2 miles from I-275; 6 miles from I-94 and I-96.

Hosts: Michael and Bernadette Van Lenten
Rooms: 3 (PB) $95-125
Full Breakfast
Credit Cards: A, B, C
Notes: 2, 3, 4, 5, 6, 7, 8, 9, 10, 11, 12, 13, 14

CHARLEVOIX

Aaron's Windy Hill Guest Lodge
202 Michigan, 49720
(616) 547-2804; (616) 547-6100

Beautiful Victorian-style home with a huge river-stone porch where guests can enjoy a homemade buffet-style breakfast. Each spacious room is beautifully decorated and has a private bath. Three rooms can accommodate up to five people. The inn is on the main street, one block north of shops, art galleries, fine restaurants, and the drawbridge. One block east of Lake Michigan's swimming. Beautiful sunsets. Open May 15 through October 30. No smoking in rooms.

Host: Nancy DeHollander
Rooms: 8 (PB) $60-115
Full Breakfast
Credit Cards: None
Notes: 2, 8, 9, 10, 11, 12, 13, 14

The Bridge Street Inn
113 Michigan Avenue, 49720
(616) 547-6606; FAX (616) 547-1812

Beautifully restored 1895 Colonial Revival cottage with English motif. Bridal suite, antique furnishings, plush beds, and lake views. Wraparound porch. Short walk to Lake Michigan's sandy beaches, Round Lake Harbor, antique shops, art galleries, and fine restaurants. Golf nearby. The Bridge Street Inn, formerly known as Baker Cottage, is housed in a three-story home in the summer resort town of Charlevoix.

Hosts: Vera and John McKown
Rooms: 9 (3 PB: 6 SB) $75-140
Continental Breakfast
Credit Cards: A, B
Notes: 5, 7, 10, 11, 12, 13, 14

DIMONDALE

Bannick's Bed and Breakfast
4608 Michigan Road, 48821
(517) 646-0224

This large ranch-style home features attractive decor with stained-glass entrances. Almost three rural acres offer a quiet escape from the fast pace of the workday world. On a main highway (M99) five miles from Lansing and close neighbor to Michigan State University.

Hosts: Pat and Jim Bannick
Rooms: 2 (SB) $25-40
Full Breakfast
Credit Cards: None
Notes: 5, 7, 8, 9, 11, 12, 13

---

7 No smoking; 8 Children welcome; 9 Social drinking allowed; 10 Tennis nearby; 11 Swimming nearby; 12 Golf nearby; 13 Skiing nearby; 14 May be booked through a travel agent; 15 Handicapped accessible.

EMPIRE

Empire House Bed and Breakfast

11015 LaCore, South, P.O. Box 203, 49630-0203
(616) 326-5524; e-mail: hrfriend@gtii.com

This 19th-century farmhouse, on picturesque acreage, is in the beautiful Sleeping Bear Dunes National Lakeshore area. Four rooms with outside entrances are available for guests. A large screened porch and a separate two-bedroom apartment for weekly use is also on premises. A quiet, homey atmosphere, freshly ground coffee, and a wonderful breakfast. Close to the beaches of Lake Michigan, golf, tennis, hiking trails in the summer and skiing trails in the winter.

Hosts: Rosemary and Harry Friend
Rooms: 4 (1 PB; 3 SB) $55
Apartment: $65
Continental Breakfast
Credit Cards: None
Notes: 2, 5, 10, 11, 12, 13

FENNVILLE

Heritage Manor Inn

2253 Blue Star Highway, 49408
(616) 543-4384; (888) 543-4384
FAX (616) 543-4711

Country hospitality is practiced daily in this lovely English manor. Enjoy homemade country breakfast, Jacuzzi/fireplaced suites, indoor pool and whirlpool, volleyball, and basketball. Hiking and horseback riding nearby. Four townhouses, two with sunken Jacuzzis. Elegant white marble fireplaces. Near Saugatuck and Lake Michigan. Ideal for family reunions and holiday retreats. Specializing in honeymoons and anniversaries.

Host: Willie Rahrig
Rooms: 14 (PB) $55-145
Townhouses: 4 (PB)
Full Breakfast
Credit Cards: A, B, D
Notes: 5, 8, 9, 10, 11, 12, 13, 14

J. Paules Fenn Inn

2254 South 58th Street, 49408
(616) 561-2836 (phone/FAX)

Nestled in the countryside of Fennville, near beautiful Hutchins Lake guests will find this traditional bed and breakfast that was built around the turn of the century. Enjoy quiet country living on this acre and one-half, yet guests are minutes from cross-country ski trails, snowmobiling, golfing, biking, hiking Fenn Valley winery, and much more. The bed and breakfast is also just minutes from Holland, Saugatuck, Allegan, and South Haven.

Hosts: Paulette J. Clouse and Ewald Males
Rooms: 5 (2 PB: 3 SB) $70-130
Full Breakfast
Credit Cards: A, B, D
Notes: 2, 5, 6, 7, 8, 9, 10, 11, 12, 13, 15

The Kingsley House

626 West Main Street, 49408
(616) 561-6425
www.laketolake.com/kingsleyhouse

An elegant Victorian inn on the edge of Fennville, near Saugatuck, Holland, and South Haven. The guest rooms are decorated in Victorian elegance. Honeymoon suite with Jacuzzi and fireplace. Beaches, shopping, fine dining, and a playhouse theater nearby. The Allegan State Forest, with miles of nature trails, is enjoyable to explore. Bicycle rides to the lake or winery

Heritage Manor Inn

NOTES: Credit cards accepted: A MasterCard; B Visa; C American Express; D Discover; E Diner's Club; F Other; 2 Personal checks accepted; 3 Lunch available; 4 Dinner available; 5 Open all year; 6 Pets welcome;

Frankenmuth, MI

The Kingsley House

available. Country lover's delight. Featured in *Innsider* magazine, "Great Lakes Getaway." Chosen one of the top 50 inns in America by *Inn Times*. A Continental plus breakfast is available for those who do not want a full breakfast.

Hosts: Gary and Kari King
Rooms: 8 (PB) $80-165
Full Breakfast
Credit Cards: A, B, C, D
Notes: 2, 4, 5, 7, 9, 10, 11, 12, 13, 14

FLINT

Avon House Bed and Breakfast
518 Avon Street, 48503
(810) 232-6861

Built in 1893, Avon House is an enchanting Victorian home with spacious rooms, beautiful warm woodwork, and antiques.

Avon House

A comfortable, homey setting for business persons, tourists, and out-of-town guests to enjoy a delicious homemade breakfast served every morning. In Flint's college and cultural area near University of Michigan (Flint) and Mott College. Playyard for children. Frankenmuth, Birch Run, and Cross Roads villages within short driving distances.

Host: Arletta E. Minore
Rooms: 3 (SB) $40
Full Breakfast
Credit Cards: F
Notes: 2, 5, 7, 8, 9, 10, 11, 12, 13

FRANKENMUTH

Bavarian Town

Bavarian Town Bed and Breakfast
206 Beyerlein Street, 48734
(517) 652-8057; e-mail: b+bedb@juno.com

Beautifully redecorated rooms in a Cape Cod dwelling just three blocks off of Main Street in the most popular tourist town of Michigan. Quiet residential district. Air conditioning. Bilingual hosts, direct descendants of original German settlers of Frankenmuth, are willing to share hospitality hour and information on Frankenmuth. Full breakfast includes fresh fruit, baked goods, and hot entreés. Private toilet and sink. Rooms share a shower. Beautiful yard.

Hosts: Kathy and Louie Weiss
Rooms: 2 (PB/SB) $65-70
Full Breakfast
Credit Cards: None
Notes: 2, 5, 7, 8, 9, 10, 11, 12, 13

---

7 No smoking; 8 Children welcome; 9 Social drinking allowed; 10 Tennis nearby; 11 Swimming nearby; 12 Golf nearby; 13 Skiing nearby; 14 May be booked through a travel agent; 15 Handicapped accessible.

Bed and Breakfast at The Pines
327 Ardussi Street, 48734
(517) 652-9019
www.tir.com/~dhodge

Frankenmuth, a Bavarian village, is Michigan's number-one tourist attraction. The hosts' ranch-style home is within walking distance of tourist areas and famous restaurants. Bedrooms tastefully decorated with heirloom quilts, antique accents, and ceiling fans. Enjoy homemade breads and rolls as part of a modified breakfast. Recipes shared. No smoking, please.

Hosts: Richard and Donna Hodge
Rooms: 3 (1 PB; 2 SB) $40-50
Full Breakfast
Credit Cards: None
Notes: 2, 5, 7, 9, 12

Bed and Breakfast at the Pines

GLEN ARBOR

Sylvan Inn
6680 Western Avenue, 49636
(616) 334-4333

The Sylvan Inn is a beautifully decorated historic landmark building in the heart of the Sleeping Bear Dunes National Lakeshore. Its easy access to Lake Michigan and other inland lakes makes a stay at the Sylvan Inn a unique experience. Closed March, April, and November. Children over seven welcome.

Hosts: Jenny and Bill Olson
Rooms: 14 (7 PB; 7 SB) $60-125
Continental Breakfast

Sylvan Inn

Credit Cards: A, B
Notes: 2, 7, 9, 10, 11, 12, 13, 14

The White Gull Inn
5926 SW Manitou Trail, 49636
(616) 334-4486; FAX (616) 334-3546

One of Michigan's most scenic areas is home to the White Gull Inn, circa 1900. With the Sleeping Bear Dunes just minutes away and alluring Lake Michigan just one block away, visitors will find no shortage of sightseeing or recreational activities during a stay here. Glen Lake is three miles away. Walk to the area's fine dining and shopping opportunities. The inn's farmhouse setting, country decor, and comfortable guest rooms offer guests a relaxing haven no matter what the season. Each room is decorated with antiques and cable TV. Breakfast consists of a variety of fruit, juices, and home-baked items.

Hosts: Bill and Dotti Thompson
Rooms: 5 (5 SB) $55-70
Continental Breakfast
Credit Cards: A, B, C, D
Notes: 2, 5, 7, 10, 11, 12, 13

GRAND HAVEN

Boyden House Inn Bed and Breakfast
301 South Fifth Street, 49417
(616) 846-3538

Built in 1874, this Victorian-style inn is in the heart of Grand Haven, within walking

NOTES: Credit cards accepted: A MasterCard; B Visa; C American Express; D Discover; E Diner's Club; F Other; 2 Personal checks accepted; 3 Lunch available; 4 Dinner available; 5 Open all year; 6 Pets welcome;

distance of shopping, restaurants, beach, and the boardwalk. Some rooms have fireplaces and balconies. Two rooms have two-person whirlpool baths. Central air conditioning. Great kitchen and two common rooms are available for guest use. Full homemade breakfast served in the beautiful dining room. Limited handicapped accessibility.

Hosts: Corrie and Berend Snoeyer
Rooms: 7 (PB) $65-100
Suites: 2 (PB) $110-120
Full Breakfast
Credit Cards: A, B, C, D
Notes: 2, 5, 7, 8, 9, 10, 11, 12, 13, 14

Seascape Bed and Breakfast

20009 Breton, Spring Lake, 49456
(616) 842-8409

On private Lake Michigan beach, scenic lakefront rooms. Relax and enjoy the warm hospitality and cozy "country living" ambiance of this nautical lakeshore home. Full country breakfast served in gathering room with fieldstone fireplace or on large wraparound deck. Both offer panoramic views of Grand Haven Harbor. Quiet residential setting. Stroll or cross-country ski through dune preserve. A charming retreat for all seasons.

Host: Susan Meyer
Rooms: 3 (PB) $75-150
Full Breakfast
Credit Cards: A, B
Notes: 2, 5, 7, 9, 10, 11, 12, 13, 14

Village Park Bed and Breakfast

60 West Park Street, Fruitport, 49415-9668
(616) 865-6289; (800) 469-1118
www.bbonline.com/mi/villagepark

Overlooking the welcoming waters of Spring Lake and Village Park where guests can picnic, play tennis, or use the pedestrian bike path and boat launch. Spring Lake has access to Lake Michigan. Relaxing common area with fireplace; guests may also relax on the decks or in the hot tub and use the exercise facility with sauna and massage table. Historic setting of mineral springs health

Village Park

resort. Serving the Grand Haven and Muskegon areas. Close to Hoffmaster Park and Gillette Sand Dune Nature Center.

Host: John Hewett
Rooms: 6 (PB) $60-90
Full and Continental Breakfast
Credit Cards: A, B, D
Notes: 2, 5, 7, 8, 9, 10, 11, 12, 13, 14

GRAND RAPIDS

Bed and Breakfast of Grand Rapids

510 Paris Avenue Southeast, 49503
(616) 451-4849; (800) 551-5126

Bed and Breakfast of Grand Rapids is a reservation service for two homestays in the 1,500-property Heritage Hill Historic District. Lovely and unique accommodations vary, which include the 1889 Georgian Revival Brayton House and 1896 Shingle-style Tobermory House. Both of these homes offer easy access to freeways, public transportation, and the downtown cultural, business, shopping, and entertainment center. Cot and crib are available. Swimming is 35 miles away.

Contact: George Seamon (reservation service)
Rooms: 6 (3 PB; 3 SB) $60-80
Full Breakfast
Credit Cards: A, B, C
Notes: 2, 5, 7, 8, 9, 10, 12, 13

---

7 No smoking; 8 Children welcome; 9 Social drinking allowed; 10 Tennis nearby; 11 Swimming nearby; 12 Golf nearby; 13 Skiing nearby; 14 May be booked through a travel agent; 15 Handicapped accessible.

Fountain Hill Bed and Breakfast

222 Fountain Northeast, 49503
(616) 458-6621; (800) 261-6621
FAX (616) 235-7536

Fountain Hill's gracious atmosphere and attention to details will sweep guests off to sheer relaxation. This 19th-century home is ideally suited for the corporate traveler and the tourist alike. Feather beds, down comforters, cable TV, VCR, soft bathrobes, Jacuzzi tubs, and candlelight breakfasts are just the beginning of the hosts' attempts to pamper their guests. The bed and breakfast is within walking distance of downtown, theaters, restaurants, convention center, museums, and night clubs. Private off-street parking.

Rooms: 4 (PB) $65-110
Full Breakfast
Credit Cards: A, B, C, D
Notes: 2, 4, 5, 7, 9, 10, 11, 12, 13, 14

HARRISON

Carriage House Inn

1515 Grant Avenue, P.O. Box 130, 48625
(517) 539-1300; FAX (517) 539-5661
e-mail: carhsinn@glccompters.com

The Carriage House Inn is nestled in a pine plantation, overlooking beautiful Budd Lake, offering its guests intimate accommodations on 127 acres. The seven guest rooms have private baths, most having whirlpool tubs, color cable TVs, VCRs, telephones, coffee makers, refrigerators, and air conditioning. Executive retreat accommodations, private retreats, receptions and training facilities are also available. Breakfast is provided featuring a wide selections of egg dishes, pancakes, quiches, coffee, tea, juice, and fruit.

Host: John
Rooms: 7 (PB) $75-135
Full Breakfast
Credit Cards: A, B, C
Notes: 2, 5, 7, 8, 9, 10, 11, 12, 13, 14, 15

HOLLAND

Dutch Colonial Inn

560 Central Avenue, 49423
(616) 396-3664; FAX (616) 396-0461
www.laketolake.com/dutchcolonialinn

The award-winning Dutch Colonial Inn, built in 1928, features elegant decor with 1930s furnishings and lovely heirloom antiques. All guest rooms have tiled private baths, some with whirlpool tubs for two, and fireplaces. Honeymoon suites available for that special getaway. Attractions include excellent shopping, Hope College, bike paths, ski trails, and Michigan's finest beaches. Business people welcome; corporate rates available. Air conditioning. Open year-round with special Christmas touches. Dutch hospitality at its finest.

Hosts: Bob and Pat Elenbaas
Rooms: 4 (PB) $60-150
Full Breakfast
Credit Cards: A, B, C, D
Notes: 2, 5, 7, 10, 11, 12, 13, 14

Dutch Colonial Inn

North Shore Inn of Holland

686 North Shore Drive, 49424
(616) 394-9050

Views of the blue waters of Lake Macatawa, gardens of colorful perennials, rich interior decor, comfortable beds, and a gourmet breakfast are all found at the

---

NOTES: Credit cards accepted: A MasterCard; B Visa; C American Express; D Discover; E Diner's Club; F Other; 2 Personal checks accepted; 3 Lunch available; 4 Dinner available; 5 Open all year; 6 Pets welcome;

North Shore Inn of Holland. Three bedrooms offer a choice of lake views, private or shared baths, balconies, king-, queen-size, or double beds. Two and one-half miles from downtown Holland and Hope College, the inn is adjacent to 25 miles of bike paths, and is five miles from Lake Michigan. Surrounded by two acres; a quiet and peaceful setting is assured. Children over 12 welcome.

Hosts: Kurt and Beverly Van Crenderen
Rooms: 3 (2 PB; 1 SB) $95-110
Full Breakfast
Credit Cards: None
Notes: 2, 7, 9, 10, 11, 12, 14

HOUGHTON

Charleston House Historic Inn

918 College Avenue, 49931
(800) 482-7404; FAX (906) 482-7068

The Charleston House Historic Inn, of 1900 Georgian architecture, is listed in the national register. Double veranda, ceiling fans, wicker furniture. Ornate woodwork, stained glass windows, library with fireplace, high ceilings, grand staircase. Comfortable reproduction furnishings, king-size canopied and twin-size beds. All guest rooms have private baths, air conditioning, color cable TV, telephones, in-room coffee/tea service. Some rooms with water views, fireplace, and private veranda. AAA-approved. Smoking limited to garden. Children 12 and older welcome.

Charleston House Historic Inn

Hosts: John and Helen Sullivan
Rooms: 5 (PB) $98-165
Full Breakfast
Credit Cards: A, B, C
Notes: 2, 5, 7, 9, 10, 11, 12, 13, 14

ITHACA

Chaffins Balmoral Farm Bed 'n Breakfast

1245 West Washington Road, 48847
(517) 875-3410

Turn-of-the-century farmhouse on cash-crop farm. Easily identified by its stone wall and large gambrel-roofed barn. Guests' stay at Balmoral Farm consists of agricultural information, overnight stay, and hot country breakfast featuring homemade blueberry muffins. The remodeled home, furnished with family antiques, had its kitchen featured in *Country Woman*. Central Michigan University and Alma College are nearby. Hiking, bicycling, bowling, and roller skating are all nearby, in addition to antique and gift boutiques in neighboring towns. Closed November 15 through April 15.

Host: Sue Chaffin
Rooms: 2 (SB) $50
Full Breakfast
Credit Cards: None
Notes: 2, 10, 11, 12

JONES

Sanctuary at Wildwood

58138 M-40, 49061
(616) 244-5910; (800) 249-5910
e-mail: wildwoodinns@voyagen.net
www.rivercountry.com/saw

The Sanctuary at Wildwood, built as a millionaire's estate, has been transformed into a unique nature-orientated bed and breakfast on 95 acres of wooded meadows that abound with wildlife. Walking trails enable guests to enjoy nature all four seasons. Each suite has a fireplace, Jacuzzi, and private bath. Enjoy golfing, canoeing, wineries, and skiing

7 No smoking; 8 Children welcome; 9 Social drinking allowed; 10 Tennis nearby; 11 Swimming nearby; 12 Golf nearby; 13 Skiing nearby; 14 May be booked through a travel agent; 15 Handicapped accessible.

nearby. Full breakfast. Innkeepers enjoy pampering the guests.

Host: Dick and Dolly Buerille
Rooms: 11 (PB) $129-159
Full Breakfast
Credit Cards: A, B, C, D, E
Notes: 2, 5, 7, 9, 10, 11, 12, 13, 14, 15

JONESVILLE

The Munro House

202 Maumee, 49250
(517) 849-9292; (800) 320-3792

This 1840 Greek Revival structure was built by George C. Munro, a brigadier general during the Civil War. Visitors can see the secret room used to hide runaway slaves as part of the Underground Railroad. The seven cozy guest rooms, all with private baths, are furnished with period antiques, many with working fireplaces and Jacuzzis. There are five common area rooms, including a library and breakfast room with open hearth fireplace. A full breakfast and evening snack are served.

Host: Joyce A. Yarde
Rooms: 7 (PB) $75-150
Full Breakfast
Credit Cards: A, B, C, D
Notes: 2, 5, 7, 8, 9, 10, 11, 12, 14

KALAMAZOO

Hall House

106 Thompson Street, 49006
(616) 343-2500; (888) 761-2525
FAX (616) 343-1374; www.hallhouse.com

"Experience the Difference" in this 14-room Georgian Revival home in a national historic district. Stay in one of the five beautifully appointed guest rooms—some with fireplaces and Jacuzzis, all with private baths, CATV/VCRs,

air conditioning, and telephones. Full hot breakfast served on weekends. Smoke-free. Near colleges and downtown. Business travelers are welcome.

Hosts: Jerry and Joanne Hofferth
Rooms: 5 (PB) $85-150
Full Breakfast
Credit Cards: A, B, C
Notes: 2, 5, 7, 9, 10, 11, 12, 13, 14

LELAND

Manitou Manor

147 North Manitou Trail, P.O. Box 864, 49654
(616) 256-7712

This century-old farmhouse, nestled among six acres of cherry orchards, makes staying on the Leelanau peninsula a peaceful experience. Manitou Manor is a historical bed and breakfast that boasts private baths and family-style breakfasts. Open year-round. From weddings to quiet getaways, it's a perfect place to celebrate the seasons.

Hosts: The Lambdins
Rooms: 5 (PB) $85-159
Full Breakfast
Credit Cards: A, B, D
Notes: 2, 5, 7, 8, 9, 10, 11, 12, 13

LOWELL

McGee Homestead Bed and Breakfast

2534 Alden Nash Northeast, 49331
(616) 897-8142

Surrounded by orchards, this 1880s brick farmhouse stands on five acres and has a barn filled with petting animals. The guest area of the bed and breakfast has its own entrance, living room with fireplace, parlor, and small kitchen. Four spacious guest rooms are individually decorated with antiques and all have private baths. A big country breakfast is served. A golf course is next door and Grand Rapids is 20 minutes away. The largest antique mall in Michigan is five miles away.

NOTES: Credit cards accepted: A MasterCard; B Visa; C American Express; D Discover; E Diner's Club; F Other; 2 Personal checks accepted; 3 Lunch available; 4 Dinner available; 5 Open all year; 6 Pets welcome;

Hosts: Bill and Ardie Barber
Rooms: 4 (PB) $38-58
Full Breakfast
Credit Cards: A, B, C, D
Notes: 2, 7, 8, 9, 10, 11, 12, 13, 14

LUDINGTON

Bed and Breakfast at Ludington
2458 South Beaune Road, 49431
(616) 843-9768

Relaxation and privacy are the order of the day here. Widely separated rooms provide homey comfort. Positioned in a beautiful creek valley on a country lane, this relaxed atmosphere is haven for nature lovers who enjoy walks, birding, star gazing, campfires, cross-country skiing, or tobogganing. Near golf course, Lake Michigan beaches, and fine restaurants. Big breakfasts, crib, tree swing, picnic table, volleyball net. Jacuzzi available September through June.

Hosts: Grace and Robert Schneider
Rooms: 3 (2 PB; 1 SB) $40-60
Full Breakfast
Credit Cards: None
Notes: 2, 5, 6, 7, 8, 9, 10, 11, 12, 13

The Inn at Ludington
701 East Ludington Avenue, 49431
(616) 845-7055

Make your own history! The Inn at Ludington has had its share of historical residents, from Hall of Famers to hometown heroes, but no one is more important than the guests who are there right now. Create your own memories while soothing oneself in an old-fashioned tub filled with bubbles, relax before a crackling fire, cuddle in a lace-covered canopied bed. Awake to sunshine and the smell of blueberry muffins baking. All the delights of this beachfront community are nearby. Beach, shops, restaurants, and crosslake car ferry within walking distance. AAA-approved.

Host: Diane Shields
Rooms: 6 (PB) $70-90
Full Breakfast
Credit Cards: A, B, C
Notes: 2, 5, 7, 8, 9, 10, 11, 12, 13, 14

The Lamplighter
602 East Ludington Avenue, 49431
(616) 843-9792; (800) 301-9792
www.laketolake.com/lamplighter

Unique centennial home in town is only minutes from beautiful, sandy Lake Michigan beaches, the car ferry to Wisconsin, and one of Michigan's most beautiful state parks. Fine antiques, original paintings and lithographs, queen-size beds, and private baths create a unique ambiance of elegance, comfort, and convenience. A whirlpool for two is the ideal setting for a romantic getaway. Gourmet breakfasts are served in the formal dining room or outdoors in the gazebo. Murder mystery weekend packages available. Smoke free.

Hosts: Judy and Heinz Bertram
Rooms: 4 (PB) $75-115
Full Breakfast
Credit Cards: A, B, C, D
Notes: 2, 5, 7, 9, 10, 11, 12, 13, 14

Snyder's Shoreline Inn
903 West Ludington Avenue, P.O. Box 667, 49431-0667
(616) 845-1261; FAX (616) 843-4441

The inn ranks among the finest in western Michigan with its tremendous views of Lake Michigan and Ludington's active deep-water harbor. Sleep comfortably in pleasant guest rooms individually decorated with a charm that reflects the owner's personal touch—stenciled walls, pieced quilts, antiques. Enjoy lake-view rooms with patios or private covered balconies, and in-room spas. Complimentary Continental breakfast served in breakfast room. Honeymoon suites and luxury barrier-free handicapped rooms. Heated outdoor pool and spa. Packages and off-season rates. Smoke free. Reservations a must. AAA. ABBA.

Hosts: Angie Snyder and Kate Whitaker
Rooms: 44 (PB) $65-229
Continental Breakfast
Credit Cards: A, B, C, D
Notes: 2, 7, 10, 11, 12, 15

---

7 No smoking; 8 Children welcome; 9 Social drinking allowed; 10 Tennis nearby; 11 Swimming nearby; 12 Golf nearby; 13 Skiing nearby; 14 May be booked through a travel agent; 15 Handicapped accessible.

MACKINAC ISLAND

Cloghaun
P.O. Box 203, 49757
(906) 847-3885

Cloghaun, a large Victorian home built in 1884, is close to shops, restaurants, and ferry lines. The name *Cloghaun* is Gaelic and means "land of little stones." Built by Thomas and Bridgett Donnelly to house their large Irish family, the Cloghaun represents the elegance and ambiance of a bygone era. "Come join us on the porch at Cloghaun and experience the Victorian charm, the romance, the serenity, and magic of Mackinac."

Host: James Bond
Rooms: 11 (9 PB; 2 SB) $80-130
Continental Breakfast
Credit Cards: None
Notes: 2, 8, 9, 10, 11, 12, 14

Cloghaun

Haan's 1830 Inn
P.O. Box 123, 49757
3418 Oakwood Avenue,
Island Lake, IL 60042 (winter address)
(906) 847-6244; (847) 526-2662 (winter)

Lovely restored Greek Revival home furnished with antiques and decorated from the period. In a quiet neighborhood three blocks from historic fort and 1900s downtown. Dining room has 12-foot harvest table for breakfast of home-baked cakes and muffins, plus cereals and fruit. A short ferry ride brings guests to this historic and beautiful island. Sightseeing, bicycling, horseback riding, fine dining, golf, tennis, and shopping

Haan's 1830 Inn

nearby. Or sit on one of the three porches and watch the horse-drawn carriages go by.

Hosts: Nicholas and Nancy Haan
Rooms: 7 (5 PB; 2 SB) $80-128
Continental Breakfast
Credit Cards: None
Notes: 2, 7, 8, 10, 11, 12

Metivier Inn
Market Street, P.O. Box 285, 49757
(906) 847 6234; www.mackinac.com/

The Metivier Inn is conveniently on Market Street in the downtown historic district. This small lovely country inn offers bedrooms with private baths and efficiency apartment. Guests may also enjoy the cozy living room and the spacious, comfortable wicker-furnished front porch. A Continental plus breakfast is served to all guests.

Hosts: George and Angela Leonard
Rooms: 21 (PB) $115-255
Continental Breakfast
Credit Cards: A, B, C, D
Notes: 2, 7, 10, 11, 12, 13, 14, 15

MANISTEE

1879 E. E. Douville House
111 Pine Street, 49660
(616) 723-8654

This Victorian home, completed with lumber from nearby forests, features ornate pine

NOTES: Credit cards accepted: A MasterCard; B Visa; C American Express; D Discover; E Diner's Club; F Other; 2 Personal checks accepted; 3 Lunch available; 4 Dinner available; 5 Open all year; 6 Pets welcome;

Muskegon, MI 73

1879 E. E. Douville House

woodwork hand-carved by area craftsmen. Interior wooden shutters on windows, a winding staircase, and elaborate archways with pocket doors are also original to the house. Antiques and collectibles fill the home. Ceiling fans in every room. Manistee Victorian Village, riverwalk to Lake Michigan, and historic buildings are nearby.

Hosts: Barbara and Bill Johnson
Rooms: 2 (SB) $55-65
Continental Breakfast
Credit Cards: None
Notes: 2, 5, 7, 9, 10, 11, 12, 13

MENDON

Mendon Country Inn

440 West Main Street, P.O. Box 98, 49072
(616) 496-8132; (800) 304-3366
FAX (616) 496-8403
e-mail: wildwoodinns@voyagen.net
www.rivercoutnry.com/mci

The historic Wakeman House, now known as the Mendon Country Inn, was originally built in 1843 and rebuilt out of brick in 1873 by Adams Wakeman. Eight-foot windows, high ceilings, and spacious rooms complement the walnut spiral staircase in the lobby. There are numerous antique shops, a local Amish settlement, flea markets, golf, and wineries nearby. There are bicycles for two and canoes available at the inn. Hosts endeavor to provide guests with the comforts of home, the friendliness of small-town life, a great Continental plus breakfast, nine Jacuzzi suites with fireplaces, and a truly enjoyable stay. Smoking not permitted in public areas.

Hosts: Dick and Dolly Buerkle
Rooms: 18 (PB) $50-159
Continental Breakfast
Credit Cards: A, B, C, D
Notes: 2, 5, 8, 9, 10, 11, 12, 13, 14, 15

MOUNT PLEASANT

Country Chalet Bed and Breakfast

723 South Meridian Road, 48858
(517) 772-9259

The Country Chalet is a comfortable Bavarian-style home atop a hill surrounded by rolling wooded farmland, 25 acres of pastures, and woods and ponds that are playgrounds to wild animals and birds. Guests in the three upper-level bedrooms share a living/dining room with fireplace, and all guests are welcome to enjoy the chalet's sauna, game room, and fireplace in the lounge. For those who love to watch good college competition, Central Michigan University is less than a 10-minute drive from the chalet.

Hosts: Ron and Carolyn Lutz
Rooms: 3 (SB) $49-69
Full Breakfast
Credit Cards: None
Notes: 2, 5, 7, 8, 9, 12

MUSKEGON

Port City Victorian Inn

1259 Lakeshore Drive, 49441
(616) 759-0205; (800) 274-3574
e-mail: pcvicinn@gte.com
www.bbonline.com/mi/portcity

An 1877 romantic Victorian getaway on the bluffs of Muskegon Lake. Just minutes from Lake Michigan beaches, state parks, downtown theaters, sports arena, and restaurants. Five-bedroom home featuring suites with

---

7 No smoking; 8 Children welcome; 9 Social drinking allowed; 10 Tennis nearby; 11 Swimming nearby; 12 Golf nearby; 13 Skiing nearby; 14 May be booked through a travel agent; 15 Handicapped accessible.

Port City Victorian Inn

lake views and private double-whirlpool baths. One room decorated with a masculine nautical look with a private bath. Other rooms are elegantly decorated with the flair of the Victorian era. The main floor is all common area for guests' enjoyment. All rooms are provided with air conditioning, cable TV, telephone jacks/computer modem ready, and desks. Fax available.

Hosts: Frederick and Barbara Schossau
Rooms: 5 (3 PB; 2 SB) $75-125
Full Breakfast
Credit Cards: A, B, C, D, E, F
Notes: 2, 5, 7, 8, 9, 10, 11, 12, 13, 14

NEW BUFFALO

Sans Souci Euro Inn

19265 South Lakeside Road, 49117
(616) 756-3141; FAX (616) 756-5511
e-mail: sans-souci@worldnetatt.net
www.sans-souci.com

The sophisticated traveler may choose a private, secluded luxury suite, a family home, or modern lakeside cottage at Sans Souci, only 70 miles from Chicago. There are 50 acres of spring-fed lakes, wildflower meadows, whispering pines, and abundant wildlife near Lake Michigan beaches. Excellent bird watching on property and in nearby parks. Cycle, fish, hike, or relax in the sun. Health club privileges. Antique and art galleries, fine restaurants nearby. Cross-country skiing.

Host: Angie Siewert (owner)
Rooms: 9 (PB) $110-220
Full Breakfast
Credit Cards: A, B, C, D
Notes: 2, 5, 8, 9, 10, 11, 12, 13, 14, 15

OSCODA

Huron House

3124 North US-23, 48750
(517) 739-9255; e-mail: huronh@oscoda.com
www.oscoda.com/huronhouse

Couples' retreat on Lake Huron. Panoramic views of Lake Huron, fireplaces, in-room whirlpool tubs, private outdoor hot tubs. Breakfast delivered to guests' room. Relax in a hot tub under the stars as Great Lakes' freighters pass in the night. The perfect escape for couples.

Hosts: Denny and Martie
Rooms: 12 (PB) $75-150
Continental Breakfast
Credit Cards: A, B
Notes: 2, 5, 7, 9, 10, 11, 12, 13

OWOSSO

R&R Farm-Ranch

308 East Hibbard Road, 48867
(517) 723-3232; (517) 723-2553

A newly remodeled farmhouse from the early 1900s, the Rossmans' ranch sits on 150 acres overlooking the Maple River Valley. The large circular drive and white board fences lead to stables of horses and cattle. Guests may use the family parlor, game room, and fireplace or stroll about the gardens and pastures along the river. Breakfast is served in the dining room or outside on the deck. Central air conditioning. Cross-country skiing nearby.

Hosts: Carl and Jeanne Rossman
Rooms: 3 (SB) $45-55
Continental Breakfast
Credit Cards: None
Notes: 2, 5, 6, 7, 8, 10, 12, 13

NOTES: Credit cards accepted: A MasterCard; B Visa; C American Express; D Discover; E Diner's Club; F Other; 2 Personal checks accepted; 3 Lunch available; 4 Dinner available; 5 Open all year; 6 Pets welcome;

PAW PAW

Carrington Country House
43799 60th Avenue, 49079
(616) 657-5321

Carrington Country House is a 150-year-old farmhouse built in the center of fruit orchards and vineyards near I-94. Just down the street is a public access to spring-fed Lake Cora. It is a short walking distance from the house. The picturesque country road leading to the house is lined with large old sugar maples that form a canopy of gold and green throughout the year. Each of the three guest rooms is uniquely decorated and filled with antiques that are family heirlooms. The guest rooms are spacious, and the glassed-in year-round front porch, where breakfast is served, looks out over a cherry orchard and a grape vineyard. Spring and fall are especially beautiful seasons to enjoy.

Host: William H. Carrington III
Rooms: 3 (SB) $45-68
Full Breakfast
Credit Cards: F
Notes: 2, 5, 6, 7, 8, 9, 11, 12

PENTWATER

The Candlewyck House Bed and Breakfast
438 East Lowell, Box 392, 49449
(616) 869-5967

This 1868 farmhouse-style inn offers a quiet setting within the historic Lake Michigan port village of Pentwater. Each of the six rooms is furnished with antiques, private bath, air conditioning, cable TV; several have fireplaces. Guests enjoy conversation in the library during winter months and relax during warmer months on the flower-filled brick patio. Walk or ride bikes to the beach and pier fishing, or browse in one of Pentwater's many boutiques. Midweek packages available. Open year-round.

Hosts: John and Mary Jo Neidow
Rooms: 6 (PB) $65-99
Full Breakfast
Credit Cards: A, B
Notes: 2, 5, 7, 8, 9, 10, 11, 12, 13, 14

Pentwater Inn

Pentwater Inn
180 East Lowell, Box 98, 49449
(616) 869-5909

Lovely 1868 Victorian Inn with English and American antiques in beautifully appointed rooms. Charter boats, marinas, international shopping, the beach on Lake Michigan, and good food and drink all within a few minutes' walk. At the inn, enjoy complimentary drinks and snacks each evening at 6:00 P.M. and a breakfast to remember. Use the hot tub, bikes, or cable TV, or relax on one of the decks. Fishing, cross-country skiing, and golf are nearby. Jacuzzi suite.

Hosts: Donna and Quintus Renshaw
Rooms: 5 (PB) $75-125
Full Breakfast
Credit Cards: A, B
Notes: 2, 5, 8, 9, 10, 11, 12, 13

PETOSKEY

Montgomery Place Bed and Breakfast
618 East Lake Street, 49770
(616) 347-1338

Montgomery Place is a magnificently preserved Victorian home sitting on a hillside in Petoskey, overlooking Lake Michigan's

---

7 No smoking; 8 Children welcome; 9 Social drinking allowed; 10 Tennis nearby; 11 Swimming nearby; 12 Golf nearby; 13 Skiing nearby; 14 May be booked through a travel agent; 15 Handicapped accessible.

Little Traverse Bay from its 80-foot grand veranda. Close to shops, galleries, and all vacation activities, Montgomery Place features four large, comfortable rooms, private baths, a full gourmet breakfast, and afternoon wine and snacks.

Hosts: Ruth Bellissimo and Diane Gillette
Rooms: 4 (PB) $95-135
Full Breakfast
Credit Cards: A, B, D
Notes: 2, 5, 7, 9, 10, 11, 12, 13, 14

Terrace Inn

1549 Glendale, P.O. Box 266, 49770
(800) 530-9898; FAX (616) 347-2407
www.freeway.net/terracei

In the heart of Victorian Bay View, a fairy-tale village of over 400 cottages adjacent to Petoskey. Unique turn-of-the-century country-inn charm. A private Lake Michigan beach, tennis courts, and hiking/cross-country ski trails are steps away. Golf and getaway packages offered. Dine outdoors on the porch or in the beautiful dining room. Excellent for romantic getaways. Complimentary use of bicycles. With 44 guest rooms, a perfect spot for retreats or conferences. Open year-round. Limited handicapped accessibility.

Hosts: Tom and Denise Erhart
Rooms: 44 (PB) $73-1039
Continental Breakfast
Credit Cards: A, B, C
Notes: 2, 4, 5, 7, 8, 9, 10, 11, 12, 13, 14, 15

PORT AUSTIN

Lake Street Manor Bed and Breakfast

8569 Lake Street, 48467
(517) 738-7720

This brick Victorian, circa 1875, has a fenced in garden back yard, pavilion with picnic tables, chairs, and a brick barbecue for guests' enjoyment. TV/VCR with movies in all rooms. Hot tub in bay room, sitting room to play cards and read. One double bed in all rooms, two persons per room. Kitchen open to guests. Special weekday rates. Two-night minimal reservations on weekends. Bikes for guests to use. Open Memorial Day weekend through Labor Day.

Hosts: Carolyn Greenwood and dog Libby
Rooms: 5 (3 PB; 2 SB) $55-65
Continental Breakfast
Credit Cards: A, B, C, D
Notes: 2, 9, 10, 11, 12, 13

PORT HOPE

The Stafford House

4489 Main Street, 48468
(517) 428-4554

With delicious full buffet-style breakfasts, afternoon refreshments, or special dinner packages, guests enjoy staying in this 1886 country Victorian home. There are also many amenities to leave guests with lasting memories. From spectacular sunrises to moonlit nights they enjoy golf, charter fishing, scenic lighthouses, antiquing, lakeshore parks, sandy beaches, and much, much more. Children over 10 welcome.

Hosts: Greg and Kathy Gephart
Rooms: 4 (PB) $60-85
Full Breakfast
Credit Cards: A, B, D
Notes: 2, 4, 5, 7, 11, 12, 13, 14

PORT SANILAC

Raymond House Inn

111 South Ridge Street, M-25, 48469
(810) 622-8800; (800) 622-7229
FAX (810) 622-9587
www.bbonline.com/mi/raymond

Luxury and comfort, 500 feet from Lake Huron harbor. Seven spacious bed chambers with warm period furnishings, private baths, and central air. Old-fashioned parlor. Fitness and "pamper" studio. Collection of original boudoir dolls. Built in 1872. Listed in register of historical sites. Original Victoriana is preserved: gingerbread facade,

---

NOTES: Credit cards accepted: A MasterCard; B Visa; C American Express; D Discover; E Diner's Club; F Other; 2 Personal checks accepted; 3 Lunch available; 4 Dinner available; 5 Open all year; 6 Pets welcome;

white icicle trim, classic moldings, and hand-crocheted trims. Highest quality rating. Nearby are lighthouse, marina, beach, swimming, restaurants, sunken wrecks, museum, barn theater, golf, tennis, and antiques.

Hosts: The Denisons
Rooms: 7 (PB) $65-85
Full Breakfast
Credit Cards: A, B
Notes: 2, 7, 9, 10, 11, 12, 14

SAGINAW

Montague Inn
1581 South Washington, 48601
(517) 752-3939; FAX (517) 752-3159
www.montagueinn.com

This restored Georgian mansion is surrounded by spacious lawns with flower and herb gardens. Summer evenings may be spent under the trees watching the wildlife. Enjoy winter evenings curled up in front of the roaring fire in the library. Fine cuisine is offered for lunch and dinner Tuesday through Saturday in the dining room overlooking the grounds. The inn is minutes from historic Frankenmuth and the outlets at Birch Run.

Rooms: 18 (16 PB; 2 SB)
Continental Breakfast
Credit Cards: A, B, C
Notes: 2, 5, 7, 8, 9, 10, 11, 12, 14, 15

ST. JOSEPH

South Cliff Inn Bed and Breakfast
1900 Lakeshore Drive, 49085
(616) 983-4881; FAX (616) 983-7391

South Cliff Inn is a beautifully renovated bed and breakfast, sitting on a bluff overlooking Lake Michigan, in the quaint village of Joseph. Several of the guest rooms have fireplaces or whirlpool tubs or both and several have balconies overlooking the lake. The innkeeper is a retired chef so get ready to enjoy the homemade breakfasts. South Cliff Inn has received the Readers Choice Award for the Best Bed and Breakfast in southwestern Michigan in 1994, 1995, 1996, and 1997.

Host: Bill Swisher
Rooms: 7 (PB) $75-165
Continental Breakfast
Credit Cards: A, B, C, D
Notes: 5, 7, 9, 10, 11, 12, 13, 14

SAUGATUCK

Beechwood Manor Bed and Breakfast
736 Pleasant Street, 49453
(616) 857-1587; FAX (616) 857-3909

Historic restored treasure on the hill. Built in 1870s as a private home for a diplomat. Listed in the national register. The finest accommodations and hospitality, heirloom furnishings. Covered veranda with rockers, the perfect relaxing setting. A waterfront cottage available. All travelers welcome. Inquire about accommodations for children. Just blocks from the heart of town. Four minutes' drive to Lake Michigan beach.

Hosts: James and Sherron Lemons
Rooms: 5 (PB) $105-185
Full and Continental Breakfast
Credit Cards: A, B
Notes: 5, 7, 9, 10, 11, 12, 13, 14

Kemah Guest House
633 Allegan Street, 49453-0389
(616) 857-2919; (800) 445-3624
www.bbonline.com/mi/kemah/

Old World elegance and charm, with a touch of Art Deco, return guests to the 1920s. Enjoy a relaxing, romantic stay "on the hill" overlooking the harbor—but only three blocks from downtown shopping and fine dining. Six guest rooms, two with whirlpool tubs, in a 5,000-plus-square-foot restored mansion await guests. Seven rooms of common area include two fireplaces, solarium with seven bayed, stained-glass

---

7 No smoking; 8 Children welcome; 9 Social drinking allowed; 10 Tennis nearby; 11 Swimming nearby; 12 Golf nearby; 13 Skiing nearby; 14 May be booked through a travel agent; 15 Handicapped accessible.

windows, rathskeller, and billiard rec-room in the old speakeasy. A Continental breakfast that is very hearty.

Owners: Terry and Cindi Tatsch
Rooms: 6 (4 PB; 2 SB) $85-140
Continental Breakfast
Credit Cards: A, B, C, D
Notes: 2, 5, 7, 9, 10, 11, 12, 13, 14

Maplewood Hotel
428 Butler Street, P.O. Box 1059, 49453
(616) 857-1771

Adjacent to the village green in the heart of downtown Saugatuck, the Maplewood Hotel is steps from shopping and restaurants. Elegant rooms with private baths, air conditioning, TVs, and telephones; some with fireplaces and Jacuzzi tubs. Gourmet breakfast is included. Enjoy the deck with a heated lap pool or the common room with a wood-burning fireplace. Conference facilities, fax, and copier are available. Rated excellent by the American Bed and Breakfast Association.

Host: Catherine L. Simon
Rooms: 15 (PB) $100-185
Full Breakfast
Credit Cards: A, B, C
Notes: 2, 5, 7, 8, 9, 10, 11, 12, 13, 14, 15

The Newnham SunCatcher Inn
131 Griffith, P.O. Box 1106, 49453
(616) 857-4249
www.bbonline.com/mi/suncatcher

Country charm with a touch of elegance. Built near the turn of the century with wraparound veranda. Inside, guests will find beautiful oak floors, graced with oval braided rugs and family antiques. One block from business district. Sun deck, hot tub, heated swimming pool, full breakfast, and air conditioning. Two suites with fireplaces and five rooms.

Hosts: Barb and Nancy
Rooms: 7 (5 PB; 2 SB) $85-120
Full Breakfast
Credit Cards: A, B
Notes: 2, 5, 7, 9, 10, 12, 13, 14

The Park House Bed and Breakfast and Cottages
888 Holland Street, 49453
(616) 857-4535; (800) 321-4535
FAX (616) 857-1065
e-mail: parkhouse@softhouse.com

Saugatuck's oldest residence (circa 1857), Susan B. Anthony once slept here and now guests can too. Full breakfast, air conditioning, close to town, beach, and cross-country trails. Three bedrooms for two, one family suite, two Jacuzzi suites, and two cottages feature fireplaces. Some offer TV/VCR, telephone, breakfast in bed. Handicapped accessible. Winter brings murder mysteries and progressive dinner packages. Inquire about their bed and breakfast in Mexico.

Hosts: Joe and Lynda Petty; Dan Osborn
Rooms: 8 (PB) $95-165
Full Breakfast
Credit Cards: A, B, C, D
Notes: 2, 5, 7, 8, 9, 10, 11, 12, 13, 14, 15

"The Porches" Bed and Breakfast
2297 Lakeshore Drive, Fennville, 49408
(616) 543-4162

Built in 1897, "The Porches" offers five guest rooms, each with private bath. Only three miles south of Saugatuck, with its own private beach and hiking trails. Large common room has TV. Inn overlooks Lake Michigan. Beautiful sunsets from the front

The Newnham SunCatcher Inn

NOTES: Credit cards accepted: A MasterCard; B Visa; C American Express; D Discover; E Diner's Club; F Other; 2 Personal checks accepted; 3 Lunch available; 4 Dinner available; 5 Open all year; 6 Pets welcome;

"The Porches"

porch. Open May 1 through November 1. Full breakfast on Sunday. Continental plus breakfast Monday through Saturday. Fully air conditioned. Inquire about accommodations for children.

Hosts: Bob and Ellen Johnson
Rooms: 5 (PB) $75-85
Full and Continental Breakfast
Credit Cards: A, B
Notes: 2, 7, 9, 10, 11, 12

The Red Dog Bed and Breakfast
132 Mason Street, 49453
(616) 857-8851; (800) 357-3250

A comfortable place to stay in the heart of downtown Saugatuck, steps away from everything. Built in 1879, it has six air-conditioned guest rooms, antiques, private baths, color cable TV, and a romantic fireplace suite with Jacuzzi for two. A full breakfast is served in the dining room. Second-floor back porch overlooks the lovely garden.

Hosts: Patrick and Kristine Clark
Rooms: 6 (PB) $70-125
Full Breakfast
Credit Cards: A, B, C, D, E
Notes: 2, 5, 7, 8, 9, 10, 11, 12, 13, 14

Rosemont Inn
83 Lakeshore Drive, P.O. Box 214, 49453
(616) 857-2637; (800) 721-2637
www.rosemontinn.com

This country inn on Lake Michigan, selected as "One of the Midwest's Top Ten Romantic Retreats" by the *Chicago Sun Times*, offers lake-view rooms with gas fireplaces and Jacuzzi suites. Other areas include a lakeside gathering room to view spectacular sunsets and a poolside great room, both with fireplaces. Enjoy the lake-viewing gazebo, complimentary bicycles, large custom-designed indoor whirlpool/sauna. Outdoor heated swimming pool. Waterfall garden. Full buffet breakfast and evening hors d'oeuvres. The inn is fully air conditioned. Direct beach access at doorstep.

Hosts: The Sajdak Family
Rooms: 14 (PB) $95-235
Full Breakfast
Credit Cards: A, B, C, D
Notes: 2, 5, 7, 9, 10, 11, 12, 13, 14, 15

Rosemont Inn

Sherwood Forest Bed and Breakfast
938 Center Street, P.O. Box 315, 49453
(800) 838-1246

This beautiful Victorian-style house is surrounded by woods. Guest rooms are decorated with antiques and traditional furnishings. Two suites are available with

---

7 No smoking; 8 Children welcome; 9 Social drinking allowed; 10 Tennis nearby; 11 Swimming nearby; 12 Golf nearby; 13 Skiing nearby; 14 May be booked through a travel agent; 15 Handicapped accessible.

Saugatuck, MI

Sherwood Forest

Jacuzzi and fireplace. Another has a large mural, along with a fireplace. The bed and breakfast has central air conditioning, a heated swimming pool, and a wraparound porch. The eastern shore of Lake Michigan and a public beach are a half-block away. The charming shops and restaurants of Saugatuck are just two miles away.

Hosts: Keith and Susan Charak
Rooms: 4 (PB) $85-165
Continental Breakfast
Credit Cards: A, B, D, E
Notes: 2, 5, 7, 9, 10, 11, 12, 13, 14

Twin Gables Country Inn
900 Lake Street, P.O. Box 881, 49453
(616) 857-4346

Overlooking Kalamazoo Lake, this historic inn is centrally air conditioned throughout and features 14 charming guest rooms, with private baths, some with fireplace, furnished in antiques and country. Cross-country skiiers relax in the large indoor hot tub and cozy up to a warm crackling fireplace, while summer guests may take a refreshing dip in the outdoor pool and enjoy glorious sunsets on the front veranda. Three separate two- and one-bedroom cottages are also available. Smoking permitted in designated areas. Continental plus breakfast is served.

Hosts: Michael and Denise Simcik
Rooms: 14 (PB) $79-119
Continental Breakfast
Credit Cards: A, B, C, D
Notes: 2, 5, 8, 9, 10, 11, 12, 13, 14, 15

Twin Oaks Inn
227 Griffith Street, P.O. Box 867, 49453
(616) 857-1600

Built in 1860, this totally renovated inn offers old English warmth and charm along with all modern amenities. Queen- or king-size beds and private baths. Air conditioning, along with cable TV, VCRs, and a library of more than 700 films, assures a wonderful stay no matter what the weather. Common areas with fireplace and outdoor hot tub, along with antiques throughout, guarantee a memorable escape. Homemade breakfast. Cottage with sleeping loft and private hot tub.

Hosts: Nancy and Jerry Horney
Rooms: 6 (PB) $65-125
Cottage: 1
Full and Continental Breakfast
Credit Cards: A, B, D
Notes: 2, 5, 7, 8, 9, 10, 11, 12, 13, 14

SOUTH HAVEN

A Country Place Bed and Breakfast
79 North Shore Drive North, 49090
(616) 637-5523

Experience gracious hospitality at this lovingly restored 1860s Greek Revival. The English country theme evident throughout is created by beautiful florals and antique treasures collected during the hosts' stay in England. A "sin"sational breakfast is served by the fireside or on the deck overlooking the garden, spacious

NOTES: Credit cards accepted: A MasterCard; B Visa; C American Express; D Discover; E Diner's Club; F Other; 2 Personal checks accepted; 3 Lunch available; 4 Dinner available; 5 Open all year; 6 Pets welcome;

lawn, and gazebo, all surrounded by six acres of peaceful woodland. Lake Michigan beach access one-half block away. Complimentary refreshments are available.

Hosts: Art and Lee Niffenegger
Rooms: 5 (PB) $75-110
Full Breakfast
Credit Cards: A, B, C, D
Notes: 2, 7, 9, 10, 11, 12, 14

Ross House

229 Michigan Avenue, 49090
(616) 637-2256

The historic Ross house was built in 1886 by lumber tycoon Volney Ross. It sits on a quiet, tree-lined street on the south side of the Black River. Lake Michigan public beaches, downtown shopping area, Kal-Haven Trail, and many fine restaurants are only blocks away. Full breakfast served on weekends; Continental breakfast served on weekdays. Cross-country skiing is nearby. Beach condos are also available.

Hosts: Cathy Hormann and Brad Wilcox
Rooms: 7 (1 PB; 6 S3B) $45-55
Full Breakfast
Credit Cards: None
Notes: 2, 5, 7, 9, 10, 11, 12, 14

Seymour House Bed and Breakfast

1248 Blue Star Highway, 49090
(616) 227-3918

On 11 acres of beautiful countryside, one-half mile from Lake Michigan and minutes to Saugatuck and South Haven. This Italianate-style 1862 mansion has original pocket doors and intricate carved woodwork. Some guest rooms with fireplace and Jacuzzi. Two-bedroom guest log cabin also available. Close to sandy beaches, wineries, three golf courses, antique shops, orchards, and restaurants. Enjoy the best of both worlds—close to activities in the area, yet in minutes return to the peaceful and tranquil setting of the Seymour House. Children are welcome in the cabin.

Hosts: Tom and Gwen Paton
Rooms: 5 (PB) $80-135
Full Breakfast
Credit Cards: A, B
Notes: 2, 5, 7, 9, 11, 12, 13, 14

Yelton Manor

Yelton Manor Bed and Breakfast

140 North Shore Drive, 49090
(616) 637-5220
www.yeltonmanor.com

Elegant, gracious Victorian mansions on the sunset shore of Lake Michigan. Seventeen gorgeous rooms, all with private bath, some with Jacuzzi and fireplace. Panoramic lake views, prize-winning gardens, two salons with fireplaces, cozy wing chairs, floral carpets, four-poster beds, and a pampering staff set the tone for relaxation and romance. Guests will never want to leave after enjoying the wonderful breakfasts, day-long treats, and evening hors d'oeuvres.

Hosts: Elaine and Rob
Rooms: 17 (PB) $90-205
Full Breakfast
Credit Cards: A, B, C
Notes: 2, 5, 7, 9, 10, 11, 12, 13

---

7 No smoking; 8 Children welcome; 9 Social drinking allowed; 10 Tennis nearby; 11 Swimming nearby; 12 Golf nearby; 13 Skiing nearby; 14 May be booked through a travel agent; 15 Handicapped accessible.

STEPHENSON

Top of the Hill
South 310 Center Street, 49887
(906) 753-4757

Clean, comfortable bilevel home in a small town in the Upper Peninsula of Michigan, close to the Wisconsin border. The lower guest room offers a large bedroom with queen-size bed, private bath, large family room with TV and pool table. The upper bedroom has a double bed and a shared bathroom. Top of the Hill's friendly hosts makes it guests' home away from home.

Hosts: Art and Phyllis Strohl
Rooms: 2 (1 PB; 1 SB)
Continental Breakfast
Credit Cards: None
Notes: 2, 5, 8, 9, 12, 13

SUTTONS BAY

Open Windows Bed and Breakfast
613 St. Mary's Avenue, P.O. Box 698, 49682
(616) 271-4300; (800) 520-3722
e-mail: openwindows@centuryinter.net
www.leelanau.com/openwindows

A charming century-old home with lovely gardens and front porch for viewing the bay. This warm, inviting home is decorated with guests' comfort in mind. Enjoy the hearty homemade breakfasts and the friendly atmosphere. The village with its beaches, unique shops, and fine restaurants is just a short walk away, or ride the bikes and explore the surrounding countryside. Fireplace, beach fires and picnics, sunsets on Lake Michigan. Fifteen miles from Traverse City.

Open Windows

Hosts: Don and Norma Blumenschine
Rooms: 3 (PB) $95-110
Full Breakfast
Credit Cards: None
Notes: 2, 3, 4, 5, 7, 10, 11, 12, 13, 14

TRAVERSE CITY

Bowers Harbor Bed and Breakfast
13972 Peninsula Drive, 49686
(616) 223-7869

Private sandy beach, West Bay sunsets, and all the fun of Traverse City are found at this bed and breakfast on Old Mission Peninsula. Three lovely bedrooms available, all with private baths and brass beds. Enjoy the beautiful sunsets from the wraparound stone front porch or from the beach. Bowers Harbor is close to restaurants and wineries. Rates include a full breakfast. No smoking is permitted inside the bed and breakfast.

Hosts: Gary and Mary Ann Verbanic
Rooms: 3 (PB) $100-130
Full Breakfast
Credit Cards: None
Notes: 2, 5, 7, 9, 10, 11, 12, 13

NOTES: Credit cards accepted: A MasterCard; B Visa; C American Express; D Discover; E Diner's Club; F Other; 2 Personal checks accepted; 3 Lunch available; 4 Dinner available; 5 Open all year; 6 Pets welcome;

Victoriana 1898

622 Washington Street, 49686
(616) 929-1009

Touch a bit of history and take home a memory to be long remembered when staying at this Victorian treasure. Magnificently crafted with tiled fireplaces, oak staircase, gazebo, and carriage house. The home is furnished with antiques and family heirlooms. In a quiet, historic district close to West Bay and downtown. Very special breakfast served.

Hosts: Flo and Bob Schermerhorn
Rooms: 3 (PB) $60-85
Full Breakfast
Credit Cards: None
Notes: 2, 5, 7, 9, 10, 11, 12, 13, 14

UNION PIER

The Inn at Union Pier

9708 Berrien Street, P.O. Box 222, 49129
(616) 469-4700
www.innatunionpier.com

Only 90 minutes from Chicago and 200 steps to the beach, the inn caters to both weekend getaways and weekday corporate retreats. Choose from 16 guest rooms, many featuring Swedish fireplaces and porches or balconies, and two luxurious whirlpool suites. Unwind in the outdoor hot tub or sauna, or enjoy Michigan wines and popcorn in the great room. "Harbor Country" offers diverse dining, antiquing, and wineries, and year-round outdoor activities from biking to cross-country skiing.

The Inn at Union Pier

Hosts: Joyce Erickson Pitts and Mark Pitts
Rooms: 16 (PB) $135-205
Full Breakfast
Credit Cards: A, B, D
Notes: 2, 5, 7, 9, 10, 11, 12, 13

---

7 No smoking; 8 Children welcome; 9 Social drinking allowed; 10 Tennis nearby; 11 Swimming nearby; 12 Golf nearby; 13 Skiing nearby; 14 May be booked through a travel agent; 15 Handicapped accessible.

Minnesota

Minnesota

Cedar Rose Inn

ALEXANDRIA

Cedar Rose Inn
422 Seventh Avenue West, 56308
(320) 762-8430; (888) 203-5333

From the wild blooming roses in the summer, to the warm crackling fire in the winter, the Cedar Rose Inn offers year-round comfort for anyone away from home. In the "silk stocking" historic district near downtown Alexandria, guests can easily access the many shops and recreational activities in this quaint city of lake. The inn was built in 1903 and retains the beautiful original structure providing a romantic escape into history.

Hosts: Aggie and Florian Ledermann
Rooms: 4 (PB) $75-125
Full Breakfast
Credit Cards: A, B
Notes: 2, 5, 7, 9, 10, 11, 12, 13

ANNANDALE

Thayer's Historic Bed and Breakfast
Highway 55–60 West Elm Street, P.O. Box 246, 55302
(320) 274-8222; (800) 944-6595
FAX (320) 274-5051
www.bbonline.com/mn/thayer

Built 1895; in the national historic register; a unique, casually elegant, gracious inn notable for comfort and good conversation. Authentic antiques, private baths, claw-foot tubs, air conditioning, hot tub, sauna, liquor lounge, gourmet dining, fireplaces, whirlpools, murder mystery dinners, and customized packages featuring satin sheets and breakfast in bed. Owner is a psychic and readings are by appointment. Location has easy access to Minneapolis and St. Cloud on Highway 55.

Host: Sharon Gammell
Rooms: 11 (PB) $48.50-147
Full or Continental Breakfast
Credit Cards: A, B, C, D
Notes: 2, 3, 4, 5, 9, 10, 11, 12, 13, 14

BATTLE LAKE

Xanadu Island
Route 2, Box 51, 56515
(800) 396-9046

Experience the relaxation and comfort of this grand old lakeside lodge set on a private 1920s island estate. Linger by a fireplace, soak in a whirlpool, or borrow a

---

NOTES: Credit cards accepted: A MasterCard; B Visa; C American Express; D Discover; E Diner's Club; F Other; 2 Personal checks accepted; 3 Lunch available; 4 Dinner available; 5 Open all year; 6 Pets welcome; 7 No smoking; 8 Children welcome; 9 Social drinking allowed; 10 Tennis nearby; 11 Swimming nearby; 12 Golf nearby; 13 Skiing nearby; 14 May be booked through a travel agent; 15 Handicapped accessible.

the lake. Battle Lake is a lake town with unique allery. Excellent golfing, ng are all close by.

Hosts: Bryan and Janet Lonski
Rooms: 5 (PB) $75-140
Full Breakfast
Credit Cards: A, B
Notes: 2, 5, 7, 9, 10, 11, 12, 13, 14

BEMIDJI

Lakewatch Bed and Breakfast
609 Lake Boulevard NE, 56601
(218) 751-8413; e-mail: lakewatch@bji.net
www.bji.net/pages/lakewatch/

Charming 1904 home overlooking Lake Bemidji. Four rooms with private baths, central air, one with two-person claw-foot soaking tub. Guest sitting room, cozy library, living room with lake views and fireplace. Cross-country skiing, biking, canoeing, Hasca State Park, Chippewa National Forest. Short walk to downtown shops and restaurants and to Bemidji State University. Generous breakfast served at time requested by guest. Member of the Minnesota Bed and Breakfast Guild.

Hosts: Sherry Mergens and Rick Toward
Rooms: 4 (PB) $55-85
Full Breakfast
Credit Cards: A, B
Notes: 2, 5, 7, 9, 10, 11, 12, 13, 14

BROOKLYN CENTER

Inn on the Farm
6150 Summit Drive North, 55430
(800) 428-8382

The Inn on the Farm at Earle Brown Heritage Center offers a bed and breakfast experience guests will never forget. Housed in a cluster of historic farm buildings, the inn is on the grounds of a beautifully restored Victorian gentlemen's country estate, just 10 minutes from the heart of downtown Minneapolis.

The Inn on the Farm is on the edge of the Green, the estate's beautifully landscaped central mall. In summer, guests will enjoy the shaded walking paths which lead them across the Green's extensive lawns.

Rooms: 10 (PB) $110-140
Full Breakfast
Credit Cards: A, B, C, D, E
Notes: 4, 5, 7, 10, 11, 12, 15

CANNON FALLS

Quill and Quilt
615 West Hoffman Street, 55009
(507) 263-5507

Colonial Revival, circa 1897. Oak woodwork; spacious, airy common areas. Decorated with delicate wallpapers, antiques, and handmade quilts. Four guest rooms. Private baths. One suite with double whirlpool. Full breakfast and evening sweets. Near biking, hiking, skiing, antiquing, and canoeing. Only 35 miles to the Mall of America. Midweek rates and gift certificates available. Inquire about accommodations for children.

Hosts: James and Staci Smith
Rooms: 4 (PB) $60-130
Full Breakfast
Credit Cards: A, B
Notes: 2, 5, 7, 9, 10, 11, 12, 13

Quill and Quilt

NOTES: Credit cards accepted: A MasterCard; B Visa; C American Express; D Discover; E Diner's Club; F Other; 2 Personal checks accepted; 3 Lunch available; 4 Dinner available; 5 Open all year; 6 Pets welcome;

CHASKA

Bluff Creek Inn
1161 Bluff Creek Drive, 55318
(612) 445-2735

Country inn (circa 1860), European elegance with country charm in Minnesota River valley. Thirty minutes to downtown Minneapolis. Designer-coordinated rooms, whirlpool, fireplace. One of top 10 Midwest inns (*Chicago Tribune*). Minutes to Mall of America, Landscape Arboretum, Chanhassen Dinner Theatre, Renaissance Festival. There are walking/biking/ski trails. Gourmet three-course breakfast, hors d'oeuvres. Children over 12 welcome. No pets. No smoking.

Hosts: Anne and Gary Delaney
Rooms: 5 (PB) $85-150
Full Breakfast
Credit Cards: A, B, C, D, E
Notes: 2, 5, 7, 10, 11, 12, 13

Bluff Creek Inn

CROOKSTON

Elm Street Inn
422 Elm Street, 56716
(218) 281-2343
e-mail:legal@beltrami.means.net

Lovingly restored 1910 home with antiques, hardwood floors, and stained- and beveled-glass windows. Private baths. Wicker-filled sun porch. Old-fashioned beds with quilts. Memorable candlelight breakfast. Indoor community pool next door. Excellent bird watching. Near the University of Minnesota campus. No pets. Smoke-free.

Hosts: John and Sheryl Winters
Rooms: 4 (PB) $55-65
Full Breakfast
Credit Cards: A, B, C, D
Notes: 2, 5, 7, 9, 10, 11, 12, 14

CROSS LAKE

Birch Hill Inne Bed and Breakfast
P.O. Box 468, 56442
(218) 692-4857; e-mail: stay@birchhillinne.com
www.birchhillinne.com

Five guest rooms, private baths, two with Jacuzzi tubs. Private wildflower gardens, hiking and cross-country ski trails. Antique furnishings. Sumptuous Continental breakfast. Spacious screened porch. Pine-paneled breakfast room with fireplace. Pontoon boat, canoe, paddle boat, fishing boat, and bicycles available. Tennis, bike path, golf nearby. On the beautiful Whitefish chain of lakes. Twenty-three miles north of Brainerd. Open year-round. No smoking. No pets. No accommodations for children.

Hosts: Steve and Heidi Engen
Rooms: 5 (PB) $72-80
Continental Breakfast
Credit Cards: A, B, C
Notes: 2, 5, 7, 9, 10, 11, 12, 13

Manhattan Beach Lodge
County Road 66, P.O. Box 719, 56442
(218) 692-3381; (800) 399-4360
FAX (218) 692-2774
e-mail: mblodge@crosslake.net
www.mblodge.com

When the Manhattan Beach Lodge was built in 1929, it brought a touch of civilization to Minnesota's lake country wilderness. The same is still true today as visitors

---

7 No smoking; 8 Children welcome; 9 Social drinking allowed; 10 Tennis nearby; 11 Swimming nearby; 12 Golf nearby; 13 Skiing nearby; 14 May be booked through a travel agent; 15 Handicapped accessible.

watch an eagle soar overhead or the sunset over the 14 lakes of the Whitefish chain. The lodge provides casual elegance in lodging and dining and a wealth of activities, such as hiking, biking, boating, fishing, golf, skiing, snowshoeing, and more. The Lodge is rustic where guests expect it to be and wonderfully restored with all the conveniences when guests want it to be.

Hosts: Mary and John Zesbaugh
Rooms: 10 (PB) $69-109
Continental Breakfast
Credit Cards: A, B, D
Notes: 2, 3, 4, 5, 7, 8, 9, 10, 11, 12, 13, 15

DULUTH

Olcott House Bed and Breakfast Inn

2316 East 1st Street, 55812
(800) 715-1339; www.visitduluth.com/olcotthouse

Historic 1904 Georgian Colonial mansion offering over 10,000 square feet of elegant living. Tastefully decorated romantic suites with working fireplaces and private baths. Carriage house is perfect for honeymoons and special occasions. Library, music room, grand porch, lake views. Smoke free. Candlelight breakfasts, antiques, gift certificates. Midweek discounts. AAA-approved. Children 12 and older welcome.

Hosts: Barb and Don Trueman
Rooms: 6 (PB) $85-135
Full Breakfast
Credit Cards: A, B, D
Notes: 2, 5, 7, 9, 10, 11, 12, 13, 14

EXCELSIOR

James H. Clark House Bed and Breakfast

371 Water Street, 55331
(612) 474-0196

Newly restored Victorian (1858) home neslted in historic village of Excelsior. Four guest rooms. Private baths. Fireplaces.

James H. Clark House

Whirlpools. Full candlelight breakfast. Three blocks from Lake Minnetonka. Twenty-five minutes from downtown Minneapolis and Mall of America, one-half block from hiking/biking trail and trolley. Near antique shops, theaters, fine restaurants, boat cruises. Home has an "English Cottage decor with the feel of summer all year around."—*Minnesota Monthly*. Children over 12 welcome.

Hosts: Betty and Skip Welke
Rooms: 4 (PB) $85-145
Full Breakfast
Credit Cards: None
Notes: 2, 5, 7, 9, 10, 11, 12, 13

FERGUS FALLS

Bakketopp Hus

Rural Route 2, Box 187 A (Long Lake), 56537
(218) 739-2915; (800) 739-2915
www.bbonline.com/mn/bakketopp

This chalet lake home is nestled in the woods with decks overlooking a scenic lake where guests can hear the call of the loon. It is decorated with antiques, handmade quilts and down comforters. Suites have a private spa, a draped canopied bed, and a fireplace. Ten minutes from I-94, guests are in the wooded hills and valleys of lake country. Nearby is a state park and scenic villages. Enjoy this relaxed, romantic getaway with breakfast served overlooking the lake.

NOTES: Credit cards accepted: A MasterCard; B Visa; C American Express; D Discover; E Diner's Club; F Other; 2 Personal checks accepted; 3 Lunch available; 4 Dinner available; 5 Open all year; 6 Pets welcome;

Pincushion Mountain Bed and Breakfast

968 Gunflint Trail, 55604
(218) 387-1276; (800) 542-1226
e-mail: pincushion@boreal.org
www.pinchionbb.com

Three miles north of Grand Marais. Secluded on forested ridge offering views of Lake Superior 1,000 feet below. Newer inn (circa 1986) decorated in country fashion. Private baths, full breakfast, sauna, beamed common area with fireplace and deck. Vast network of hiking, biking, cross-country skiing, and snowshoeing trails maintained to doorstep. BWCA canoe entry close by.

Hosts: Scott and Mary Beattie
Rooms 4 (PB) $90-99
Full Breakfast
Credit Cards: A, B
Notes: 2, 3, 5, 7, 9, 10, 11, 12, 13, 14

Bakketopp Hus

Hosts: Judy and Dennis Nims
Rooms: 3 (PB) $70-105
Full Breakfast
Credit Cards: A, B, D
Notes: 2, 5, 7, 9, 10, 11, 12, 13

GRAND MARAIS

Old Shore Beach Bed and Breakfast

1434 Old Shore Road, 55604
(218) 387-9707; (888) 387-9707
FAX (218) 387-9811
e-mail: visit@oldshorebeach.com

Old Shore Beach Bed and Breakfast sits along a pebble beach on the shore of Lake Superior. This newly built lakeshore home began welcoming guests in 1997. Four guest rooms have private baths, queen- or king-size beds, in-room seating areas, and many views of Lake Superior. The grand cobblestone fireplace and its comfortable living room welcome all visitors. Full breakfast is served in the lake-view dining room. A large deck and lakeside seating, sauna, rental of mountain bikes and snowshoes, cozy terry-cloth robes and slippers in each room contribute to relaxation. Picnic-style lunch available.

Pincushion Mountain

HIBBING

Adams House

201 East 23rd Street, 55746
(218) 263-9742; (888) 891-9742

The Adams House is a quiet, smoke-free accommodation in the center of the city and its attractions. A brief distance to lakes, woods, golf, and skiing. The English Tudor-style house features antique- and chintz-decorated bedrooms, a guest lounge with a kitchenette, and a charming flower garden. Continental breakfast served in the sunny

Host: Paulette Anholm
Rooms: 4 (PB) $95-115
Full Breakfast
Credit Cards: A, B
Notes: 2, 5, 7, 11, 12, 13

---

7 No smoking; 8 Children welcome; 9 Social drinking allowed; 10 Tennis nearby; 11 Swimming nearby; 12 Golf nearby; 13 Skiing nearby; 14 May be booked through a travel agent; 15 Handicapped accessible.

dining room includes Swedish coffee and warm conversation.

Hosts: Marlene and Merrill Widmark
Rooms: 5 (1 PB; 4 SB) $43-48
Continental Breakfast
Credit Cards: B
Notes: 2, 5, 7, 8, 9, 10, 11, 12, 13

HOUSTON

Addie's Attic Bed and Breakfast
117 South Jackson, P.O. Box 677, 55943
(507) 896-3010

This beautiful turn-of-the-century home, circa 1903, has a cozy front parlor with curved glass window. Games, TV, and player piano available. Guest rooms are decorated and furnished with "attic finds." Hearty country breakfast served in dining room. Near hiking, biking, cross-country skiing trails, canoeing, and antique shops. Weekday rates.

Hosts: Fred and Marilyn Huhn
Rooms: 3 (SB) $45-50
Full Breakfast
Credit Cards: None
Notes: 2, 5, 7, 9, 10, 11, 12, 13

KENYON

Grandfather's Woods
3640-450th Street. 55946
(507) 789-6414

Charming 1860s fifth-generation working farmstead showcases family antiques and memorabilia used to distinctively decorate three cozy guest rooms, one with fireplace. A large inviting guest area consists of parlor, hearthside dining room (fruit and treats always available), sitting porches. Several garden swings and small pond are tucked into the colorful cottage garden. Guests hike or cross-country ski through 65 acres of wooded trails. The Percheron draft horse team provides hay- or sleighrides.

Hosts: Judy and George Langemo
Rooms: 3 (2 PB; 1 SB) $60-70
Full and Continental Breakfast

Credit Cards: None
Notes: 2, 3, 4, 5, 7, 8, 11, 12, 13, 14

LAKE CITY

Victorian Bed and Breakfast
620 South High Street, 55041-1757
(651) 345-2167; (888) 345-2167

Built in 1896, this Stick-style Victorian overlooks beautiful Lake Pepin, which is part of the Hiawatha Valley of the Mississippi River. Noted for its scenic bluffs and high concentration of eagles, swans, and waterfowl, Lake Pepin can be seen from every room. Original stained-glass windows and carved butternut woodwork are outstanding features of this house. The adjacent guest house features rooms with whirlpools and fireplaces as well as lake views.

Hosts: Bernie and Ione Link
Rooms: 5 (PB) $65-135
Full Breakfast
Credit Cards: None
Notes: 2, 5, 7, 9, 10, 11, 12, 13

Victorian

LAKE KABETOGAMA

Bunt's Kabinns
12497 Burma Road, 56669
(218) 875-2691; (888) 741-1020
FAX (218) 875-3008

Three private cabins and a four-room inn one-half mile apart. Two cabins are near

---

NOTES: Credit cards accepted: A MasterCard; B Visa; C American Express; D Discover; E Diner's Club; F Other; 2 Personal checks accepted; 3 Lunch available; 4 Dinner available; 5 Open all year; 6 Pets welcome;

the Canadian border and Voyageurs National Park, on the shores of Lake Kabetogama. Another is on 80 secluded acres. The small inn is in a converted school and church building. Private baths, full kitchens, fireplaces, whirlpool, Jacuzzis, saunas, many decks, beach, dock, satellite, color TVs, VCRs, and washers and dryers. Truly four touches of class in the midst of the wilderness.

Host: Bob Buntrock
Rooms: 4 (PB) $60-150
Continental Breakfast
Credit Cards: A, B, C, D
Notes: 2, 3, 4, 5, 8, 9, 10, 11, 12, 13, 14, 15

LANESBORO

Mrs. B's Historic Lanesboro Inn and Restaurant

101 Parkway North, P.O. Box 411, 55949
(507) 467-2154; (800) 657-4710

On the bank of the Root River nestled in a deep forested valley of southeast Minnesota's bluff country sits Mrs. B's Lanesboro Inn, an 1872 limestone snuggery with 10 special country Victorian rooms and an acclaimed restaurant. Mrs. B's is in the historic downtown of Lanesboro (pop. 850) directly on a spectacular 60-mile paved bike and ski trail. Lanesboro is an unspoiled, activity-based area offering a great variety of both indoor and outdoor things to do.

Hosts: Bill Sermeus and Mimi Abell
Rooms: 10 (PB) $50-95
Full Breakfast
Credit Cards: F
Notes: 2, 3, 4, 5, 7, 8, 9, 10, 12, 13, 15

LUTSEN

Lindgren's Bed and Breakfast

Lindgren's Bed and Breakfast

5552 County Road 35, P.O. Box 56, 55612-0056
(218) 663-7450

A 1920s log home in Superior National Forest on walkable shoreline of Lake Superior. Massive stone fireplaces, Finnish sauna, whirlpool, baby grand piano, TVs, VCR, and CD player. A hearty Northwoods breakfast is served. In center of area known for skiing, golf, stream and lake fishing, skyride, mountain biking, snowmobiling, horseback riding, alpine slide, kayaking, fall colors, Superior Hiking Trail, Boundary Waters Canoe Area entry point, and state parks. Spacious manicured grounds. One-half mile off scenic Highway 61 on the Lake Superior Circle Tour. AAA-approved. Children 12 and older welcome.

Host: Shirley Lindgren
Rooms: 4 (PB) $85-125
Full Breakfast
Credit Cards: A, B
Notes: 2, 3, 5, 7, 9, 10, 11, 12, 13, 14

MINNEAPOLIS

Evelo's Bed and Breakfast

2301 Bryant Avenue South, 55405
(612) 374-9656

This 1897 house is in the Lowry Hill East neighborhood and has a well-preserved

---

7 No smoking; 8 Children welcome; 9 Social drinking allowed; 10 Tennis nearby; 11 Swimming nearby; 12 Golf nearby; 13 Skiing nearby; 14 May be booked through a travel agent; 15 Handicapped accessible.

Victorian interior. The three guest rooms are on the third floor, each furnished in period furniture. The entire first floor is done in original dark oak millwork. A small refrigerator, coffee maker, telephone, fax, and TV are available for guest use. Air conditioned. The bed and breakfast is within walking distance of downtown, Lake of the Isles, Upton shopping area, Walker Art Center, Guthrie Theater, and the Minneapolis Institute of Arts. Established in 1979. Cross-country skiing nearby.

Hosts: David and Sheryl Evelo
Rooms: 3 (SB) $60
Continental Breakfast
Credit Cards: A, B, C, D, E
Notes: 2, 5, 7, 9, 10, 11, 12, 13

Nan's Bed and Breakfast

2304 Fremont Avenue South, 55405
(612) 377-5118; (800) 214-5118
e-mail: zosel@mn.mcad.edu

Comfortable urban 1890s Victorian family home offering guest rooms furnished with antiques. Friendly, outgoing hosts will help guests find their way around town. Near downtown, lakes, theaters, galleries, restaurants, and shopping. One block from buses.

Hosts: Nan and Jim Zosel
Rooms: 3 (SB) $55-60
Full Breakfast
Credit Cards: A, B, C, D, E
Notes: 2, 5, 8, 9, 10, 11, 12

MORRIS

The American House

410 East Third Street, 56267
(320) 589-4054

Victorian home decorated with antiques and country charm. Ride the tandem bike on scenic trails. Within walking distance of area restaurants and shops. One block from the University of Minnesota-Morris campus.

Host: Karen Berget
Rooms: 3 (SB) $40-60
Full Breakfast
Credit Cards: A, B
Notes: 2, 5, 7, 8, 9, 10, 11, 12, 14

NEVIS

The Park Street Inn

Route 3, Box 554, 56467-9704
(218) 652-4500; (800) 797-1778

This 1912 home is richly furnished with antiques, stained glass, carved oak woodwork, and a Mission-style fireplace. Suite features a double whirlpool and a sunroom that overlooks Lake Belle Taine. The new Grotto has a huge whirlpool and king-size bed. City park and beach across the street. Heartland Trail one block away for hiking, bicycling, and snowmobiling. Close to restaurants, antique and gift shops, golfing, and horseback riding. Older children welcome. Pets by arrangement.

Hosts: Irene and Len Hall
Rooms: 4 (PB) $70-125
Full Breakfast
Credit Cards: A, B
Notes: 2, 5, 9, 11, 12, 13, 14

PARK RAPIDS

Dickson Viking Huss Bed and Breakfast

202 East Fourth Street, 56470
(218) 732-8089

"Aunt Helen" invites guests to this charming contemporary home with vaulted ceiling and fireplace in the living room that features a watercolor exhibit. Big breakfast. Bicycle or snowmobile the Heartland Trail. Visit Itasca Park and the source of the Mississippi or cross-country ski. Unique shop and restaurant attractions. State inspected.

Host: Helen K. Dickson
Rooms: 3 (1 PB; 2 SB) $38.50-51.50
Full Breakfast
Credit Cards: A, B
Notes: 2, 5, 7, 8, 9, 10, 11, 12, 13, 14

NOTES: Credit cards accepted: A MasterCard; B Visa; C American Express; D Discover; E Diner's Club; F Other; 2 Personal checks accepted; 3 Lunch available; 4 Dinner available; 5 Open all year; 6 Pets welcome;

WildWood Lodge Bed and Breakfast

HC 06, Box 45A, 56470
(218) 732-1176; (888) WWLODGE
FAX (218) 732-8434; www.wildwoodbb.com

An elegant northwoods lodge that is nestled among majestic pines and towering birch trees. A *Better Homes & Gardens* award winner as well as quality assurance rating by the Minnesota B & B Guild. This charming lodge is decorated in an English country, Ralph Lauren style. Three luxurious rooms with private baths—some with whirlpools. Country club golf course down the lane, biking on the Heartland Trail, Itasca State Park 20 miles, and private swimming beach right out the door. Cross-country skiing nearby.

Hosts: Liz and Phil Smith
Rooms: 3 (PB) $95-145
Full Breakfast
Credit Cards: A, B
Notes: 2, 5, 7, 9, 10, 11, 12, 13

ROCHESTER

Inn at Rocky Creek Bed and Breakfast

2115 Rocky Creek Drive Northeast, 55906
(507) 288-1019

Just 10 minutes from downtown and the Mayo Clinic, this bed and breakfast offers all the comforts of home. A special place to relax and escape. Spacious rooms all include private baths. Queen-size beds, central air, and a collection of comfortable antiques. Golf courses abound—walking paths and biking and cross-country ski trails at nearby Quarry Hill Nature Center.

Hosts: Robert and Jane Hanson
Rooms: 3 (PB) $70-125
Full and Continental Breakfast
Credit Cards: A, B
Notes: 2, 5, 7, 10, 11, 12, 13, 14

ST. CHARLES

Victorian Lace Inn Bed and Breakfast with TeaRoom and Gift Shop

1512 Whitewater Avenue, 55972-1234
(507) 932-4496

Be surrounded with the ambiance of the Victorian era at this inn, fully restored in 1990. After guests step from the street of this small town and turn the crank-style doorbell, they are greeted by a curved staircase which takes them up to the four guest rooms. With many original features remaining, it takes guests back in time—a respite from the hustle and bustle of today's world—where even the clocks seem to stand still.

Host: Sharon Vreeman
Rooms: 4 (4 SB) $70-85
Full Breakfast
Credit Cards: A, B, C
Notes: 2, 3, 5, 7, 10, 11, 12, 13, 14

Victorian Lace

ST. PAUL

At Home

538 Laurel Avenue, 55102
(612) 227-7170
www.U.S.WestDex.com"AtHome"b&b
www.b&bsmpls/st.paul

At Home is in the historic Ramsey Hill area of St. Paul. Built in 1906 and renovated in

---

7 No smoking; 8 Children welcome; 9 Social drinking allowed; 10 Tennis nearby; 11 Swimming nearby; 12 Golf nearby; 13 Skiing nearby; 14 May be booked through a travel agent; 15 Handicapped accessible.

1991, the rooms contain many family antiques. Bedrooms are airy and sunny and two of the baths have deep claw-foot tubs. Amenities include a private living room with gas fireplace, breakfast served in the dining room or front porch, in-room telephones, fresh flowers, and massage therapy on premises by appointment. Eclectic shops and many fine restaurants within walking distance. Only five minutes from the capitol and downtown. Twenty minutes from Minneapolis-St. Paul International Airport. Continental plus breakfast served.

Host: Sharon Dexter
Rooms: 3 (PB) $55-65
Continental Breakfast
Credit Cards: None
Notes: 2, 5, 7, 9, 10, 11, 12, 13

Chatsworth Bed and Breakfast
984 Ashland Avenue, 55104
(612) 227-4288; FAX (612) 225-8217

Take refuge from the hustle and bustle of daily life at the spacious 1902 Victorian inn in a beautiful and serene wooded setting. Whether guests seek a convenient haven for business travel or a destination for a romantic getaway, they enjoy the lovely gardens and experience the warm and comfortable elegance of Chatsworth. Three blocks from the many excellent restaurants and unique shops on Grand Avenue. Also in the vicinity are numerous colleges and churches. Only minutes away from the Chatsworth is the Twin Cities' international airport, the Mall of America, and the downtown areas of both St. Paul and Minneapolis.

Room: 5 (3 PB; 2 SB) $70-130
Full Breakfast
Credit Cards: A, B, C, D
Notes: 2, 4, 5, 7, 9, 10, 11, 12, 13, 14

The Rose Bed and Breakfast
2129 Larpenteur Avenue West, 55113
(612) 642-9417

This 1925 English Tudor is in a large wooded area between a historic farm museum and a golf course in the center of the Twin Cities' metro area, beside the University of Minnesota-St. Paul campus. Fresh flowers, large private yard with prairie and stream, cross-country skiing, art, books, and privacy or conversation. Continental plus breakfasts accommodating any personal dietary preferences or requirements.

Hosts: Carol Kindschi and Larry Greenberg
Suites: 2 (PB) $100
Continental Breakfast
Credit Cards: None
Notes: 2, 5, 7, 9, 10, 11, 12, 13

SHERBURN

Four Columns Inn
668 140th Street, 56171
(507) 764-8861

Built in 1884 as a stagecoach stop, this lovingly remodeled Greek Revival inn welcomes travelers. Four antique-filled guest bedrooms, claw-foot tubs, and working fireplaces welcome guests. A library, circular stairway, living room with a grand piano, and a solarium with a redwood hot tub make a stay here memorable. A hideaway bridal suite with access to a roof deck with a super view of the countryside is perfect for honeymooners. There is also a romantic getaway Victorian gazebo. Near lakes, antiques, amusement park, and

Chatsworth

NOTES: Credit cards accepted: A MasterCard; B Visa; C American Express; D Discover; E Diner's Club; F Other; 2 Personal checks accepted; 3 Lunch available; 4 Dinner available; 5 Open all year; 6 Pets welcome;

Four Columns Inn

live theater. Two miles north of I-90 on Highway 4, between Chicago and the Black Hills. Call for brochure. AAA three-diamond-rated.

Hosts: Norman and Pennie Kittleson
Rooms: 4 (3 PB; 1 SB) $55-75
Full Breakfast
Credit Cards: None
Notes: 2, 5, 7, 10, 11, 12, 13, 14

SIDE LAKE

McNair's Bed and Breakfast Country Inn
7694 Highway 5, P.O. Box 155, 55781
(218) 254-5878

Impressive French Colonial inn on sunny knoll of manicured lawns and gardens. Surrounded by state forest, numerous lakes, snowmobile and cross-country trails, and a year-round recreational paradise. Hibbing-Chisholm area, 90 minutes from Duluth, 3.5 hours from Twin Cities. Elegant guest rooms, fine antiques, sumptuous bedding, and private baths. Spacious, romantic private apartment suites, kitchens, brick fireplaces, and a Jacuzzi for two. Full multicourse gourmet breakfast experience. Homemade desserts. Pampering is hosts' speciality. Discount for two- or three-night stays.

Hosts: Don and Louise McNair
Rooms: 4 (PB) $80-130
Full Breakfast
Credit Cards: None
Notes: 2, 5, 7, 9, 10, 11, 12, 13, 14

SPRING VALLEY

Chase's
508 North Huron Avenue, 55975
(507) 346-2850
e-mail: chasebnb@deskmedia.com
www.bbonline.com/mn/chases

Listed in the National Register of Historic Places. Built in 1879. Enjoy the comfort and quiet solitude or enjoy the beauty, trails, park, golf course, and rural pleasures. Each of the five bedrooms has a style of its own. Furnished in antiques, which are for sale, the large rooms have small, cozy sitting areas and private baths in the room. Breakfast is hearty but subject to the whims of the cook.

Room: 5 (PB) $85
Full or Continental Breakfast
Credit Cards: A, B, D
Notes: 2, 7, 8, 9, 10, 11, 12

Chase's

STILLWATER

Ann Bean House
319 West Pine Street, 55082
(612) 430-0355; (800) 933-0355

Built in 1878, this towering four-story lumber baron's mansion still retains the finest in Victorian design: ornately carved

7 No smoking; 8 Children welcome; 9 Social drinking allowed; 10 Tennis nearby; 11 Swimming nearby; 12 Golf nearby; 13 Skiing nearby; 14 May be booked through a travel agent; 15 Handicapped accessible.

‑ior shutters that fold in two stately towers with ..s of the St. Croix River ⌐uest rooms are spacious and quiet, with cozy chairs and private baths. The large double parlor is available for guests to read, relax, or play the grand piano in. Guests will be welcomed at the door with wine and homemade bread. Morning arrives with a four-course breakfast.

Host: John Wubbels
Rooms: 5 (PB) $79-159
Full Breakfast
Credit Cards: A, B, C, D
Notes: 2, 5, 7, 9, 10, 12, 13

Aurora Staples Inn

303 North Fourth Street, 55082
(612) 351-1187

Lovely Queen Anne Victorian home in a historic rivertown. Built by a lumber baron for his daughter. Includes formal gardens, air conditioning, whirlpools, and fireplaces. Furnished and decorated appropriate to the Victorian era. Guests are served a full breakfast. Close to antique shops, book stores, and wonderful restaurants.

Hosts: Carol Hendrickson and Jenny Roesler
Rooms: 5 (PB) $105-150
Full Breakfast
Credit Cards: A, B, C
Notes: 2, 5, 7, 9, 12, 13, 14

James Mulvey Residence Inn

622 West Churchill Street, 55082
(612) 430-8008; FAX (612) 430-2801
www.contn/bb

This is an enchanting place. Built in 1878 by lumberman James A. Mulvey, the Italianate residence and stone carriage house grace the most visited historic rivertown in the upper Midwest. Exclusively for guests are the grand parlor, formal dining room, Victorian sun porch, and seven fabulously decorated guest rooms filled with exquisite art and antiques. Four-course breakfast, double whirlpools, mountain bikes, fireplaces, and air conditioning. Grace-filled service from innkeepers who care.

Hosts: Jill and Truett Lawson
Rooms: 7 (PB) $99-179
Full Breakfast
Credit Cards: A, B, C, D
Notes: 2, 5, 7, 9, 10, 11, 12, 13, 14

WABASHA

Eagles on the River Bed and Breakfast

1000 Marina Drive, P.O. Box 185, 55981
(651) 565-3509; (800) 684-6813
e-mail: eagles@wabasha.net
www.luminet.net/~eagles

Mississippi River views from Wabasha's landmark contemporary bed and breakfast. Marina one-half block away. Whirlpool, romantic fireplace, sauna, full breakfast, TV, VCR, private baths. Game room has

Eagles on the River

NOTES: Credit cards accepted: A MasterCard; B Visa; C American Express; D Discover; E Diner's Club;
F Other; 2 Personal checks accepted; 3 Lunch available; 4 Dinner available; 5 Open all year; 6 Pets welcome;

pool table, darts, board games, refrigerator, and microwave. Mall of America is 90 minutes away. Nearby are kayak, canoe, bike, cross-country and downhill ski, boat, and pontoon rentals. Eagle watching. State parks and hiking. Six area golf courses. Honeymooners love the privacy. Patio area and sandy beach. River mile marker 759.4.

Rooms: 2 (PB) $109-159
Full Breakfast
Credit Cards: A, B
Notes: 2, 5, 7, 9, 10, 11, 12, 13, 14

WINONA

Carriage House Bed and Breakfast

420 Main Street, 55987
(507) 452-8256; FAX (507) 452-0939
www.fsnw.com/bb

The Carriage House Bed and Breakfast is in the center of Winona, a historic town on the mighty Mississippi River. All of the beautifully decorated rooms have private baths and two rooms have gas-fired fireplaces and Jacuzzi whirlpool baths. Built in 1870, the Carriage House features a four-season porch, tandem bicycles, and a wonderful breakfast. Hosts' 1929 Model A Ford is available for special occasions. Continental plus breakfast served.

Hosts: Deb and Don Salyards
Rooms: 4 (PB) $80-150
Continental Breakfast
Credit Cards: A, B, C, D
Notes: 2, 5, 7, 9, 10, 11, 12, 13, 14

Carriage House

7 No smoking; 8 Children welcome; 9 Social drinking allowed; 10 Tennis nearby; 11 Swimming nearby; 12 Golf nearby; 13 Skiing nearby; 14 May be booked through a travel agent; 15 Handicapped accessible.

Missouri

Missouri

Borgman's

ARROW ROCK

Borgman's Bed and Breakfast
706 Van Buren, 65320
(816) 837-3350

The hosts invite guests to experience the historic town of Arrow Rock in the warmth of the century-old home. Choose one of four spacious guest rooms that share three baths, and relax in the sitting room or on the porch. Wind up the old Victrola for a song, choose a game or puzzle, browse through a book, or just sit for a spell and listen to the sounds of Arrow Rock. In the morning guests will enjoy a family-style breakfast of freshly baked bread, juice or fruit, coffee, and tea.

Hosts: Kathy and Helen Borgman
Rooms: 4 (S3B) $50-55
Continental Breakfast
Credit Cards: None
Notes: 2, 5, 7, 8

BONNE TERRE

Victorian Veranda Bed and Breakfast
207 East School Street, 63628
(573) 358-1134; (800) 343-1134

Elegant 1880 Victorian mansion overlooking the town Bicentennial Park. Choose from four romantic guest rooms, all with own private baths. Three have thermal massage baths for two. Guests may relax in the parlor or cozy up to the fireplace in the gathering room. The aroma of freshly ground coffee and variety of home-baked goodies will guide the guest to the large dining room for a candlelight breakfast. "So come enjoy the porch swing on this large wraparound veranda and escape to a quiet getaway."

Hosts: Galen and Karen Forney
Rooms: 4 (PB) $70-90
Full Breakfast
Credit Cards: A, B, D
Notes: 2, 5, 7, 8, 9, 10, 11, 12, 14

BRANSON

The Barger House Bed and Breakfast
621 Lakeshore Drive, 65616
(417) 335-2134; (800) 266-2134

On Lake Taneycomo in the beautiful Ozark Mountains, the Barger House is a charming version of an 18th-century Colonial home. A deck with a hot tub and large pool provides a beautiful view of the lake and downtown Branson. Trout fishing off the private

---

NOTES: Credit cards accepted: A MasterCard; B Visa; C American Express; D Discover; E Diner's Club; F Other; 2 Personal checks accepted; 3 Lunch available; 4 Dinner available; 5 Open all year; 6 Pets welcome; 7 No smoking; 8 Children welcome; 9 Social drinking allowed; 10 Tennis nearby; 11 Swimming nearby; 12 Golf nearby; 13 Skiing nearby; 14 May be booked through a travel agent; 15 Handicapped accessible.

boat dock. Delicious breakfast served in the dining room or on the deck. Wedding and honeymoon packages available.

Host: Ralph Barger
Rooms: 3 (PB) $75-95
Full Breakfast
Credit Cards: A, B, D
Notes: 2, 3, 4, 5, 8, 9, 10, 11, 12, 14

Cameron's Crag

P.O. Box 295, Point Lookout, 65615
(800) 933-8529

Perched high on a bluff overlooking Lake Taneycomo and Branson, Cameron's Crag offers three guest suites featuring spectacular scenery, a hearty breakfast, and easy access to area attractions. All suites have private entrances, king-size beds, hot tubs, private baths, and cable TV/VCR. One suite has full kitchen, whirlpool, and hot tub.

Hosts: Kay and Glen Cameron
Rooms: 3 (PB) $75-95
Full Breakfast
Credit Cards: A, B, C, D
Notes: 2, 5, 7, 8, 9, 11, 12, 14

Josie's Peaceful Getaway

Indian Point, HCR. 1, Box 1104, 65616
(417) 338-2978; (800) 289-4125

A pristine, gorgeous lakefront view awaits guests at Josie's on famous Table Rock Lake. Sunsets and moonlit nights lace the sky. Contemporary design with cathedral ceilings and a 15-foot-high stone fireplace. Victorian touches include stained glass, china dishes, crystal goblets, candlelight, and fresh flowers. Experience cozy wood-burning fireplaces, lavish Jacuzzi spas, or a secluded picnic lunch in the gazebo. Air-conditioned. Celebrate honeymoons/anniversaries in style. Five minutes to marina and Silver Dollar City. Eight miles to the music shows in Branson. Inquire about accommodations for children. Continental breakfast served Wednesdays and Thursdays.

Hosts: Bill and JoAnne Coats
Rooms: 2 (PB) $60-110
Suite: 1

Full and Continental Breakfast
Credit Cards: A, B, C, D
Notes: 2, 5, 7, 9, 11, 12, 14

Red Bud Cove

Red Bud Cove Bed and Breakfast Suites

162 Lakewood Drive (Lake Road 65-48, County Road 65-180), Hollister, 65672
(800) 677-5525

On beautiful Table Rock Lake and just 15 minutes from Branson. Spend the evening in comfort in a spacious suite with lakefront patio and deck. Eight suites with private entrances have living rooms (some with fireplaces), bedrooms with king- or queen-size beds, bathrooms (some with spas), fully equipped kitchenettes and dining areas, air conditioning, TV, and telephone. Full breakfast is served in the main dining room. Outdoor hot tub, rental boats, and dock space are available for guests' added enjoyment.

Hosts: Rick and Carol Carpenter
Rooms: 8 (PB) $77-107
Full Breakfast
Credit Cards: A, B, D
Notes: 2, 5, 7, 9, 11, 12, 14, 15

CALIFORNIA

Memory Lane Bed and Breakfast

102 South Oak, 65018
(573) 796-4233

Memory Lane is an 1894 home that has been renovated carefully to retain its Victo-

---

NOTES: Credit cards accepted: A MasterCard; B Visa; C American Express; D Discover; E Diner's Club;
F Other; 2 Personal checks accepted; 3 Lunch available; 4 Dinner available; 5 Open all year; 6 Pets welcome;

Cameron, MO   101

Memory Lane

rian character. Guest bedrooms feature antique furnishings while the remainder of the house is decorated with a blend of antique and modern furniture. Antique lovers can enjoy the nostalgia of using an authentic crank telephone or listening to a Thomas Edison crank phonograph. There are more than 50 antique shops within a 35-mile radius of California.

Hosts: Joe and Mary Ellen Laprise
Rooms: 3 (3 SB) $38
Full Breakfast
Credit Cards: None
Notes: 2, 5, 7, 8, 10, 11, 12

CAMERON

Cook's Country Cottage

7880 Northeast Bacon Road, 64429
(816) 632-1776

This country estate, nestled in 40 acres of hardwood timber, offers a serene getaway spot. A private lake, walking trails, water garden, fountains, and a host of wildlife and songbirds entertain and delight guests as they enjoy the peaceful atmosphere. Private entrances and baths assure guests of their privacy while they choose to relax in beautiful rooms furnished in country decor. Shopping and tours to local historical sites including Missouri's largest Amish settlement are available. Warm baked cookies and fresh flowers awaiting guests in their rooms make them feel like "coming home."

Hosts: Don and Loura Cook
Rooms: 2 (PB) $50-75
Full Breakfast
Credit Cards: None
Notes: 2, 3, 4, 5, 7, 10, 11, 12, 13

Cook's Country Cottage

7 No smoking; 8 Children welcome; 9 Social drinking allowed; 10 Tennis nearby; 11 Swimming nearby; 12 Golf nearby; 13 Skiing nearby; 14 May be booked through a travel agent; 15 Handicapped accessible.

DIXON

Rock Eddy Bluff
HCR 62, Box 241, 65459
(573) 759-6081; (800) 335-5921

This rural inn is a nature-lover's dream. Perched atop an Ozark river bluff it provides two scenic guest rooms. They feature unpretentious, old-time furnishings, comfortable, antique, queen-size beds, and a spectacular view of the river valley. Turkey Ridge Cottage is popular with groups of two to six people. Or step back in time at secluded Line Camp, where modern contraptions are prohibited. Canoes are provided for guests. Explore the river, fish, or swim. Just relax or hike the wooded hills. Accompany hosts in an Amish horse-drawn wagon. A place to discover. Reservations only.

Hosts: Kathy and Tom Corey
Rooms: 4 (1 PB; 3 SB) $65-95
Full Breakfast
Credit Cards: A, B, D
Notes: 2, 5, 6, 8, 9, 11, 12

HANNIBAL

Fifth Street Mansion Bed and Breakfast Inn
213 South Fifth Street, 63401
(573) 221-0445; (800) 874-5661
www.hanmo.com/fifthstreetmansion

This Italianate mansion, built in 1858, is one of the remnants of "Millionaires Row," an impressive block of grand homes built and owned by some of Hannibal's wealthiest and most influential citizens. The interior features unique fireplaces, stained glass, and original chandeliers, with large rooms featuring antiques and period decor. Whether seeking a romantic hideaway or a homelike setting on business trips, guests will find Fifth Street Mansion offers a blend of Victorian charm and contemporary comforts with plenty of old-fashioned hospitality.

Fifth Street Mansion

Hosts: Mike and Donalene Andreotti
Rooms: 7 (PB) $75-90
Full Breakfast
Credit Cards: A, B, C, D
Notes: 2, 5, 7, 9, 10, 12, 14

Garth Woodside Mansion
Rural Route 3, Box 578, 63401
(573) 221-2789; www.hanmo.com/garth

Stay at this award-winning 1871 Victorian country estate for the ultimate experience. Original furnishings span more than 150 years with potpourri-scented air, canopied beds, and nightshirts. Spacious bedchambers are a careful selection of lace, fabrics, and textures chosen to blend with an eye toward every detail and comfort. Stroll on 39 magnificent wooded acres or rock and relax on the veranda. Judged one of the Midwest's "Ten Best Inns." Two-night min-

Garth Woodside Mansion

NOTES: Credit cards accepted: A MasterCard; B Visa; C American Express; D Discover; E Diner's Club; F Other; 2 Personal checks accepted; 3 Lunch available; 4 Dinner available; 5 Open all year; 6 Pets welcome;

imum stay required during holidays. Children over 12 are welcome.

Hosts: Irv and Diane Feinberg
Rooms: 8 (PB) $67-110
Full Breakfast
Credit Cards: A, B
Notes: 2, 5, 7, 9, 10, 12

INDEPENDENCE

Woodstock Inn Bed and Breakfast
1212 West Lexington, 64050
(816) 833-2233; (800) 276-5202
FAX (816) 461-7226

Nestled within Independence's famous historical district, the Woodstock Inn Bed and Breakfast is just a short stroll away from all the sites one comes to Independence to see. Eleven warm and inviting rooms, each with a distinct personality and private bath. And after a restful night's sleep, wake up to a piping-hot cup of coffee and take a seat at the long oak dining table. Tempt one's palate with the house's specialty, gourmet Belgium waffles topped with powdered sugar and smothered with specialty syrups or fresh fruit sauce. The full breakfast is exactly what is needed to start off a wonderful day of sightseeing. Inquire about accommodations for children.

Hosts: Todd and Patricia Justice
Rooms: 11 (PB) $59-99
Full Breakfast
Credit Cards: A, B, C, D
Notes: 2, 5, 7, 10, 11, 12, 14, 15

JACKSON

Trisha's Bed and Breakfast, Tea Room and Gifts
203 Bellevue, 63755
(573) 243-7427; (800) 651-0408
www.rosecity.net

Innkeepers Gus and Trisha welcome guests to their 1905 Victorian home in Cape

Trisha's

Girardeau's county seat. Near a historic steam train, parks, historic grist-mill and covered bridge, museums, murals, and much more. Four delightfully decorated guest rooms with private baths are available. Breakfast is a three-course gourmet meal with home-baked goodies, home-grown and hand-picked fruits, jams, plus delicious entrées. Tea room available for parties and special events. Children over five are welcome.

Hosts: Gus and Trisha
Rooms: 4 (PB) $55-80
Full Breakfast
Credit Cards: A, B
Notes: 2, 3, 4, 5, 7, 10, 11, 12, 14

JAMESPORT

Nancy's Guest Cottage Bed and Breakfast
Rural Route 1, Box 3, 64648
(660) 684-6156

The guest cottage is within walking distance of 16 antique shops and 27 craft and specialty shops. Guests will receive the use of an entire house filled with antique memories of yesteryear. A full country breakfast is included. There is also a large selection of country dinner menus available. Country horse and buggy rides available. Jamesport

---

7 No smoking; 8 Children welcome; 9 Social drinking allowed; 10 Tennis nearby; 11 Swimming nearby;
12 Golf nearby; 13 Skiing nearby; 14 May be booked through a travel agent; 15 Handicapped accessible.

is the largest Amish community in Missouri. Homemade cookies always ready for guests' arrival.

Hostess/owner: Nancy Eads
Rooms: 4 (4 SB) $75
Full Breakfast
Credit Cards: A, B
Notes: 2, 3, 4, 5, 6, 8, 9, 12, 14

KANSAS CITY

Bed and Breakfast Kansas City
P.O. Box 14781, Lenexa, KS 66285
(913) 888-3636

Forty Victorian turn-of-the-century contemporary homes and three inns for great getaways. Accommodations near Country Club Plaza, Kansas City, Independence, or adjacent historic towns. All sizes of beds and all with private bath. Some with fireplace, Jacuzzi, pool, or hot tub. Accommodations also available in the country. Two accommodations are handicapped accessible.

Agent: Edwina Monroe
Accommodations: (PB) $60-160
Full Breakfast
Credit Cards: None
Notes: 2, 5, 7

The Doanleigh Inn
217 East 37th Street, 64111
(816) 753-2667; FAX (816) 531-5185

In the heart of the city, the Doanleigh Inn stands between the famed Country Club Plaza and Hallmark Crown Center. Lovely European and American antiques enhance the Georgian architecture of the inn. Wine and hors d'oeuvres await guests each evening and a full gourmet breakfast is served each morning. Fireplaces and Jacuzzis provide the ultimate in relaxation. Other amenities include afternoon cookies, daily newspapers, free local calls and faxes, and in-room computer modem access.

Hosts: Cynthia Brogdon and Terry Maturo
Rooms: 5 (PB) $95-150

The Doanleigh Inn

Full Breakfast
Credit Cards: A, B, C, D
Notes: 2, 5, 7, 9, 10, 14

Hotel Savoy
219 West 9th Street, 64105
(816) 842-3575

Hotel Savoy is one of the finest European bed and breakfast hotels in the United States. Built in 1888, it offers the opportunity to drift back in time in suites filled with antiques and Victorian decor. Breakfast consists of more than 32 items, such as lobster bisque, salmon and caviar, medallions of beef, or even oysters Rockefeller. In the heart of Kansas City's historic garment district. A very romantic getaway.

Hotel Savoy

NOTES: Credit cards accepted: A MasterCard; B Visa; C American Express; D Discover; E Diner's Club; F Other; 2 Personal checks accepted; 3 Lunch available; 4 Dinner available; 5 Open all year; 6 Pets welcome;

Host: Larry Green
Rooms: 110 (PB) $79-120
Full Breakfast
Credit Cards: A, B, C, D, E, F
Notes: 2, 3, 4, 5, 7, 8, 9, 14

Pridewell

600 West 50th Street, 64112
(816) 931-1642

A fine Tudor residence in a residential area on the site of the Civil War battle of Westport. Near the Nelson Art Gallery, University of Missouri-Kansas City, Missouri Repertory Theatre, and Rockhurst College. Adjacent to Country Club Plaza shopping district, including several four-star restaurants, public transportation, public tennis courts, and park.

Hosts: Edwin and Louann White
Rooms: 2 (1 PB; 1 SB) $75-80
Full Breakfast
Credit Cards: None
Notes: 2, 5, 7, 8, 9, 14

Southmoreland on the Plaza

116 East 46th Street, 64112
(816) 531-7979

A two-time winner of the ABBA's four-crown award, recognized for "Outstanding Achievement in Preservation" by the Association of American Historic Inns, and named "Most Romantic New Urban Inn" by *Romantic Hideaways* newsletter, this classic New England Colonial between Country Club Plaza and the Nelson-Atkins Museum of Art presents an elegant bed-and-breakfast atmosphere with small-hotel amenities. Rooms offer private decks, fireplaces, or Jacuzzi baths. Special services designed for business travelers. Privileges at Plaza Health Club and Spa. Mobil Travel Guide four-star winner since 1993.

Hosts: Penni Johnson and Susan Moehl
Rooms: 12 (PB) $115-170
Full Breakfast
Credit Cards: A, B, C
Notes: 2, 5, 7, 9, 10, 14, 15

NEOSHO

Southmoreland on the Plaza

The Heaton House

The Heaton House

335 South Wood Street, 64850
(417) 455-0788; FAX (417) 455-0494

A three-story Queen Anne Victorian built in 1902. The house has its original oak and pine woodwork throughout and features five fireplaces. Get acquainted with other guests in the sitting room, relax in the main parlor, or swing on the large wraparound porch. In the morning guests are invited downstairs to the dining room to enjoy a full country breakfast.

---

7 No smoking; 8 Children welcome; 9 Social drinking allowed; 10 Tennis nearby; 11 Swimming nearby; 12 Golf nearby; 13 Skiing nearby; 14 May be booked through a travel agent; 15 Handicapped accessible.

Host: Brenda Brewer
Rooms: 3 (PB) $55-70
Full Breakfast
Credit Cards: A, B
Notes: 2, 5, 7, 8, 11, 12

ROCHEPORT

School House Bed and Breakfast Inn
504 Third Street, 65279
(573) 698-2022

This historic three-story brick building was once a school house. Now luxuriously appointed as a country inn, it features 13-foot-high ceilings, custom-made plantation shutters, beautiful antiques, and two suites with private spa. Each room is accented with a few reminders of the inn's simple past like the large framed prints of the famous *Dick and Jane Primer*. The basement houses an antique shop. Within walking distance are cafés, a winery, galleries, antique shops, and a 200-mile-long hiking and biking trail.

Hosts: Vicki and John Ott; Penny Province
Rooms: 10 (PB) $85-155
Full Breakfast
Credit Cards: A, B
Notes: 2, 5, 7, 8, 9, 10, 11, 12, 14, 15

ST. CHARLES

Boone's Lick Trail Inn
1000 South Main Street, 63301
(314) 947-7000; FAX (314) 946-2637

The Boone's Lick Trail Inn is named for the road blazed by the sons of Daniel Boone for transporting salt. The inn, circa 1840, is now the southern anchor of the St. Charles National Historic District, a delightful 10-block area filled with historic buildings, cobblestone streets, gas lamps, and more than 100 shops, boutiques, and restaurants. At the doorstep, lie the historic 230-mile hiking and biking Katy Trail State Park, *Goldenrod* showboat, Casino St. Charles,

Boone's Lick Trail Inn

Lewis and Clark Center, a certified site on the Lewis and Clark Trail, Missouri's first state capitol, and Frenchtown, with the St. Rose Philippine Duchesne Shrine. Closed Christmas Day and Easter Saturday.

Hosts: V'Anne and Paul Mydler
Rooms: 5 (PB) $85-175
Full Breakfast
Credit Cards: A, B, C, D, E
Notes: 2, 7, 8, 9, 10, 11, 12, 14, 15

STE. GENEVIEVE

Inn St. Gemme Beauvais
78 North Main, 63670
(314) 883-5744

This magnificent structure has been redecorated and updated recently. It boasts of being the oldest continuously operated inn in Missouri and is in the historic district. Each room has a unique theme and most are two-room suites. A three-course breakfast is served in the elegant Victorian living room, and all historic buildings are within walking distance. Lunch, high tea, and hors d'oeuvres are served daily. Dinner is served by special arrangement.

Host: Janet Joggerst
Rooms: 7 (PB) $69-149
Full Breakfast
Credit Cards: A, B, D
Notes: 2, 3, 4, 5, 7, 8, 9, 10, 11, 12

NOTES: Credit cards accepted: A MasterCard; B Visa; C American Express; D Discover; E Diner's Club; F Other; 2 Personal checks accepted; 3 Lunch available; 4 Dinner available; 5 Open all year; 6 Pets welcome;

Southern Hotel

Southern Hotel

146 South Third Street, 63670
(800) 275-1412
e-mail: southernhotelbb@ldd.net
www.southernhotelbb.com

This graceful 1790s Federal building began operating as a hotel in 1805 and was known for the finest accommodations between Natchez and St. Louis. Each of the romantic guest rooms contains a collection of country Victorian antiques and delightful "whimsies." Here the past is carefully blended with modern comforts to make guests' stay a very special experience. Named "One of the Ten Best Inns in the Midwest." Oldest, longest operating hotel or lodging in the United States west of the Mississippi.

Hosts: Mike and Barbara Hankins
Rooms: 8 (PB) $80-125
Full Breakfast
Credit Cards: A, B, D
Notes: 2, 5, 7, 9, 10, 11, 12

ST. LOUIS

Fleur-de-Lys Inn, Mansion at the Park

3500 Russell Boulevard, 63104
(314) 773-3500; (888) 969-3500
FAX (314) 773-6546

The city's most luxurious inn, famous for its special accommodations for business travelers. This elegant, historic mansion in the heart of St. Louis was built in 1912. It features 12-foot ceilings and rich wood moldings and trim. Restored and furnished in antique and period reproduction furnishings, the inn's individual suites and rooms all boast private baths, designer fabrics, telephones, data ports, and cable TVs. Two suites feature Jacuzzi tubs. Full gourmet breakfasts plus evening appetizers served daily. Total pampering and sumptuous surroundings for sophisticated business and leisure travelers are the inn's specialties.

Host: Kathryn Leep
Rooms: 4 (PB) $80-175
Full Breakfast
Credit Cards: A, B, C, D, E
Notes: 2, 4, 5, 7, 9, 10, 11, 12, 14

Lafayette House Bed and Breakfast

2156 Lafayette Avenue, 63104-2543
(314) 772-4429; (800) 641-8965
FAX (314) 664-8965
www.bbonline.com/mo/lafayette/

This 1876 Queen Anne mansion is in historic Lafayette Square. The Lafayette House is only minutes from downtown St. Louis. Attend a baseball or football game, shop at historic Union Station, visit the Gateway Arch, science center, zoo, or simply stroll through lovely Lafayette

Lafayette House

---

7 No smoking; 8 Children welcome; 9 Social drinking allowed; 10 Tennis nearby; 11 Swimming nearby; 12 Golf nearby; 13 Skiing nearby; 14 May be booked through a travel agent; 15 Handicapped accessible.

Square Park. The suite, on the third floor that can accommodate four, has a private bath and kitchen. For the business guests, there are a fax, in-room telephones, and flexible breakfast hours. AAA-inspected and -approved. Resident cats.

Hosts: Nancy Buhr and Annalise Millet
Rooms: 6 (3 PB; 3 SB) $60-150
Full Breakfast
Credit Cards: A, B, C, D, E
Notes: 2, 5, 7, 8, 9, 12, 14

Napoleon's Retreat Bed and Breakfast

1815 Lafayette Avenue, 63104
(314) 772-6979; (800) 700-9980

Built in 1880 in historic Lafayette Square, recently chosen as one of America's "Prettiest Painted Places," this elegant, fully restored French Second Empire Victorian offers stunning accommodations in an exquisite, yet comfortable, setting. Furnished with fine antiques and artwork, all air-conditioned guest rooms feature private baths, cable TV, and private telephones. The Carriage House suite features a kitchen as well as balcony overlooking the garden courtyard, while another room boasts a fireplace and oversize whirlpool tub. A two-minute walk to several restaurants, Napoleon's Retreat is just one and one-half miles from downtown St. Louis, including the convention center, sports stadiums, and the arch.

Hosts: Michael Lance and Jeff Archuleta
Rooms: 5 (PB) $75-150
Full Breakfast
Credit Cards: A, B, C, D, E
Notes: 2, 5, 7, 9, 12, 14

Somewhere!! A Bed and Breakfast Guesthouse

2049 Sidney Street, 63104-2828
(314) 664-4PAM (4726)
(800) 730-2PAM (2726)

This three-story Victorian brick boasts many original 1881 architectural features, including marble fireplaces, 14-foot ceilings, pocket doors, and a Victorian garden. The two guest suites have Jacuzzi baths, crystal chandeliers, cable TV/VCR units, and CD/cassette players, coffee makers, robes, freshly cut flowers, chocolates, and complimentary "welcome home" snacks. The full breakfast features the owner's homemade yeast rolls made from scratch or enjoy a Continental breakfast in bed. "Spoil me rotten" packages and weekend specials available. Close to downtown, Soulard market area, Anheuser-Busch Brewery, Cherokee Antique Row; 30 minutes from airport. Off-street parking.

Host: Pam Pullman
Rooms: 2 (PB) $175
Full or Continental Breakfast
Credit Cards: A, B, C, D
Notes: 2, 5, 9

The Winter House

3522 Arsenal Street, 63118
(314) 664-4399
e-mail: kmwinter@swbell.net

Nine-room Victorian built in 1897 features pressed-tin ceiling in lower bedroom, a suite with TV, and the Rose Room with king-size bed on second floor. Live piano music complimentary at breakfast with advance notice. Fruit, candy, and fresh flowers are provided in bedrooms. Nearby attractions include a Victorian

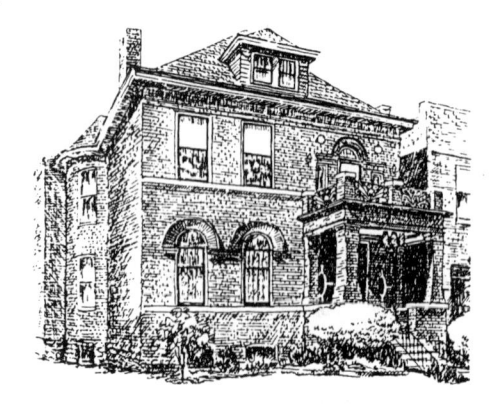

The Winter House

NOTES: Credit cards accepted: A MasterCard; B Visa; C American Express; D Discover; E Diner's Club; F Other; 2 Personal checks accepted; 3 Lunch available; 4 Dinner available; 5 Open all year; 6 Pets welcome;

walking park in the national register and the Missouri Botanical Garden. Within six miles are the Gateway Arch, Busch Stadium, St. Louis Science Center, Trans World Dome, zoo, symphony, and Union Station. Walk to fine dining. Reservations required. Additional fee of $20 for one-night stays.

Host: Kendall Winter
Rooms: 2 (PB) $85-105
Suite: 1 (PB) $100
Full Breakfast
Credit Cards: A, B, C, D, E, F
Notes: 2, 5, 7, 8, 9, 10, 14

SPRINGFIELD

Virginia Rose Bed and Breakfast
317 East Glenwood, 65807
(417) 883-0693; (800) 345-1412
e-mail: vrosebb@mocom.net

This two-story farmhouse built in 1906 offers a country atmosphere and hospitality right in town. On a tree-covered acre, the home is complete with red barn, rockers on the porch, lovely period furnishings, and quilts on queen-size beds. Guests can relax in the parlor with a glass of iced tea or snickerdoodle coffee as they read or watch TV. Hearty homemade breakfasts are served with freshly baked muffins or biscuits on Virginia Rose dishes that have been lovingly collected for years.

Virginia Rose

Walnut Street Inn

Hosts: Jackie and Virginia Buck
Rooms: 5 (PB) $50-100
Full Breakfast
Credit Cards: A, B, C, D
Notes: 2, 5, 7, 8, 11, 12, 14

Walnut Street Inn
900 East Walnut, 65806
(417) 864-6346; (800) 593-6346

This award-winning 1894 Queen Anne Victorian inn, in the historic district, invites guests to escape. Friendly innkeepers, flickering fireplaces, European antiques, four-poster beds, feather comforters, Jacuzzis, skylights, and Victorian flower gardens abound. Walk to performing arts centers, theaters, cafés, boutiques, and antique shops. Near Bass Pro Shops Outdoor World, Branson music shows, with the glorious Ozark Mountains at the back door.

---

7 No smoking; 8 Children welcome; 9 Social drinking allowed; 10 Tennis nearby; 11 Swimming nearby; 12 Golf nearby; 13 Skiing nearby; 14 May be booked through a travel agent; 15 Handicapped accessible.

Hosts: Gary and Paula Blankenship
Rooms: 12 (PB) $84-159
Full Breakfast
Credit Cards: A, B, C, D, E, F
Notes: 2, 5, 7, 8, 9, 10, 11, 12, 14

WARRENSBURG

Cedarcroft Farm

431 Southeast County Road Y, 64093-8316
(660) 747-5728; (800) 368-4944
e-mail: bwayne@cedarcroft.com
www.cedarcroft.com

Cedarcroft Farm offers old-fashioned country hospitality, country quiet, and more-than-you-can-eat country cooking on an 1867 family farm listed in the National Register of Historic Places. Guests may explore the 80 acres of secluded woods, meadows, and streams, and savor a full country breakfast. Hosts are Civil War re-enactors who demonstrate 1860s soldiers' life. Home of Old Star Fertilizer, as featured on CNN.

Hosts: Sandra and Bill Wayne
Suite: 1 (PB) $75-90
Full Breakfast

Credit Cards: A, B, C, D
Notes: 2, 4, 5, 7, 8, 9, 11, 12, 14

WASHINGTON

Schwegmann House Bed and Breakfast Inn

438 West Front Street, 63090
(314) 239-5025; (800) 949-2262
FAX (314) 239-3920
www.SchwegmannHouse.com

In the heart of Missouri River wine country, the Schwegmann House rekindles the local flour miller's gracious hospitality of 137 years ago. Nine elegant guest rooms, river views, private baths, antique furnishings, and handmade quilts await guests' stay. Relax by the fireside or stroll perennial gardens. Savor a generous breakfast. Relish the Miller's Suite massage tub for two. Walk to excellent restaurants, antique and gift shops. Mobil Travel Guide-approved. In the National Register of Historic Places.

Hosts: Cathy and Bill Nagel
Rooms: 9 (PB) $75-150
Full Breakfast

Cedarcroft Farm

NOTES: Credit cards accepted: A MasterCard; B Visa; C American Express; D Discover; E Diner's Club; F Other; 2 Personal checks accepted; 3 Lunch available; 4 Dinner available; 5 Open all year; 6 Pets welcome;

Washington House Bed and Breakfast

100 West Front Street, 63090
(314) 742-4360

Washington House, built circa 1837, is in a national historic district. This authentically restored inn on the Missouri River features river views, canopied beds, antiques, and full breakfast. Washington House is in the heart of Missouri's wine country, only 45 minutes west of St. Louis.

Hosts: Terry and Sue Black
Rooms: 2 (PB) $75
Full Breakfast

Washington House

Credit Cards: A, B
Notes: 2, 5, 7, 8, 9, 10, 11, 12, 13

---

7 No smoking; 8 Children welcome; 9 Social drinking allowed; 10 Tennis nearby; 11 Swimming nearby; 12 Golf nearby; 13 Skiing nearby; 14 May be booked through a travel agent; 15 Handicapped accessible.

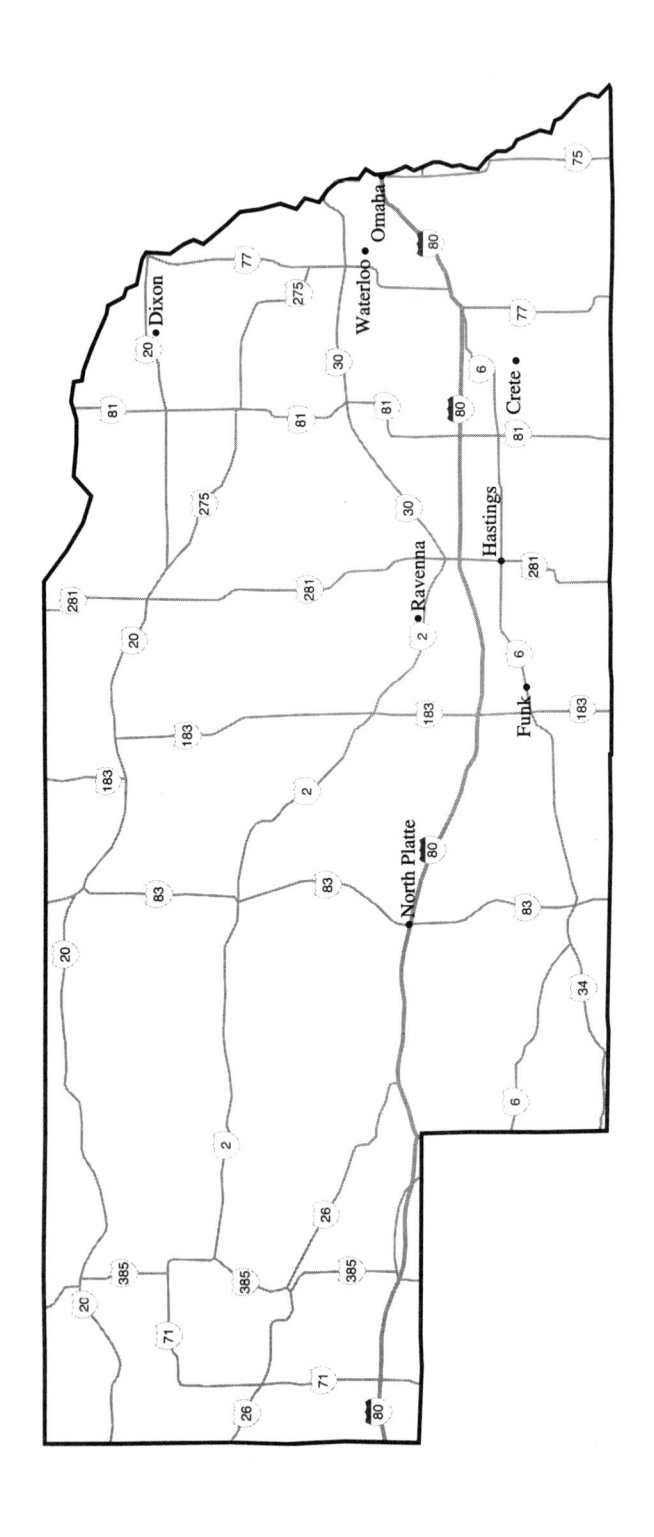

Nebraska

Nebraska

CRETE

The Parson's House
638 Forest Avenue, 68333
(402) 826-2634

Enjoy warm hospitality in a restored four-square home built at the turn of the century in a quiet neighborhood near Doane College and its beautiful campus. Furnished with much antique furniture and a modern whirlpool bathtub. A full breakfast is served in the formal dining room.

Host: Sandy Richardson
Rooms: 2 (SB) $45
Full Breakfast
Credit Cards: None
Notes: 2, 5, 7, 10, 11, 12

DIXON

The George's
57759-874 Road, 68732-3024
(402) 584-2625; e-mail: DixonMom@aol.com

Spacious, air-conditioned farmhouse 35 miles west of Sioux City, Iowa. Enjoy country hospitality, hearty breakfasts, hiking, bird watching, and hunting during pheasant season. Table games, relaxing with a book, local fairs and celebrations. Many recreational activities within easy driving distance. Quiet and relaxing setting. Pets welcome by prior arrangement.

Host: Mrs. Marie George
Rooms: 6 (6 SB) $40-45
Full Breakfast
Credit Cards: None
Notes: 2, 7, 8, 9, 10, 11, 12

FUNK

Uncle Sam's Hilltop Lodge
Rural Route 1, Box 110, 68940
(308) 995-5568 (evenings)
(308) 995-2204 (answering machine)

Uncle Sam says "we want you for our guest." Only five minutes from I-80 and a suburb of Kearney. Sandhill cranes are nearby in spring. This 1979 solar home is built into Nebraska's Sandhills with four levels; all are ground level. An indoor sand pile and game room are available. Enjoy the view or relax in the tub for two. Free full breakfasts and farm tours.

Hosts: Sam and Sharon Schrock
Rooms: 2 (1 PB; 1 SB) $40-60
Full Breakfast
Credit Cards: None
Notes: 2, 5, 6, 7, 8, 10, 11, 12

HASTINGS

Grandma's Victorian Inn Bed and Breakfast
1826 West 3rd Street, 68901
(402) 462-2013

Built circa 1886, this Victorian home has an open staircase and outstanding woodwork. For guests' comfort, each room has a private bath. Antique furniture is exhibited in the home with an accent on rocking chairs and a queen-size bed is in each room. Breakfast is served in the dining room; breakfast in bed can be arranged at additional charge. Return to the memories of yore and "whispers of yesterday." Children over 12 are welcome.

NOTES: Credit cards accepted: A MasterCard; B Visa; C American Express; D Discover; E Diner's Club; F Other; 2 Personal checks accepted; 3 Lunch available; 4 Dinner available; 5 Open all year; 6 Pets welcome; 7 No smoking; 8 Children welcome; 9 Social drinking allowed; 10 Tennis nearby; 11 Swimming nearby; 12 Golf nearby; 13 Skiing nearby; 14 May be booked through a travel agent; 15 Handicapped accessible.

Manager/Innkeeper: Tim Sassman
Rooms: 5 (PB) $60
Full Breakfast
Credit Cards: A, B, D
Notes: 5, 7, 10, 11, 12, 15

NORTH PLATTE

Knoll's Country Inn

Route 2, Box 458, 69101
(308) 368-5634; (800) 337-4526
www.bbonline.com/ne/knolls

Knoll's Country Inn, circa 1974, is in the country on 20 acres surrounded by peace and quiet. The hostess loves to cook and offers delicious breakfasts. The four guest rooms have queen-size beds. Relax in a whirlpool bathtub or under the stars in the outdoor hot tub. There are four golf courses nearby, hunting in season, and two lakes for fishing and water sports. For railroad buffs, North Platte has the Union Pacific Railroad's Bailey Yard, the largest classification yard in the world. The *Challenger* locomotive is at Cody Park in North Platte. The inn is on I-80 and Highway 83, halfway between Omaha and Denver. Children 12 and older are welcome.

Hosts: Arlene and Bob Knoll
Rooms: 4 (1 PB: 3 SB) $55-75
Full Breakfast
Credit Cards: None
Notes: 2, 5, 10, 11, 12, 13

OMAHA

The Offutt House

140 North 39th Street, 68131
(402) 553-0951

This comfortable mansion, built in 1894, is in the section of large homes built around the same time by Omaha's most wealthy residents. Rooms are comfortably spacious and furnished with antiques. Some feature fireplaces. The house is near downtown Omaha and the historic Old Market area, which offers many beautiful shops and excellent restaurants. Full breakfast offered. Reservations requested.

The Offutt House

Hosts: Janet and Paul Koenig
Rooms: 6 (PB) $65-105
Full Breakfast
Credit Cards: A, B, C, D
Notes: 2, 5, 6, 7, 8, 9, 10, 11, 12, 14

RAVENNA

Aunt Betty's Bed and Breakfast

804 Grand Avenue, 68869
(308) 452-3739

Enjoy the peacefulness of a small midwestern town in a Victorian three-story bed and breakfast. Four guest rooms, sitting room with coffee, hot chocolate, soft drinks, tea, TV, and books. Each room is tastefully decorated in antiques. Hunter's loft on third floor, with special accommodations for hunters, including guide, dogs, and suggestions for places to hunt. Enjoy a full Nebraska breakfast with special features such as German pancakes, egg dishes of all kinds, fresh fruit, juice, cottage fries, and Aunt Betty's sticky buns. Breakfast is served in the formal dining room or in the garden when weather permits.

Hosts: Harvey and Betty Shrader
Rooms: 4 (4 SB) $49-59
Full Breakfast
Credit Cards: A, B, D
Notes: 2, 5, 7, 8, 10, 11, 12

NOTES: Credit cards accepted: A MasterCard; B Visa; C American Express; D Discover; E Diner's Club; F Other; 2 Personal checks accepted; 3 Lunch available; 4 Dinner available; 5 Open all year; 6 Pets welcome;

WATERLOO

The J.C. Robinson House
102 East Lincoln Avenue, 68069-0190
(402) 779-2704; (800) 779-2705

This wonderful bed and breakfast was built in 1905 and is in the national historic register. The 21-room mansion retains its original appointments including hardwood floors, carved paneling, stained and leaded glass, tiled fireplaces, and pocket doors. Antique furnishings, including an extensive clock collection dating from 1735, create an atmosphere of relaxation and rest. The house invites guests to step back in time to an earlier, gracious era.

The J.C. Robinson House

Hosts: Bill and Linda Clark
Rooms: 4 (1 PB; 3 SB) $50-80
Full and Continental Breakfast
Credit Cards: None
Notes: 2, 5, 7, 9, 11, 12, 14

7 No smoking; 8 Children welcome; 9 Social drinking allowed; 10 Tennis nearby; 11 Swimming nearby; 12 Golf nearby; 13 Skiing nearby; 14 May be booked through a travel agent; 15 Handicapped accessible.

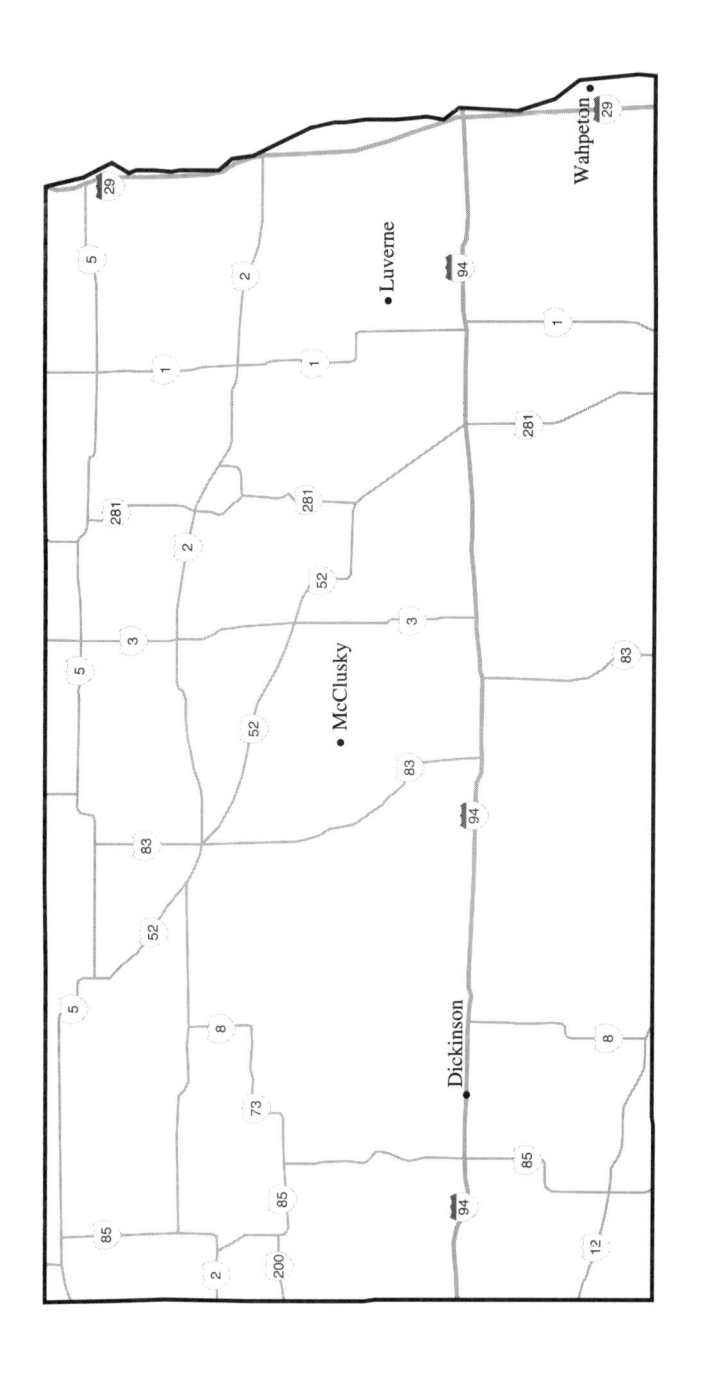

North Dakota

North Dakota

DICKINSON

Hartfiel Inn
509 Third Avenue West, 58601
(701) 225-6710; FAX (701) 225-1184

The Hartfiel Inn was originally built in 1908. Decorating of the inn was inspired by travels to Europe. Every room holds many cultural surprises. Special features include candlelight breakfast and dining in the formal dining room or on the terrace. Large private back yard with waterfall and garden. Large fireplace and formal library. Private hot tub room. The inn is designed to spoil the most discriminating of tastes. Close to many tourist sites.

Hosts: Rick and Quita Hartfiel
Rooms: 4 (PB) $59-89
Full Breakfast
Credit Cards: A, B
Notes: 2, 5, 6, 8, 9, 10, 11, 12, 14

LUVERNE

Volden Farm Bed and Breakfast
Rural Route 2, Box 50, 58056
(701) 769-2275

A retreat in the real sense of the word. Peace, quiet, beauty, good books, art, nature, and animals join with home comforts, good food, great coffee, and conversation for an ideal stay on the Volden farm. Four guest rooms available with shared and private baths. Separate house available for privacy with deck, feather bed, and more. Inquire about accommodations for pets. Outdoor smoking permitted.

Volden Farm

Hosts: Jim and JoAnne Wold
Rooms: 4 (1 PB; 3 SB) $50-95
Full Breakfast
Credit Cards: None
Notes: 2, 3, 4, 5, 7, 8, 9, 10, 11, 12, 13, 14

MCCLUSKY

Midstate Bed and Breakfast
980 Highway 200 Northeast, 58463-9281
(701) 363-2520 (phone/FAX); (888) 434-2520

An easy location to find! This 1980s home is on a working farm at mile marker 232 on Highway 200, the highway known to be the most economical passage through the northern U.S. Guests enter through a plant-filled atrium to a private lower level that also includes guests' own TV lounge. In an area of abundant upland game, waterfowl, and deer. Guests are allowed hunting privilege on over 4,000 acres. Air conditioning. Elegance and excellence in hospitality, yet economical.

Hosts: Grace and Allen Faul
Rooms: 4 (1 PB; 3 SB) $35
Full Breakfast
Credit Cards: None
Notes: 2, 3, 4, 5, 7, 8, 9, 10, 11

NOTES: Credit cards accepted: A MasterCard; B Visa; C American Express; D Discover; E Diner's Club; F Other; 2 Personal checks accepted; 3 Lunch available; 4 Dinner available; 5 Open all year; 6 Pets welcome; 7 No smoking; 8 Children welcome; 9 Social drinking allowed; 10 Tennis nearby; 11 Swimming nearby; 12 Golf nearby; 13 Skiing nearby; 14 May be booked through a travel agent; 15 Handicapped accessible.

WAHPETON

Abercrombie Country Inn

6855 177 Avenue Southeast, 58075
(701) 553-9235; (800) 383-5071

Just one-half hour from Fargo, this contemporary bed and breakfast inn is in the Red River Valley. Guest quarters include lobby, balcony with open staircase, fireplace, and four exterior decks. Rooms are equipped with queen-size beds, TVs, and telephones. An indoor hot tub and outdoor spa are available. Many Canada geese return each spring to nest in interesting places on the acreage, including in a barbecue grill on a deck. Guests may take photographs.

Host: Rich Holm
Rooms: 4 (PB) $50-75
Full Breakfast
Credit Cards: A, B, D
Notes: 2, 3, 4, 5, 7, 8, 9, 12, 15

---

7 No smoking; 8 Children welcome; 9 Social drinking allowed; 10 Tennis nearby; 11 Swimming nearby; 12 Golf nearby; 13 Skiing nearby; 14 May be booked through a travel agent; 15 Handicapped accessible.

Ohio

ARCHBOLD

Sauder Heritage Inn
State Route 2, P.O. Box 235, 43502
(800) 590-9755

In northwest Ohio's rural corner, the Sauder Heritage Inn is ideal for a getaway or retreat. Each of the 33 smoke-free, oversized rooms features private bath and refrigerator. Upscale Continental breakfast served each morning in the majestically timber-framed lobby. Featured in October 1995 issue of *Country Inns* magazine. Historic village adjacent. Lunch and dinner available at the adjacent restaurant.

Host: Orlyss Sauder
Rooms: 33 (PB) $89-129
Continental Breakfast
Credit Cards: A, B, C
Notes: 2, 5, 7, 8, 11, 12, 14, 15

ASHTABULA

Michael Cahill Bed and Breakfast
1106 Walnut Boulevard, 44004
(440) 964-8449

The Cahill home is a Stick-style Victorian structure built in 1887. Completely restored in the mid-1980s, the whole house is used for the bed and breakfast, with four bedrooms and three large sitting rooms. Guests enjoy walking access to Lake Erie, nature museum, marine museum, Hubbard House, charter boat fishing, Bridge Street shops, and eateries. Or they may relax on the large wraparound porch.

Hosts: Pat and Paul Goode
Rooms: 4 (PB) $55-65
Full Breakfast
Credit Cards: None
Notes: 2, 5, 8, 9, 10, 11, 12, 14

BELLVILLE

The Frederick Fitting House
72 Fitting Avenue, 44813
(419) 886-2863

An 1863 Victorian home in a quaint country village between Columbus and Cleveland. Near Mohican and Malabar Farm State Parks, downhill and cross-country skiing, bike trail, canoeing, and Kenyon College. Gourmet breakfast served in the formal dining room, or garden gazebo. Closed Thanksgiving and Christmas.

Host: Barbara Lomax
Rooms: 3 (PB) $69-79
Full Breakfast
Credit Cards: None
Notes: 2, 7, 10, 11, 12, 13

---

7 No smoking; 8 Children welcome; 9 Social drinking allowed; 10 Tennis nearby; 11 Swimming nearby; 12 Golf nearby; 13 Skiing nearby; 14 May be booked through a travel agent; 15 Handicapped accessible.

Ohio

BERLIN

The Oaks Bed and Breakfast
4752 US 62, P.O. Box 421, 44610
(330) 893-3061; (800) 246-2504

Within walking distance to all Berlin shops and eateries. Two country decor rooms with large common room and gas fireplace. A lofted Victorian master suite with skylights, whirlpool/shower, and private sitting room. All accommodations have private baths, cable TV/VCR, and air conditioning. Continental breakfast and smoke free. Open Sunday and year-round. Amish-Mennonite hosts.

Rooms: 3 (PB) $55-95
Continental Breakfast
Credit Cards: A, B, D
Notes: 2, 5, 7, 8, 10, 11, 12, 14

CENTERVILLE

Yesterday Bed and Breakfast
39 South Main Street, 45458
(937) 433-0785; (800) 225-0485

Ten miles south of the center of Dayton, in the Centerville historic district, this house adjoins a group of fine antique shops. The house was built in 1882 and is tastefully furnished with antiques. Near restaurants and two museums. Easy driving distance of the U.S. Air Force Museum in Dayton, Kings Island theme park, and historic Lebanon and Waynesville, both major antique centers. The University of Dayton and Wright State University are 15 to 20 minutes away.

Hosts: Judy and Chuck
Rooms: 3 (PB) $70-75
Full Breakfast
Credit Cards: F
Notes: 2, 5, 7, 9, 12, 14

CHARDON

Bass Lake Inn

Bass Lake Inn
426 South Street, 44046
(216) 285-3100

Tastefully decorated rooms provide guests with a queen-size bed, gas fireplace, Jacuzzi bath, and a kitchenette with refrigerator, microwave, and coffee maker. Adjacent to the inn is the Bass Lake Taverne where guests can enjoy indoor dining by brickwork fireplaces or on a spacious outdoor patio. Banquet and meeting facilities available. Call for reservations and price information.

Host: Jodie Davis
Rooms: 12 (PB)
Continental Breakfast
Credit Cards: A, B, C, D, E
Notes: 2, 3, 4, 5, 9, 12, 13

Yesterday

NOTES: Credit cards accepted: A MasterCard; B Visa; C American Express; D Discover; E Diner's Club; F Other; 2 Personal checks accepted; 3 Lunch available; 4 Dinner available; 5 Open all year; 6 Pets welcome; 7 No smoking; 8 Children welcome; 9 Social drinking allowed; 10 Tennis nearby; 11 Swimming nearby; 12 Golf nearby; 13 Skiing nearby; 14 May be booked through a travel agent; 15 Handicapped accessible.

CHILLICOTHE

The Greenhouse Bed and Breakfast
47 East Fifth Street, 45601
(614) 775-5313

A Queen Anne-style home built in 1894 and listed in the National Register of Historic Places. Leaded-glass doors and stained-glass windows, parquet floors, and cherry beamed ceilings. The guest rooms are large, quiet, comfortable, and furnished with antiques. A full breakfast is served in the formal cherry dining room. In the historic district close to museums, antique and specialty shops, restaurants, and the Majestic Theatre in downtown Chillicothe. No smoking in the bedrooms. AAA three-diamond rating.

Hosts: Tom and Dee Shoemaker
Rooms: 4 (PB)
Full Breakfast
Credit Cards: A, B, C
Notes: 2, 8, 9, 10, 11, 12

The Greenhouse

Victoria Manor Bed and Breakfast
30 Western Avenue, 45601
(740) 775-6424; (800) 852-1093

This 1859 Victorian vernacular Italianate-style home is in a country-like setting with

Victoria Manor

woods on one side. Rooms are furnished with antiques and have air conditioning, telephones, and TV/VCR. A full breakfast is served in the dining room. Conveniently two blocks west of the center of historic downtown Chillicothe (Ohio's first capital). Near Tecumseh Outdoor Drama, Adena, and Hopewell Cultural Center. Reservations recommended. The inn also has Ohio's Champion American Elm tree as a corner marker of the property. Smoking permitted in designated areas only.

Host: Kathryn Galloway
Rooms: 4 (2 PB; 2 SB) $65-70
Full Breakfast
Credit Cards: A, B, C, D, F
Notes: 2, 5, 8, 9, 10, 11, 12, 13

CINCINNATI

Prospect Hill Bed and Breakfast
408 Boal Street, 45210
(513) 421-4408

Nestled into a wooded hillside, this Italianate Victorian townhouse was built in 1867 on Prospect Hill, a national historic district. The bed and breakfast has been restored, keeping original woodwork, doors, hardware, and light fixtures. Each room is furnished with period antiques and offers fireplaces, skeleton keys, and

---

NOTES: Credit cards accepted: A MasterCard; B Visa; C American Express; D Discover; E Diner's Club; F Other; 2 Personal checks accepted; 3 Lunch available; 4 Dinner available; 5 Open all year; 6 Pets welcome;

spectacular views. A full buffet breakfast is served. Hot tub. Ample free parking. The only bed and breakfast downtown. Sixteen blocks to convention center.

Hosts: Gary Hackney and Tony Jenkins
Rooms: 4 (2 PB; 2 SB) $89-139
Full Breakfast
Credit Cards: A, B, C, D
Notes: 5, 7, 9, 11, 12, 13

The Victoria Inn of Hyde Park

3567 Shaw Avenue, 45208
(513) 321-3567; (888) 422-4629
FAX (513) 321-3147

The Victoria Inn of Hyde Park is an elegant and comfortable bed and breakfast in the heart of Cincinnati's most charming neighborhood. The inn received a *Better Homes & Gardens* award for outstanding renovation. Perfect for business or romantic getaway. Fifteen minutes from downtown, Riverfront Stadium, the zoo, and numerous local universities. The only bed and breakfast in the area that supplies private telephones, a fax, copier, and in-ground swimming pool. Voted Best B&B, *Cincinnati* magazine, October 1993.

Hosts: Tom Possert and Debra Moore
Rooms: 4 (PB) $89-149
Full Breakfast
Credit Cards: A, B, C
Notes: 2, 5, 7, 10, 11, 12

The Victoria Inn of Hyde Park

CLEVELAND

Private Lodgings, Inc. A-1

P.O. Box 18590, 44118
(216) 321-3213 (phone/fax)
e-mail: privatlodg@aol.com

A variety of accommodations including bed and breakfast lodgings, homeshare for longer stays, or short-term rentals in houses and apartments in the greater Cleveland area. Near the Cleveland Clinic, Case Western Reserve University, major museums and galleries, metro park system, downtown Cleveland business district, and Lake Erie. No credit cards. President: Jean Stanley. $45-125.

COLUMBUS

Columbus Bed and Breakfast

769 South Third Street, 43206
(614) 444-8888; FAX (614) 444-1911
e-mail: tholdridge@aol.com

This reservation service will provide comfortable lodgings in historic German Village, a registered national historic area. Close to downtown Columbus. All connecting lines of all the thruways lie on the village's edge, making it easily accessible to visitors. Private or shared baths. Continental breakfast offered at each house. Ten-dollar fee per additional person per room. Does not accept credit cards. $65-75.

Henderson House Bed and Breakfast

1544 Atcheson Street, 43203
(614) 258-3463

A Georgian 19th-century home once the farmhouse of Ohio governor and president Rutherford B. Hayes with an attached coach house suite with private entrance, kitchen, telephone, and cable TV. On five acres in the heart of the city with off-street parking, five minutes from airport, downtown business

---

7 No smoking; 8 Children welcome; 9 Social drinking allowed; 10 Tennis nearby; 11 Swimming nearby; 12 Golf nearby; 13 Skiing nearby; 14 May be booked through a travel agent; 15 Handicapped accessible.

district, convention center, OSU, restaurants, shopping malls, and less than a mile from major highways. Also, perfect for small business meetings, retreats, and social functions. Three rooms share one bath. A Continental plus breakfast served.

Host: Lee Henderson-Johnson
Rooms: 4 (1 PB; 3 S1B) $70-85
Full Breakfast
Credit Cards: None
Notes: 2, 5, 7, 9, 10, 11, 12, 15

Lansing Street

Lansing Street Bed and Breakfast

180 Lansing Street, 43206
(614) 444-8488; (800) 383-7839

Lansing Street Bed and Breakfast is in the heart of German Village, a popular historic area adjacent to downtown. The village is famous for restored homes with slate roofs, wrought-iron gates, and secluded courtyards. Quaint shops and great restaurants along cobblestone streets add to the charm of the village. This large home is tastefully furnished and is decorated with carefully selected artwork. The great room, with brick fireplace, overlooks the courtyard with birds, wind chimes, and a fountain. Two spacious suites have all the desired amenities, including private baths. Creative gourmet breakfasts are served each morning by a hostess who loves to cook.

Host: Marcia A. Barck
Rooms: 2 (PB) $80
Full Breakfast
Credit Cards: None
Notes: 2, 5, 7, 8, 9, 10

Shamrock Bed and Breakfast

5657 Sunbury Road, Gaharina, 43230-1147
(614) 337-9849

The Shamrock is a brick split-level ranch on over an acre of professionally landscaped grounds with perennial beds, roses, grape arbor, and flowering bushes. Guests enjoy the entire first floor, fireplace, Florida room, and patio with gas grill. All rooms are furnished with original art and antiques. Large library. CDs and videos are available. Easy freeway access to most attractions and close to airport and Easton. Large traditional Irish breakfast. Generally handicapped accessible. Smoking restricted.

Host: Tom McLaughlin
Rooms: 2 (PB) $60
Full Breakfast
Credit Cards: None
Notes: 2, 3, 5, 7, 8, 10, 11, 12, 13, 15

Shamrock

COLUMBUS (WESTERVILLE)

Priscilla's Bed and Breakfast

5 South West Street, 43081
(614) 882-3910; (888) 882-3910

Priscilla's 1854 home is surrounded by one-half acre of white picket fence. Lovely perennial gardens, bird feeders, and birdbaths accompany the one-time log cabin in

---

NOTES: Credit cards accepted: A MasterCard; B Visa; C American Express; D Discover; E Diner's Club; F Other; 2 Personal checks accepted; 3 Lunch available; 4 Dinner available; 5 Open all year; 6 Pets welcome;

the historic setting adjacent to Otterbein College. Borrow bicycles, cook on the patio, and enjoy the water garden and adjoining Alum Creek Park. Leisurely browse through 15 shops. At the rear of the house, Priscilla operates a miniature dollhouse shop. Robes are provided. Two miles north of Columbus. Free airport pickup is available.

Host: Priscilla H. Curtiss
Rooms: 3 (PB) $50-70
Full Breakfast
Credit Cards: A, B
Notes: 2, 5, 7, 8, 9, 10, 11, 12

The White Oak Inn

CRESTLINE

Bethel

4885 State Route 39, 44827
(419) 347-3054 (business)
(419) 347-8377 (reservations)
e-mail: spry641365@aol.com

Six acres in farm country surrounded by fields. Stocked pond for fishing and swimming. Horseshoes, sand volleyball, herb gardens, fruit trees, vegetable garden, and flower beds. Large common living room with deck, games, magazines, books, guitar, and plenty of sitting room. Speciality is hot fresh yeast breads for breakfast. Sitting porches and bicycles to ride. Air conditioned. Inspected by Ohio Bed and Breakfast Association. Lunch and dinner available by prior arrangement. Inquire about accommodations for children. Skiing 25 miles away.

Host: Sue Pry
Rooms: 3 (1 PB; 2 SB) $45-110
Full Breakfast
Credit Cards: None
Notes: 2, 5, 7, 9, 11, 12, 14

DANVILLE

The White Oak Inn

29683 Walhonding Road, 43014
(740) 599-6107

This turn-of-the-century farmhouse in a rolling wooded countryside features antiques and natural oak woodwork. Guests read, play board games, or socialize in the common room with a fireplace, or relax on the 50-foot-long front porch. An outdoor enthusiast's haven. Three rooms have fireplaces. Near the world's largest Amish population and historic Roscoe Village.

Hosts: Yvonne and Ian Martin
Rooms: 10 (PB) $70-140
Full Breakfast
Credit Cards: A, B, C, D
Notes: 2, 4, 5, 7, 9, 10, 11, 12, 13, 14

DELLROY (ATWOOD LAKE REGION)

Whispering Pines Bed and Breakfast

P.O. Box 340, 44620
(330) 735-2824; FAX (330) 735-7006
www.bbonline.com/oh/whispering/

Come to this 1880 Victorian home overlooking Atwood Lake. Filled with elegant antiques of the period, each guest room has a breathtaking view of the lake and a private bath. Two rooms have a wood-burning fireplace. The Honeymoon Suite features a two-person Jacuzzi, balcony, king-size bed, and wood-burning fireplace. Central air. Brick courtyard and gardens. A scrumptious breakfast served on the enclosed porch makes this a perfect romantic getaway. Pontoon with deluxe seating

7 No smoking; 8 Children welcome; 9 Social drinking allowed; 10 Tennis nearby; 11 Swimming nearby; 12 Golf nearby; 13 Skiing nearby; 14 May be booked through a travel agent; 15 Handicapped accessible.

Whispering Pines

is available for rental. Golf, boating, nature, and relaxation.

Hosts: Bill and Linda Horn
Rooms: 5 (PB) $90-140
Honeymoon Suite: $175
Full Breakfast
Credit Cards: A, B, C, D
Notes: 2, 5, 7, 9, 10, 11, 12, 14

FREDERICKTOWN

Heartland Country Resort

2994 Township Road 190, 43019
(800) 230-7030

The Heartland Country Resort is a beautifully remodeled, spacious 1878 farmhouse and a new secluded log home, both with scenic views of rolling fields, pastures, and woods. There is a variety of things to do, including horseback riding on wooded trails with streams and hills or riding in one of the arenas. Guests can go swimming in the heated pool in the summer, go skiing in the winter, play pool in the large recreation room, or just relax on the comfortable screened porch or deck. Continental plus breakfast served. Lunch and dinner available by prior arrangement. Inquire about pets. Smoking permitted only on the porches.

Host: Dorene Henschen
Rooms: 6 (PB) $80-175
Continental Breakfast
Credit Cards: A, B, D
Notes: 2, 5, 8, 9, 11, 12, 13, 14, 15

GENEVA-ON-THE-LAKE

The Lakehouse Inn

5653 Lake Road, 44041
(440) 466-8668; FAX (440) 466-1549
e-mail: lakehouseinn@alltel.net

The Lakehouse Inn is a family-run business on two acres of lakefront property. There are eight cottages and a 12-room bed and breakfast overlooking Lake Erie. Also on the grounds are a game room, sand volleyball court, three lighted decks, and bonfires on the beach nightly. Within walking distance to Geneva State Park and Marina, Firehouse Winery, Adventure Zone, and the Strip where there are games, rides, and an array of restaurants.

Hosts: Dan and Shelley Wolfe
Rooms: 12 (8 PB; 4 SB) $64.50
Full Breakfast
Credit Cards: A, B
Notes: 2, 5, 7, 8, 9, 10, 11, 12

GEORGETOWN

Bailey House Bed and Breakfast

112 North Water Street, 45121-1332
(937) 378-3087; (937) 378-6237

The Bailey House is a Greek Revival brick home built in 1830. The spacious

Heartland Country Resort

NOTES: Credit cards accepted: A MasterCard; B Visa; C American Express; D Discover; E Diner's Club; F Other; 2 Personal checks accepted; 3 Lunch available; 4 Dinner available; 5 Open all year; 6 Pets welcome;

rooms have Federal-style mantels, woodwork, and original ash flooring. Guest rooms have antique beds, chests of drawers, and washstands. Bailey House offers small-town friendliness, a restful setting in a historic area, and a full breakfast to start the day. U. S. Grant home and school, art gallery, and antique shops are within walking distance. Boating, fishing, hiking are available nearby. No smoking in the guest rooms.

Hosts: Nancy Purdy and Jane Sininger
Rooms: 4 (SB) $55
Full Breakfast
Credit Cards: None
Notes: 2, 5, 8, 9, 10, 12

GRANVILLE

Buxton Inn

Buxton Inn

313 East Broadway, 43023
(740) 587-0001; FAX (740) 587-1460

Ohio's oldest continuously operating inn in its original building. A complex of four buildings has 26 period guest rooms, seven dining rooms (seating up to 250 people), meeting rooms that can accommodate up to 60, a tavern, and wine cellar. Formal gardens, brick walks, and sparkling fountains provide an elegant setting for a leisurely stay. Nonsmoking rooms available.

Hosts: Orville and Audrey Orr
Rooms: 26 (PB) $80-90
Full and Continental Breakfast
Credit Cards: A, B, C, D, E
Notes: 2, 3, 4, 5, 8, 9, 10, 11, 12, 14

The Follett Wright House

The Follett Wright House

403 East Broadway, 43023
(614) 587-0941

Built in 1860 and listed in the National Register of Historic Places, this gracious bed and breakfast overlooks the historic village of Granville. Within walking distance of Dennison University, shopping, and restaurants. Breakfast consists of homemade Danish rolls and other delicious specialties.

Hosts: Kirsten and Jurgen Pape
Rooms: 2 (PB) $60
Full Breakfast
Credit Cards: None
Notes: 2, 5, 6, 7, 8, 9, 10, 11, 12

HANOVERTON

The Spread Eagle Tavern

10150 Plymouth Street, P.O. Box 277, 44423
(330) 223-1583

The Spread Eagle Tavern is an artfully restored Federal-style three-story historic brick inn that features a gourmet restaurant, a unique rathskeller, seven dining rooms, and six guest rooms for overnight lodging. All rooms are tastefully decorated with antiques that give insight into Ohio's canal-period

7 No smoking; 8 Children welcome; 9 Social drinking allowed; 10 Tennis nearby; 11 Swimming nearby; 12 Golf nearby; 13 Skiing nearby; 14 May be booked through a travel agent; 15 Handicapped accessible.

history. Listed in the National Register of Historic Places. Quiet, romantic, and unique.

Hosts: Peter and Jean Johnson
Rooms: 6 (4 PB; 2 SB) $75-125
Continental Breakfast
Credit Cards: A, B, D
Notes: 3, 4, 5, 7, 8, 9, 12

HIGGINSPORT

Ohio River House Bed and Breakfast

101 Brown Street, P.O. Box 188, 45131
(937) 375-4395; FAX (937) 375-4394
e-mail: FDSINC@bright.net

Thirty-five miles east of Cincinnati on scenic US 52, the antique-filled Ohio River House offers a truly outstanding view while capturing the ambiance of years past. The hosts offer very large rooms with an adjacent antique shop and gallery for guests' browsing pleasure. Come, enjoy a full family-style breakfast in the brick-floored kitchen as well as evening snacks at either the river's edge, in the comfort of the parlor, or in the spacious living room which is boldly decorated in a manner reminiscent of an old paddle-wheel riverboat.

Hosts: Andy and Judy Lloyd
Rooms: 5 (3 PB; 2 SB) $65-100
Full Breakfast
Credit Cards: A, B
Notes: 2, 5, 6, 8, 9, 10, 11, 12

HIRAM

The Lily Ponds

6720 Route 82, 44234
(330) 569-3222; (800) 325-5087
FAX (330) 569-3223

This spacious, lovely antique-filled home in a quiet country setting is surrounded by woods and ponds. Five-minute walk to Hiram College campus; 15-minute drive to SeaWorld, Geauga Lake, and Aurora Farms and Outlet Center; 45 minutes to Cleveland, Akron, and Youngstown. Charming guest rooms with

The Lily Ponds

private baths. Central air conditioning. Cross-country skis and skiing on property. Eight miles from Ohio Turnpike, exit 13A.

Host: Marilane Spencer
Rooms: 3 (PB) $55-85
Full Breakfast
Credit Cards: A, B
Notes: 2, 5, 6, 7, 8, 9, 10, 11, 12, 13, 14

HURON

Captain Montague's Bed and Breakfast

229 Center Street, 44839
(419) 433-4756; (800) 276-4756
e-mail: judytann@aol.com
www.innsandouts.com/inns/p208270.html

The Captain's is that perfect romantic retreat in a stately southern Colonial manor that radiates Victorian charm. Experience a bygone era of lace, luster, and love. Nestled in the heart of vacationland on the shores of Lake Erie, the Captain's is within minutes of golf courses, estuaries, boating, and shopping. Cedar

NOTES: Credit cards accepted: A MasterCard; B Visa; C American Express; D Discover; E Diner's Club; F Other; 2 Personal checks accepted; 3 Lunch available; 4 Dinner available; 5 Open all year; 6 Pets welcome;

Point and the Lake Erie islands are nearby. Enjoy the in-ground swimming pool and impeccable gardens. The Captain's is truly in the heart of Ohio. Minimum weekend stay is two nights, Memorial Day through Labor Day. Continental plus breakfast. Showcased in *Midwest Living*, August 1995.

Hosts: Judy and Mike Tann
Rooms: 7 (PB) $75-150
Continental Breakfast
Credit Cards: A, B, D
Notes: 2, 5, 7, 9, 10, 11, 12, 14

LEBANON

Burl Manor Bed and Breakfast
230 South Mechanic Street, 45036
(513) 934-0400; FAX (513) 934-0402
e-mail: jor@your-net.com

In historic Lebanon, the Burl Manor was built in the mid 1800s by William H. P. Denney, the editor and publisher of Ohio's oldest weekly newspaper. This historical Italian home reflects days of the past with the spacious parlor, formal dining room, and features a unique sunroom in the center-court staircase. The bedrooms are decorated with turn-of-the-century decor. Each queen-size bedroom has a private bath. Enjoy time indoors with a game room or bumper pool, board games, TV, VCR with a film library. Outdoor activities include an in-ground swimming pool, volleyball, and croquet. A golf center with tennis is just a block away.

Hosts: Liz and Jay Jorling
Rooms: 4 (PB) $80
Full Breakfast
Credit Cards: A, B
Notes: 2, 5, 7, 8, 10, 11, 12

White Tor
1620 Oregonia Road, 45036
(513) 932-5892

White Tor was built as a farmhouse in 1862. It stands on seven acres in a country setting.

Easily accessible from I-71 and I-75. The furniture and furnishings reflect the eclectic taste of its English hosts, and the gardens are ablaze with color from spring to fall. Guests occupy a two-room suite on the second floor with all modern amenities.

Hosts: Eric and Margaret Johnson
Rooms: 1 (PB) $75
Full Breakfast
Credit Cards: None
Notes: 2, 7, 9, 10, 11, 12

LOGAN

The Inn at Cedar Falls
21190 State Route 374, 43138
(740) 385-7489; (800) 65-FALLS
FAX (740) 385-0820
www.innatcedarfalls.com

Settled on 60 acres surrounded by Hocking Hills State Parks, the Inn features the harmony of nature and the simple joys of earth's beauty. Relax in a setting formed during the ice age. Mammoth rock formations, caves, and waterfalls share their breathtaking beauty. The Inn offers antique-furnished rooms and renovated, fully equipped, and secluded 19th-century log cabins. Dining awaits guests in 1840s log houses where they can watch gourmet meals being prepared in the open kitchen. Smoking permitted in designated areas only.

Host: Ellen Grinsfelder
Rooms: 15 (PB) $60-185
Full Breakfast
Credit Cards: A, B
Notes: 2, 3, 4, 5, 8, 9, 11, 12, 14, 15

LOUDONVILLE

Blackfork Inn
303 North Water Street, 44842
(419) 994-3252

The Blackfork Inn is a Victorian townhouse in a small-town setting, offering an elegant getaway and a convenient location for exploring the beauties of Mohican

---

7 No smoking; 8 Children welcome; 9 Social drinking allowed; 10 Tennis nearby; 11 Swimming nearby; 12 Golf nearby; 13 Skiing nearby; 14 May be booked through a travel agent; 15 Handicapped accessible.

country. Nearby are two state parks, Mohican and Malabar, and the wonderful Amish settlements with good down-home cooking and cottage industries: quilts, cabinets, clocks, dolls. The 1865 inn has two Victorian parlors for guests' use and six guest rooms, each with private bath. All are furnished in antiques and are accurate in detail. A newly restored 1847 house has two suites, one with fireplace. Complimentary breakfast includes homegrown raspberries, Amish specialties. Pets welcome with prior arrangements.

Rooms: 8 (PB) $65-125
Full Breakfast
Credit Cards: A, B
Notes: 2, 5, 7, 9, 10, 11, 12,1 3, 14

MARIETTA

*Buckley House
Bed and Breakfast*
332 Front Street, 45750
(740) 373-3080; FAX (740) 373-8000
e-mail: dnicholas@wscc.edu

Built in 1879 and in the downtown historic district within walking distance to museums, antique shopping, and the best restaurants in southeast Ohio. Relax on one of the two front porches while watching the river traffic go by on the beautiful Muskingum River. Enjoy the peace and tranquility of the southern-style garden. Stroll its brick paths, watch the fish in the pond or just enjoy the birds while sitting in the gazebo. The spa offers a wonderful view of the stars in the evening.

Hosts: Dell and Alf Nicholas
Rooms: 3 (PB) $75-85
Full Breakfast
Credit Cards: A, B, D
Notes: 2, 5, 7, 9, 12

MARION

Buckley House

Olde Towne Manor

Olde Towne Manor
245 St. James Street, 43302
(614) 382-2402; (800) 341-6163

This elegant stone home is on a beautiful acre of land on a quiet street in Marion's historic district. Enjoy a quiet setting in the gazebo or relax while reading a book from the library. A leisurely stroll will take guests to the home of President Warren G. Harding and the Harding Memorial. Guests can unwind in the hot tub or sauna or enjoy a glass of local wine in the pub while shooting a game of pool.

Hosts: Steve and Marsha Adams
Rooms: 4 (PB) $55-65
Continental Breakfast
Credit Cards: A, B, C
Notes: 2, 5, 9, 10

NOTES: Credit cards accepted: A MasterCard; B Visa; C American Express; D Discover; E Diner's Club; F Other; 2 Personal checks accepted; 3 Lunch available; 4 Dinner available; 5 Open all year; 6 Pets welcome;

MEDINA

Spitzer House Bed and Breakfast
504 West Liberty Street, 44256
(330) 725-7289

Historical 1890 "painted lady," with two cherry staircases, stained-glass windows, and cherry and oak woodwork throughout. A gentle reminder of the past, filled with warm antiques, lacy linens, and Victorian charm. The honeymoon/anniversary suite includes a charming pink Jacuzzi for two. Beautiful English rose garden. Walking distance to candle outlet, coffee shops, specialty stores, tea room, antique shops, and restaurants. Event calendar available. Four blocks from historical downtown Medina.

Hosts: Janet and Dale Rogers
Rooms: 3 (PB) $70-115
Full Breakfast
Credit Cards: A, B
Notes: 2, 5, 7, 9, 10, 11, 12

Spitzer House

MESOPOTAMIA

Old Stone House Bed and Breakfast
8505 Route 534, Box 177, 44439
(440) 693-4186

Welcome to this 200-year-old sandstone home on 25 acres amidst historical

Old Stone House

Mesopotamia and its Amish. Enjoy a country room with fireplace and the expanse of windows that let nature unfold around one. Forty-one miles east of Cleveland; 30 minutes from Sea World, factory outlets, wineries, cheese outlets. Amish dinner and buggy ride available.

Hosts: Sam and Darcy Miller
Rooms: 3 (PB) $95
Full Breakfast
Credit Cards: None
Notes: 2, 5, 7, 10, 11, 12, 13

MILLERSBURG

Fields of Home Guest House
7278 County Road 201, 44654
(330) 674-7152

Log cabin bed and breakfast four miles northwest of Berlin, in the heart of the world's largest Amish community, surrounded by the rolling hills and fields farmed with horses. Spacious rooms include private baths with whirlpool tubs, telephones, clock radios with CD players, some with fireplaces and kitchenettes. Breakfast includes fruit, muffins, rolls, cereals, juice, tea, and coffee. Relax on the front porch rockers or take a stroll around the fish pond and perennial gardens.

Hosts: Mervin and Ruth Yoder
Rooms: 5 (PB) $65-125
Continental Breakfast
Credit Cards: A, B, D
Notes: 2, 5, 7, 8, 9, 12, 14, 15

---

7 No smoking; 8 Children welcome; 9 Social drinking allowed; 10 Tennis nearby; 11 Swimming nearby; 12 Golf nearby; 13 Skiing nearby; 14 May be booked through a travel agent; 15 Handicapped accessible.

MOUNT VERNON

The Russell-Cooper House
115 East Gambler Street, 43050
(740) 397-8638

The hostess is the fifth-generation to have lived in the house that now is a four-time national award-winning bed and breakfast inn. History lives in this national register inn, and all around Mount Vernon—"America's Hometown." Grand and comfortable, the Russell-Cooper House will refresh the spirit, ease the mind, stimulate the curiosity, and generally warm the cockles of the heart. Private baths, full delicious candlelit breakfasts, and a friendly "welcome home" will make a visit a memory guests will always cherish.

Hosts: Tom and Mary Dvorak
Rooms: 6 (PB) $55-75
Full Breakfast
Credit Cards: A, B, C
Notes: 2, 5, 7, 9, 12, 14

NEW PLYMOUTH

Ravenwood Castle
65666 Bethel Road, 45654
(740) 596-2606; (800) 477-1541
FAX (740) 596-5818
www.hockinghills.com/ravenwood

The most unique and romantic place to stay! A medieval castle in Ohio's most beautiful vacation area—the Hocking Hills. Caves, waterfalls, lakes, outdoor activities, antique and craft malls, scenic railway are all nearby. Enchanting rooms, suites, and cottages, some with Jacuzzis. Experience a bit of Britain in the seasonal Tea Room and gift shops. Theme weekends, murder mysteries, "fairytale weddings," and plenty of romance. Children over 10 welcome.

Rooms: 12 (PB) $95-175
Full Breakfast
Credit Cards: A, B, D
Notes: 2, 3, 4, 5, 12, 14, 15

Ravenwood Castle

OXFORD

The Duck Pond
6391 Morning Sun Road, State Road 732 North
P.O. Box 504, 45056 (mailing)
(513) 523-8914

An 1863 Civil War farmhouse on five and one-half acres. Furnished in country antiques and collectibles. Full country-style breakfast, including such specialties as Hawaiian French toast, German pancakes, and breakfast casseroles. Three miles north of Miami University, two miles south of Hueston Woods State Park with golf, nature trails, boating, swimming, and fishing. Enjoy antiquing in several nearby towns. Certified and approved by Ohio Bed and Breakfast Association. Closed Christmas.

Hosts: Don and Toni Kohlstedt
Rooms: 4 (1 PB; 3 SB) $67-75
Full Breakfast
Credit Cards: None
Notes: 2, 7, 9, 10, 11, 12

PAINESVILLE

Rider's Inn Bed and Breakfast
792 Mentor Avenue, 44077
(440) 354-8200 (phone/FAX); (440) 942-2742

This historic stagecoach inn built in 1812 is one mile west of downtown Painesville

NOTES: Credit cards accepted: A MasterCard; B Visa; C American Express; D Discover; E Diner's Club; F Other; 2 Personal checks accepted; 3 Lunch available; 4 Dinner available; 5 Open all year; 6 Pets welcome;

Rider's Inn

on Route 20. Choose from 10 guest rooms, each with private bath, air conditioning, queen-size beds, and fine antique furnishings that are for sale. Area attractions include Lake Erie College, Fairport Harbor, Grand River Winery, Indian Museum, golf, tennis, horseback riding, water sports, and Amish country tours. Continental breakfast in bed available. Full breakfast is without eggs. A full service restaurant and separate English pub offer additional meals and a Sunday stagecoach brunch. Facilities for meetings and social functions are also available. Inquire about accomodations for pets. Restaurant is handicapped accessible.

Hosts: Elaine Crane, Gary Herman, Dick Lawrenz
Rooms: 10 (8 PB; 2 SB) $75-99
Full Breakfast
Credit Cards: A, B, C, D
Notes: 2, 3, 4, 5, 7, 8, 9, 10, 11, 12, 13, 14

POLAND (YOUNGSTOWN)

Inn at the Green
500 South Main Street, 44514
(330) 757-4688

A classically proportioned Victorian townhouse on the south end of the green in preserved Connecticut Western Reserve village. Featuring beautiful large moldings, 12-foot ceilings, five lovely working Italian marble fireplaces, interior-shuttered windows, the original poplar floors, and a relaxing patio garden. Children over seven are welcome.

Hosts: Ginny and Steve Meloy
Rooms: 4 (PB) $55-60
Continental Breakfast
Credit Cards: A, B, D
Notes: 2, 5, 9, 10, 11, 12, 14

Inn at the Green

RAVENNA

Rocking Horse Inn
248 West Riddle Avenue, 44266
(330) 297-5720; (800) 457-0439

This Victorian home is 128 years. It sits on land that was part of the western reserve. After a sheriff sale, the home was completed by Quincy Cook, the owner of the mill which still exists today. It was purchased by Immaculate Conception Church and used as a convent for more than 30 years. Purchasing the home in 1991, Jim and Carolyn have filled it with antiques and opened it as a bed and breakfast.

Hosts: James and Carolyn Leffler
Rooms: 4 (PB) $55-85
Continental Breakfast
Credit Cards: D
Notes: 2, 5, 7, 9, 12

---

7 No smoking; 8 Children welcome; 9 Social drinking allowed; 10 Tennis nearby; 11 Swimming nearby; 12 Golf nearby; 13 Skiing nearby; 14 May be booked through a travel agent; 15 Handicapped accessible.

RIPLEY

Misty River Bed and Breakfast

206 North Front Street, 45167
(937) 392-1556 (phone/FAX)

Each of the guest rooms in this charming riverfront home has its own private bath. The decor is a comfortable mix of country and antique, with a wood-burning fireplace in the living room and a big front porch where guests can relax and enjoy the river boats and the gorgeous sunsets. In the morning, guests will be served a delicious home-cooked breakfast, including Dotty's wonderful yeast cinnamon rolls. Ulysses S. Grant boarded here when he was 16. Ripley is also famous for its involvement in the Underground Railroad. Smoking permitted outside on the porch only.

Hosts: Dorothy Prevost and Lanny Warren
Rooms: 2 (PB) $75
Full Breakfast
Credit Cards: None
Notes: 2, 5, 7, 9, 14

The Signal House

234 North Front Street, 45167
(937) 392-1640 (phone/FAX)

Share historic charm and hospitality while visiting this 1830s home on the scenic Ohio River. View spectacular sunsets from three porches or elegant parlors. Enjoy spacious rooms furnished with family antiques. The area offers antique and craft shops, restaurants, winery, herb farms, covered bridges, history (early pioneers and the Underground Railroad), and lots of friendly people. River nearby for swimming and water skiing.

Hosts: Vic and Betsy Billingsley
Rooms: 2 (SB) $75
Full Breakfast
Credit Cards: A, B, D, F
Notes: 2, 5, 9, 10, 11, 12, 13, 14

ROCKBRIDGE

Glenlaurel: A Scottish Country Inn and Cottages

14940 Mount Olive Road, 43149-9736
(740) 385-4070; (800) 809-7378
FAX (740) 385-9669
www.glenlaurelinn.com

Glenlaurel, a Scottish country inn with wooded cottages, has been labeled the premier romantic getaway in the Midwest. The 130-acre estate offers walking trails, rock cliffs, and waterfalls. The Manor House, which overlooks Camusfearna Gorge, has two guest rooms and two guest suites. Each room offers a lavish two-person whirlpool tub in the bathroom, gas log fireplace in the bedroom, and private balcony. Four wooded cottages are a 10-minute walk from the Manor House. They offer kitchenette, living room, bedroom, gas log fireplace, screened porch, and hot tub on a private deck overlooking the gorge. Dinner in one of the two dining rooms is available by reservation. The estate is totally smoke free.

Host: Michael Daniels
Rooms: 2 (PB) $110-240
Suites: 2 (PB)
Cottages: 4
Full Breakfast
Credit Cards: A, B, C, D, E
Notes: 2, 5, 7, 9, 11, 12, 14, 15

The Signal House

NOTES: Credit cards accepted: A MasterCard; B Visa; C American Express; D Discover; E Diner's Club; F Other; 2 Personal checks accepted; 3 Lunch available; 4 Dinner available; 5 Open all year; 6 Pets welcome;

Thunder Ridge Cabins Bed and Breakfast
11309 Starner Road, 43149
(614) 385-1386; (800) 600-0584

Secluded hilltop setting surrounded by trees. Close to all Hocking Hills state parks. The bed and breakfast offers one-room cabins. The Otter Lodge has a private deck with hot tub, beautiful view, and full private bath. The smaller cabins are like bedrooms in the woods and tastefully decorated. All cabins have their own full private baths. Communal fire pit for marshmallow roasting and star gazing. Picnic tables and grill. Hiking, canoeing, horseback riding, and swimming nearby. Smoking permitted outside.

Hosts: Micah and Susan Freeman
Rooms: 3 (PB) $65-105
Full Breakfast
Credit Cards: A, B, D, F
Notes: 2, 5, 7, 8, 9, 11, 12, 14

SANDUSKY

1890 Queen Anne Bed and Breakfast
714 Wayne Street, 44870-3507
(419) 626-0391; FAX (419) 626-3064

A family home for 36 years. The hosts have enjoyed sharing this home and community with guests. Three bedrooms furnished with family antiques, a lovely porch overlooking lawn and gardens, and a patio for breakfast in the warm months make a stay here unforgettable. Close to ferries for Cedar Point and Lake Erie islands. Air conditioning. TV. Continental plus breakfast is served.

Host: Dr. Robert Kromer
Rooms: 3 (PB) $105-115
Continental Breakfast
Credit Cards: A, B, D
Notes: 2, 5, 7

The Red Gables

1890 Queen Anne

The Red Gables Bed and Breakfast
421 Wayne Street, 44870
(419) 625-1189
www.bbonline.com/oh/redgables/

Circa 1907 Tudor Revival in the Old Plat District. The great room, where breakfast is served, features a massive fireplace, large bay window, and plenty of oak woodwork. The style is eclectic, from oriental artifacts in the great room to flowered chintz in the bedroom. Slipcovers, curtains, and comforters have been made by the innkeeper, a semiretired theatrical costume maker. Guests have access to a refrigerator and coffee maker. Air conditioned. Inquire about accommodations for children. Four blocks from Sandusky Bay.

---

7 No smoking; 8 Children welcome; 9 Social drinking allowed; 10 Tennis nearby; 11 Swimming nearby; 12 Golf nearby; 13 Skiing nearby; 14 May be booked through a travel agent; 15 Handicapped accessible.

Guests have said, "It's like going to Grandma's house."

Host: Jo Ellen Cuthbertson
Rooms: 4 (2 PB; 2 SB) $50-100
Continental Breakfast
Credit Cards: A, B
Notes: 2, 5, 7, 9, 10, 11, 12

Wagner's 1844 Inn
230 East Washington Street, 44870
(419) 626-1726
e-mail: wagnersinn@sanduskyohio
www.lrbcg.com/wagnersinn

Elegantly restored, antique-filled Victorian home. Built in 1844 and listed in the National Register of Historic Places. Features a Victorian parlor with antique Steinway piano, living room with wood-burning fireplace, billiard room, screened porch, and enclosed courtyard. Air conditioning. In downtown Sandusky within walking distance of parks, historic buildings, antique shops, museums, and ferries to Cedar Point and Lake Erie islands. Inquire about accommodations for pets. Limited accessibility for handicapped.

Hosts: Walt and Barb Wagner
Rooms: 3 (PB) $60-100
Continental Breakfast
Credit Cards: A, B, D
Notes: 5, 7, 9, 10, 11, 12

SOUTH BLOOMINGVILLE

Steep Woods
24830 State Route 56, 43152
(614) 332-6084; (800) 900-2954

Hillside log home with two guest rooms, shared bath, full breakfast. Nearby is the Hocking State Park with its famous recessed caves, waterfalls, and unusual rock formations. New at Steep Woods is an authentic railroad caboose! Fully equipped, can sleep five. Continental breakfast is provided. Open year-round.

Hosts: Barbara and Brad Holt
Rooms: 2 (SB) $40

Steep Woods

Full and Continental Breakfast
Credit Cards: B
Notes: 2, 5, 7, 8, 9, 11

SUGAR GROVE

Hickory Bend Bed and Breakfast
7541 Dupler Road Southeast, 43155
(740) 746-8381

Hickory Bend Bed and Breakfast is on 10 acres of woods in the Hocking Hills of southeastern Ohio. "It is so quiet out here," Pat says, "we take a chair out to the road on Sundays and watch the cars go by." The approach road often offers guests a sight of deer grazing or a flock of wild turkey feeding on the hill side. The bird feeder invites, among other species, cardinals, chickadees, nuthatches, a Carolina wren, red-bellied woodpeckers, and, of course, the local squirrels. The guest room is decorated in country primitive, totally private with own bath. Patty is a spinner and weaver. At no extra cost to guests, included are fresh air, delightful sounds of birds, an occasional hoot of an owl, an array of stars, plus the feeling of embracing the universe.

Host: Patty Peery
Rooms: 1 (PB) $45
Full Breakfast

NOTES: Credit cards accepted: A MasterCard; B Visa; C American Express; D Discover; E Diner's Club; F Other; 2 Personal checks accepted; 3 Lunch available; 4 Dinner available; 5 Open all year; 6 Pets welcome;

Credit Cards: None
Notes: 2, 7, 10, 12

TIPP CITY

Willow Tree Inn
1900 West Street, Route 571, 45371
(513) 667-2957

This restored 1830 Federal manor home has four fireplaces. There are ducks, a pond, and the original 1830 barn on the premises, as well as a working springhouse and smokehouse, and beautiful gardens to stroll in. Just minutes north of Dayton in a quiet location complete with attentive personal service.

Hosts: Chuck and Jolene Sell
Rooms: 4 (1 PB; 3 SB) $50-79
Full Breakfast
Credit Cards: A, B
Notes: 2, 5, 7, 9, 10, 11, 12, 15

VALLEY CITY

Reutter's Roost Bed and Breakfast
2267 Columbia Road, 44280
(330) 483-4145; FAX (330) 483-7001
e-mail: halaluja@apk.net
www.quikpage.com/R/reutter

Open daily, full breakfast, fresh fruit, farm maple syrup, gourmet coffees or teas, dietary accommodations available; private baths, one double whirlpool, one suite (queen-size bed), one guest room with king-size bed, one guest room with queen-size bed; select comfort mattress, individually adjusted to guests' preference in firmness; 102 acres, woods, streams, hiking trails; built in 1913, wraparound porch, heated outdoor pool, fireplace, Steinway grand piano; 40 minutes to Rock and Roll Hall of Fame, Football Hall of Fame, and Amish country.

Hosts: Hal and Alice Krull
Rooms: 3 (2 PB; 1 SB) $65-85
Full Breakfast
Credit Cards: F
Notes: 2, 5, 7, 8, 9, 11, 12

WAVERLY

Governor's Lodge
171 Gregg Road, 45690
(614) 947-2266

Governor's Lodge is a place like no other. Imagine a beautiful shimmering lake, an iridescent sunset, and a quiet calm. A friendly atmosphere in an eight-room bed and breakfast on Lake White. Open year-round. Magnificent views can be enjoyed from every room. An affiliate of Bristol Village Retirement Community, it offers a meeting room and group rates for gatherings using the whole lodge.

Host: Shirley Widdig
Rooms: 8 (PB) $45-54
Continental Breakfast
Credit Cards: A, B, C, D, E
Notes: 2, 5, 8, 11, 12, 13, 14, 15

WEST ALEXANDRIA

Twin Creek Country Bed and Breakfast
5353 Enterprise Road, 45381
(937) 787-3990; (937) 787-4264; (937) 787-3279

This 1830s farmhouse has been remodeled to offer a quiet getaway for families and couples. The entire house, upper or lower level, or individual rooms are available. There are three bedrooms, two bathrooms,

Twin Creek Country

---

7 No smoking; 8 Children welcome; 9 Social drinking allowed; 10 Tennis nearby; 11 Swimming nearby; 12 Golf nearby; 13 Skiing nearby; 14 May be booked through a travel agent; 15 Handicapped accessible.

a furnished kitchen, and a living room. The owners live 100 yards away. Guests can roam the 170 acres, which include 70 acres of woods. Restaurants and antique shops are nearby. Local catering is available. Suitable for two families at once. Close to the I-70/I-75 interchange.

Hosts: Dr. Mark and Carolyn Ulrich
Suites: 2 (PB) $79-89
Full Breakfast
Credit Cards: A, B, C, D
Notes: 2, 5, 7, 8, 12

WEST LIBERTY

Liberty House Bed and Breakfast
208 North Detroit Street, 43357-0701
(937) 465-1101; (800) 437-8109
e-mail: wrpent@loganrec.com

Liberty House, in a scenic rural and peaceful village, offers a blend of the past and present. Nestled in the Mad River Valley, it has historic and natural beauty to give guests a pleasurable and memorable day. Built in the early 1900s, Liberty House has patterned oak floors and woodwork, oriental rugs, antique furnishings, and three spacious air-conditioned bedrooms with private baths. Colorful gardens and a wraparound porch with an old-fashioned swing beckon guests into Liberty House. Near Ohio Caverns and Piatt Castles. Trout fishing nearby.

Liberty House

Hosts: Sue and Russ Peterson
Rooms: 3 (PB) $55-75
Full Breakfast
Credit Cards: A, B, D
Notes: 2, 5, 7, 8, 9, 11, 12, 13

WILMOT

Hasseman House Bed and Breakfast
925 US 62, P.O. Box 215, 44689
(330) 359-7904; FAX (330) 359-7159

At the door to Ohio's Amish country is the Hasseman House Bed and Breakfast. This charming and warm, early 1900s Victorian bed and breakfast invites guests to unpack their bags and relax. Furnished with antiques, the bed and breakfast is indeed a step back into a bygone era. The Hasseman House features four cozy rooms complete with private baths and air conditioning. Guests will fall in love with the intricate woodwork and original stained glass. Amish restaurant and shops are nearby. Walk-ins are welcome!

Hosts: Milo and Kathryn Miller
Rooms: 4 (PB) $69-110
Full Breakfast
Credit Cards: A, B, D
Notes: 2, 5, 7, 11, 12

WORTHINGTON

The Worthington Inn
649 High Street, 43085
(614) 885-2600

Historic inn, built in 1831 and refurbished in 1983 and 1990. Ohio's second oldest inn. Four-star Mobil rating. Has 26 exquisitely appointed hotel suites furnished with stunning period antiques. Highly acclaimed restaurant featuring regional American cuisine. Banquet facilities accommodate 150 guests. A stay at the Worthington includes cocktails upon arrival, twice-daily housekeeping, and full breakfast. Details large and small taken care of professionally and

NOTES: Credit cards accepted: A MasterCard; B Visa; C American Express; D Discover; E Diner's Club; F Other; 2 Personal checks accepted; 3 Lunch available; 4 Dinner available; 5 Open all year; 6 Pets welcome;

personally. One mile south of I-270 at the corner of High and New England.

Hosts: Stephen and Susan Hanson
Rooms: 26 (PB) $140-215
Full Breakfast
Credit Cards: A, B, C, D
Notes: 3, 4, 5, 7, 8, 9, 10, 11, 12, 14

ZOAR

The Cider Mill Bed and Breakfast

198 East 2nd Street, P.O. Box 438, 44697
(330) 874-3240; FAX (330) 339-7505

The Cider Mill was originally a barn used by the community of Separatists to make and store cider. It has been converted to living quarters featuring a three-floor spiral staircase. Furnished with antiques and decorated country style. Built in 1863, it has received a historic marker and is listed in the national register. Rooms are available with shared or private baths. Reservations are encouraged. Central to outdoor dramas, the Pro Football Hall of Fame, Ohio's largest antique mall, historic sites, golf courses, canoe livery, horse academy, making it quick to travel to entertainment and excellent dining facilities.

Hosts: Vernon and Dorothy Furbay
Rooms: 3 (PB or SB) $60-75
Full Breakfast
Credit Cards: A, B, D
Notes: 2, 5, 7, 11, 12, 13

---

7 No smoking; 8 Children welcome; 9 Social drinking allowed; 10 Tennis nearby; 11 Swimming nearby; 12 Golf nearby; 13 Skiing nearby; 14 May be booked through a travel agent; 15 Handicapped accessible.

Oklahoma

ALINE

Heritage Manor
Rural Route 3, Box 33, 73716
(405) 463-2563; (405) 463-2566; (800) 295-2563

Heritage Manor is a country getaway on 80 acres that was settled in the land run of 1893 in northwest Oklahoma. Two pre-statehood homes have been joined together and restored by the innkeepers using a Victorian theme. Beautiful sunrises, sunsets, and stargazing from the rooftop decks. Guests can relax in the hot tub or read a book from the 5,000-volume library. Ostriches, donkeys, and Scotch Highland cattle roam a fenced area. Close to homesteader's 1894 Sod House, selenite crystal digging area, and several other attractions. Lunch and dinner available by reservation. Pets and children welcome by prior arrangements. Smoking permitted in designated areas only.

Hosts: Carolyn and A.J. Rexroat
Rooms: 4 (S3B) $75-150
Full Breakfast
Credit Cards: None
Notes: 2, 5, 9, 10, 11, 12, 13, 15

CHECOTAH

Sharpe House
301 Northwest Second, 74426
(918) 473-2832

Sharpe House is in a one-stoplight town in eastern Oklahoma just eight miles north of Lake Eufaula. The house was built in 1911 and is filled with antiques and family heirlooms. Each room has a paddle fan and air conditioning. Breakfast is served in the formal dining room or on the huge screened porch. Enjoy a few days of peace and quiet and southern hospitality. Inquire about accommodations for pets.

Host: Kay Kindt
Rooms: 3 (PB) $50
Full and Continental Breakfast
Credit Cards: None
Notes: 2, 5, 7, 8, 9, 10, 11, 12

CHICKASHA

Campbell-Richison House Bed and Breakfast
1428 West Kansas, 73018
(405) 222-1754

A red brick three-story home awaits guests with an antique-filled parlor and formal dining room with an antique glass window. Three guest rooms on the second floor provide a welcome retreat to guests or business persons for overnight or extended visits.

Hosts: David and Kami Ratcliff
Rooms: 3 (1 PB; 2 SB) $39-59
Full Breakfast
Credit Cards: None
Notes: 2, 5, 7, 8, 9, 10, 12

CLAREMORE

Country Inn Bed and Breakfast
20530 East 430 Road, 74017
(918) 342-1894

Fifteen minutes from Claremore in the quiet countryside. This small inn has a

---

NOTES: Credit cards accepted: A MasterCard; B Visa; C American Express; D Discover; E Diner's Club; F Other; 2 Personal checks accepted; 3 Lunch available; 4 Dinner available; 5 Open all year; 6 Pets welcome; 7 No smoking; 8 Children welcome; 9 Social drinking allowed; 10 Tennis nearby; 11 Swimming nearby; 12 Golf nearby; 13 Skiing nearby; 14 May be booked through a travel agent; 15 Handicapped accessible.

Country Inn

tranquil friendly atmosphere. Separate from the main house, each smoke-free room has a private bath. Guests can swim in the in-ground pool, walk the five-acre grounds, or just swing in a hammock. A full breakfast with gourmet coffee is served daily. Guests may visit numerous antique shops. Davis Gun Museum and Will Rogers Memorial are close by.

Hosts: Dennis and Linda Coons
Rooms: 2 (PB) $69
Suite: 1 (PB) $75
Full Breakfast
Credit Cards: None
Notes: 2, 5, 9, 11, 12

EDMOND (OKLAHOMA CITY)

The Arcadian Inn Bed and Breakfast
328 East First Street, 73034
(405) 348-6347; (800) 299-6347
FAX (405) 348-8100

Escape the everyday at the Arcadian Inn. Take time to savor the small pleasures of life...a long soak in the Jacuzzi for two right in one's room, a delicious cookie, a lazy morning with a candlelit breakfast served privately, or an evening of cuddling in front of the fireplace...enjoy TVs, VCRs, stereos, king- and queen-size beds, and telephones.

Hosts: Gary and Martha Hall
Rooms: 8 (PB) $75-170
Full Breakfast
Credit Cards: A, B, C, D
Notes: 2, 5, 7, 9, 10, 11, 12

The Arcadian Inn

OKLAHOMA CITY

Country House Bed and Breakfast
10101 Oakview Road, 73165
(405) 794-4008

A romantic, quiet country getaway on five beautiful acres. Some of the furnishings in the home include 19th-century antiques, heirloom quilts, an 1817 grandfather clock, and country collectibles. One mile from water sports and riding stables at Lake Draper. Start the day with a full, homemade breakfast served on antique Spode china in the dining room, or on the balcony. Guests arc pampered with fresh fruit, Godiva chocolates, and sparkling drinks in their rooms. Ask about the Honeymoon Suite that features a red heart-shaped whirlpool. Pets are wel-

NOTES: Credit cards accepted: A MasterCard; B Visa; C American Express; D Discover; E Diner's Club; F Other; 2 Personal checks accepted; 3 Lunch available; 4 Dinner available; 5 Open all year; 6 Pets welcome;

Country House

comed outside only. Smoking in designated areas only. Inquire about accommodations for children.

Hosts: Dee and Nancy Ann Curnutt
Rooms: 2 (PB) $70-90
Full Breakfast
Credit Cards: None
Notes: 2, 5, 9, 10, 11, 12, 13

Flora's Bed and Breakfast
2312 Northwest Forty-sixth, 73112
(405) 840-3157

In a quiet neighborhood, this home is furnished with antiques and collectibles and includes an elevator. Guests may relax in front of the large wood-burning fireplace or enjoy the outdoors on a 1,500-square-foot balcony with a large spa. There is covered parking, and the hosts enjoy square dancing. Easy access to the National Cowboy Hall of Fame, Remington Park racetrack, Kirkpatrick Center, and other points of interest. Many good eating places in the vicinity. Children over 11 are welcome.

Hosts: Newton W. and Joann Flora
Rooms: 2 (PB) $50-55
Continental Breakfast
Credit Cards: None
Notes: 2, 5, 7, 12, 15

Willow Way
27 Oakwood Drive, 73121-5410
(405) 427-2133; FAX (405) 427-8907

A wooded town retreat in English Tudor style with antique decor and genuine country charm. Guests enjoy breakfast on their schedule in the great hall with fireplace, lofty beamed ceiling, and a large picture window for bird and fish pond watching. Guests may choose Willow Way's newest addition: a cottage greenhouse suite complete with fireplace and a jetted tub for two under glass. Comfortable and safe with off-street parking, guests are near the National Cowboy Hall of Fame and many other area attractions. One easy mile east of I-35 in Forest Park, six minutes to downtown Oklahoma City. Business rates are available.

Hosts: Johnita and Lionel Turner
Rooms: 3 (2 PB; 1 SB) $50-125
Full or Continental Breakfast
Credit Cards: A, B
Notes: 2, 5, 7, 8, 9, 12, 14

STILLWATER

Thomasville
4115 North Denver, 74075
(405) 372-1203

A historical, century-old home, where Stillwater's first mayor lived. Tastefully furnished with period pieces from around the world.

Thomasville

---

7 No smoking; 8 Children welcome; 9 Social drinking allowed; 10 Tennis nearby; 11 Swimming nearby; 12 Golf nearby; 13 Skiing nearby; 14 May be booked through a travel agent; 15 Handicapped accessible.

Host: Virginia H. Thomas
Rooms: 4 (S2B) $60
Full Breakfast
Credit Cards: None
Notes: 2, 5, 7, 10, 12

SULPHUR

The Artesian Bed and Breakfast

1022 West 12th Street, 73086
(580) 622-5254; (888) 557-5254
FAX (580) 622-6521; e-mail: artesian@brightok.net

The cares of busy life fade upon entering this 1904 Victorian bed and breakfast which offers a glimpse of the grandeur and romance of a bygone era. Spacious rooms/suites include private baths. Full breakfast; recently refurbished with antiques and new furnishings; large wrap-around porch with swing and rockers; back deck view of water garden; afternoon refreshments. The beautiful locale of Arbuckle Wilderness provides opportunities for hiking, picnicking, water sports, and other nearby attractions. Smoking is permitted outside only. Children over 12 are welcome.

Host: Sylvia Belitz (owner/innkeeper)
Rooms: 3 (PB) $65-80
Full Breakfast
Credit Cards: A, B
Notes: 2, 5, 7, 9, 11, 12

NOTES: Credit cards accepted: A MasterCard; B Visa; C American Express; D Discover; E Diner's Club; F Other; 2 Personal checks accepted; 3 Lunch available; 4 Dinner available; 5 Open all year; 6 Pets welcome;

South Dakota

CANOVA

Skoglund Farm
Route 1, Box 45, 57321
(605) 247-3445

Enjoy the prairie: cattle, fowl, peacocks, a home-cooked evening meal, and full breakfast. Visit nearby attractions: Little House on the Prairie, Corn Palace, Doll House, and Prairie Village. Relax, hike, and enjoy a family farm. Rate includes evening meal and breakfast: $30 for adults; $20 for teens; $15 for children; children five and under free.

Hosts: Alden and Delores Skoglund
Rooms: 5 (SB) $30
Full Breakfast
Credit Cards: None
Notes: 2, 3, 4, 5, 6, 8, 9, 10, 11, 12, 14

CHAMBERLAIN

Cable's Riverview Ridge
HC69 Box 82A, 57325
(605) 734-6084

Contemporary home built on a bluff overlooking a scenic bend in the Missouri River. On the Lewis and Clark Trail. King- and queen-size beds, full breakfast, and secluded country peace and quiet are all available. Just three and one-half miles north of downtown Chamberlain on Highway 50. Enjoy outdoor recreation; visit museums, Indian reservations, and casinos; or just make this a home away from home. Smoking is permitted in designated areas only.

Hosts: Frank and Alta Cable
Rooms: 3 (1 PB; 2 SB) $60-75
Full Breakfast
Credit Cards: A, B
Notes: 2, 5, 8, 9, 11, 12

CUSTER

Custer Mansion Bed and Breakfast
35 Centennial Drive, 57730
(605) 673-3333

Historic 1891 Victorian Gothic house of seven gables is listed in the national register. A blend of Victorian elegance, country charm, and western hospitality. Awake to aroma of delicious home-cooked breakfast. Two honeymoon or anniversary suites, one with Jacuzzi, and one family suite. Near all of Black Hills attractions: Mount Rushmore, Custer State Park, Crazy Horse Memorial, National Caves. Recommended by *Bon Appétit* and Mobil Travel Guide. Member of BBISD. Two-night minimum stay during peak season.

Hosts: Mill and Carole Seaman
Rooms: 5 (PB) $68-98
Family Suite: $115
Full Breakfast

Custer Mansion

7 No smoking; 8 Children welcome; 9 Social drinking allowed; 10 Tennis nearby; 11 Swimming nearby; 12 Golf nearby; 13 Skiing nearby; 14 May be booked through a travel agent; 15 Handicapped accessible.

South Dakota

Credit Cards: None
Notes: 2, 5, 7, 8, 10, 11, 12, 13, 14

FREEMAN

Farmers Inn

28193 US Highway 81, 57029
(605) 925-7580

The Farmers Inn is in a rural setting along US 81. It is a midwestern four-square built in 1914 furnished with antiques. Features a fitness center, sauna, and crafts. Accommodations include a three-room Victorian suite with refrigerator, the Country Room with two single beds, the Native American Room with double bed and private balcony, and an attic hideaway with double whirlpool tub. The rooms are furnished with telephones, TVs, and private baths and are air conditioned.

Hosts: MarJean and Russell Waltner
Rooms: 4 (PB) $40-65
Full Breakfast
Credit Cards: None
Notes: 2, 3, 4, 5, 7, 8, 9, 10, 11, 12

GETTYSBURG

Harer Lodge Bed and Breakfast

Rural Route 1, Box 87A, 57442
(605) 765-2167; (800) 283-3356
www.bbonline.com/sd/harerlodge/

Set on the prairie where buffalo once roamed, this modern cedar lodge has a miniature golf course, miniature horses, and farm animals. Five lovely guest rooms have fresh flowers, private baths, bathrobes, and coffee and cookies when guests arrive. An authentic Native American tipi is available for campers, and a separate honeymoon cottage with an oversized Jacuzzi is available for newlyweds and anniversaries. TV, VCR, and lots of privacy. Country store with crafts, antiques, and a sweet shop is in a cream station/store restored on premises. Boating and fishing at beautiful Lake Oahe. Member of Chamber of Commerce and inspected by South Dakota Department of Health and BBISD. Smoking is permitted in designated areas only. Inquire about accommodations for pets. Inquire about permission for social drinking.

Hosts: Norma Hockesson Harer and Don Harer
Rooms: 5 (PB) $45-65
Cottage: 1 (PB) $85
Full Breakfast
Credit Cards: A, B
Notes: 2, 3, 4, 5, 8, 11, 12, 14

INTERIOR

Badlands Ranch Resort

HCR 53, Box 3, 57750
(605) 433-5599; FAX (605) 433-5598

Open year-round. A new log ranch-style home. Three floors with 12 beds. Each floor has its own bath and double locks between each floor with whirlpool tub. Horseback riding. Pool. Jacuzzi. Bike trails. Rock hunting. Two hundred acres to roam. Cabins and motel units are heated and air conditioned and are completely furnished. Thirty-five complete RV hook-ups. Laundromat. Cookouts and entertainment nightly by reservation. Ideal spot for family reunions, weddings, and youth projects. Two ponds for fishing. Free full breakfast. Winter and group rates available. Bring a camera to remember the beautiful views of the Badlands.

Host: Jake Sharp
Rooms: 5 (PB) $65-125
Full Breakfast
Credit Cards: A, B, C, D, E
Notes: 2, 3, 4, 5, 6, 7, 8, 9, 10, 11, 12, 13, 14, 15

LEAD

Deer Mountain Bed and Breakfast

HC 37, Box 1214, 57754
(605) 584-2473; FAX (605) 584-3045

Unique log home. Skiing and snowmobiling minutes away. Near historic Deadwood

---

NOTES: Credit cards accepted: A MasterCard; B Visa; C American Express; D Discover; E Diner's Club; F Other; 2 Personal checks accepted; 3 Lunch available; 4 Dinner available; 5 Open all year; 6 Pets welcome; 7 No smoking; 8 Children welcome; 9 Social drinking allowed; 10 Tennis nearby; 11 Swimming nearby; 12 Golf nearby; 13 Skiing nearby; 14 May be booked through a travel agent; 15 Handicapped accessible.

Deer Mountain

gambling town. Mount Rushmore, hunting, fishing, Homestake Gold Mine all nearby. Hot tub, pool table, videos, fireplace, and game rooms for guests' enjoyment. Box lunches available upon request. Inquire about accommodations for pets. Smoking is permitted in designated areas only.

Hosts: Vonnie and Bob Ackerman
Rooms: 4 (2 PB; 2 SB) $65-75
Full Breakfast
Credit Cards: A, B, D
Notes: 2, 5, 8, 9, 11, 12, 13, 14

RAPID CITY

Abend Haus Cottages and Audrie's Bed and Breakfast
23029 Thunderhead Falls Road, 57702-8524
(605) 342-7788
www.pahasapa.com/wp/audries

Abend Haus Cottages

The Black Hills "inn place." Ultimate in charm and Old World hospitality, this country home and six-acre estate is surrounded by thousands of acres of national forest. Thirty miles from Mount Rushmore and seven miles from Rapid City. Each quiet, comfortable suite and cottage has a private entrance, private bath, hot tub, patio, cable TV, and refrigerator. Free trout fishing, biking, and hiking on-site.

Hosts: Hank and Audry Kuhnhauser
Rooms: 6 (PB) $95
Cottages: 4 (PB) $145
Full Breakfast
Credit Cards: None
Notes: 2, 5, 7, 9, 10, 11, 12, 13

Carriage House Bed and Breakfast
721 West Boulevard, 57701
(888) 343-6415; www.carriagehouse-bb.com

The stately, three-story pillared Colonial house is on the historic, tree-lined boulevard of Rapid City. Fine antique furnishings reflect an era of Victorian romance. Experience warm and gracious hospitality reminiscent of days gone by. Scenic Mount Rushmore is only 26 miles away. Downtown Rapid City is within walking distance.

Hosts: Jay and Janice Hrachovec
Rooms: 5 (PB) $89-149
Full Breakfast
Credit Cards: A, B, C
Notes: 2, 5, 7, 9, 10, 11, 12, 13

Domivara Bed and Breakfast
12760 Domivara Road, 57702-6008
(605) 574-4207

This log home, in the Black Hills, is between two major recreational lakes: Pactola and Sheridan. With the breathtaking scenery, guests can spend their time exploring, sightseeing, swimming, boating, hiking, etc. Dessert and coffee served to guests upon arrival and a full breakfast is served each morning. Approx-

NOTES: Credit cards accepted: A MasterCard; B Visa; C American Express; D Discover; E Diner's Club; F Other; 2 Personal checks accepted; 3 Lunch available; 4 Dinner available; 5 Open all year; 6 Pets welcome;

imately 12 miles from Mount Rushmore National Monument and Crazy Horse Memorial. Personal checks are accepted for reservations only. Inquire about accommodations for pets. Smoking permitted outside only.

Host: Betty Blount
Rooms: 4 (3 PB: 2 SB) $70-75
Full Breakfast
Credit Cards: None
Notes: 2, 5, 7, 8, 9, 11, 12, 13

Historic Hotel Alex Johnson

523 Sixth Street, P.O. Box 20, 57701
(800) 888-2539

Visit the Hotel Alex Johnson and stay at a historic landmark. There are 143 historically restored guest rooms. With Old World charm combined with award-winning hospitality, this legend offers a piece of Old West history in the heart of downtown Rapid City. Listed in the National Register of Historic Places. Nonsmoking rooms available. Skiing is one hour away.

Rooms: 143 (PB) $58-88
Full Breakfast
Credit Cards: A, B, C, D, E
Notes: 2, 3, 4, 5, 6, 8, 9, 10, 11, 12, 13, 14, 15

Madison Ranch

8800 Nemo Road, 57702
(605) 342-6997

Honored with an Award of Excellence, this turn-of-the-century working horse ranch is in the beautiful Black Hills. Surrounded by timber and wildlife, the ranch once served as a rodeo guest lodge, hosted rodeos and movie productions. It features a private museum of heirloom rodeo memorabilia, western and Indian artifacts. Boarding available for guest horses. Member of and inspected by BBISD.

Hosts: Stanley and Marilynn Madison
Rooms: 4 (S2B) $65-70
Full Breakfast
Credit Cards: None
Notes: 2, 7, 9, 11, 12

Willow Springs Cabins

11515 Sheridan Lake Road, 57702
(605) 342-3665

Private one-room log cabins in the beautiful Black Hills National Forest. This secluded setting offers privacy like no other retreat. Each cabin is charmingly decorated with many antique treasures and extras. Breakfast is wonderful, featuring freshly ground coffee, juices, baked goods, and egg dishes. Hiking, swimming, private hot tub, and fishing abound. Featured in *Vacations* magazine as one of America's Best Romantic Inns.

Hosts: Joyce and Russell Payton
Cabins: 2 (PB) $95-110
Full Breakfast
Credit Cards: None
Notes: 2, 5, 7, 8, 9, 10, 11, 12, 13, 14

SIOUX FALLS

Steever House Bed and Breakfast

46850 276th Street, Lennox, 57039
(605) 647-5055

Surrounded by gently rolling farmland under a vast prairie sky, this restored Queen

Steever House

---

7 No smoking; 8 Children welcome; 9 Social drinking allowed; 10 Tennis nearby; 11 Swimming nearby; 12 Golf nearby; 13 Skiing nearby; 14 May be booked through a travel agent; 15 Handicapped accessible.

Anne home welcomes guests to the plains of eastern South Dakota. Porch offers spectacular sunsets and celestial theater, or cozy up to the fireplace, or relax in the Jacuzzi. Private parties and fine dining by reservation. Queen-size beds, cable TV. Just two miles off I-29 and 10 minutes from all the amenities of Sioux Falls.

Hosts: Sara and John Steever
Rooms: 3 (PB) $65-75
Full Breakfast
Credit Cards: None
Notes: 2, 4, 5, 7, 8, 9, 12

STURGIS

Dakota Shepherd Bed and Breakfast
Route 3, Box 25C, Vale, 57788
(605) 456-2836

Experience country life at its best on an authentic South Dakota sheep farm/ranch. Twenty miles north of Sturgis, along Highway 79. Modern ranch house with three guest rooms, 1940s furnishings, family heirlooms, and country charm. Near historic Bismarck Trail and Bear Butte State Park. Perfect for artists and photographers.

Hosts: Robert and Sheryl Trohkimoinen
Rooms: 3 (2 PB; 2 SB) $60-70
Full Breakfast
Credit Cards: A, B
Notes: 2, 4, 5, 7, 8, 9, 14

VERMILLION

The Goebel House Bed and Breakfast
102 Franklin, 57069
(605) 624-6691

A friendly old home built in 1916 and furnished with antiques and collectibles. Vermillion is home of the nationally known Shrine to Music Museum and the University of South Dakota. Four bedrooms have both private and shared baths. Each room is individually decorated with mementos of the past.

Hosts: Don and Pat Goebel
Rooms: 4 (2 PB; 2 SB) $45-55
Full Breakfast
Credit Cards: None
Notes: 2, 5, 9, 10, 11, 12

WEBSTER

Lakeside Farm Bed and Breakfast
Rural Route 2, Box 52, 57274
(605) 486-4430

Guests are invited to sample a bit of country life at Lakeside Farm. Feel free to explore the grove, barns, and pastures, or just relax with a cup of tea in the farmhouse. Accommodations for four to five guests on the second floor. The second-floor bathroom and shower serve both guest rooms. Children are welcome. In northeastern South Dakota with museums featuring pioneer and Native American culture. Fort Sisseton nearby. Smoking is not permitted. Alcoholic beverages are not permitted.

Hosts: Glenn and Joy Hagen
Rooms: 2 (SB) $45
Full Breakfast
Credit Cards: None
Notes: 2, 5, 8, 11, 12, 13

Lakeside Farm

NOTES: Credit cards accepted: A MasterCard; B Visa; C American Express; D Discover; E Diner's Club; F Other; 2 Personal checks accepted; 3 Lunch available; 4 Dinner available; 5 Open all year; 6 Pets welcome;

YANKTON

Mulberry Inn
512 Mulberry Street, 57078
(605) 665-7116

This beautiful inn was built in 1873 and offers the ultimate in comfortable lodging with historic charm. Included in the National Register of Historic Places. Features parquet floors, six guest rooms furnished with antiques, two parlors with marble fireplaces, and a large porch for evening relaxation. In a quiet residential area, and within walking distance to the Missouri River, downtown, and fine restaurants. Only minutes from the beautiful Lewis and Clark Lake and Gavins Point Dam. Full breakfast at additional cost.

Mulberry Inn

Host: Millie Cameron
Rooms: 6 (2 PB; 4 SB) $35-52
Continental Breakfast
Credit Cards: A, B
Notes: 2, 5, 7, 8, 10, 11, 12

---

7 No smoking; 8 Children welcome; 9 Social drinking allowed; 10 Tennis nearby; 11 Swimming nearby; 12 Golf nearby; 13 Skiing nearby; 14 May be booked through a travel agent; 15 Handicapped accessible.

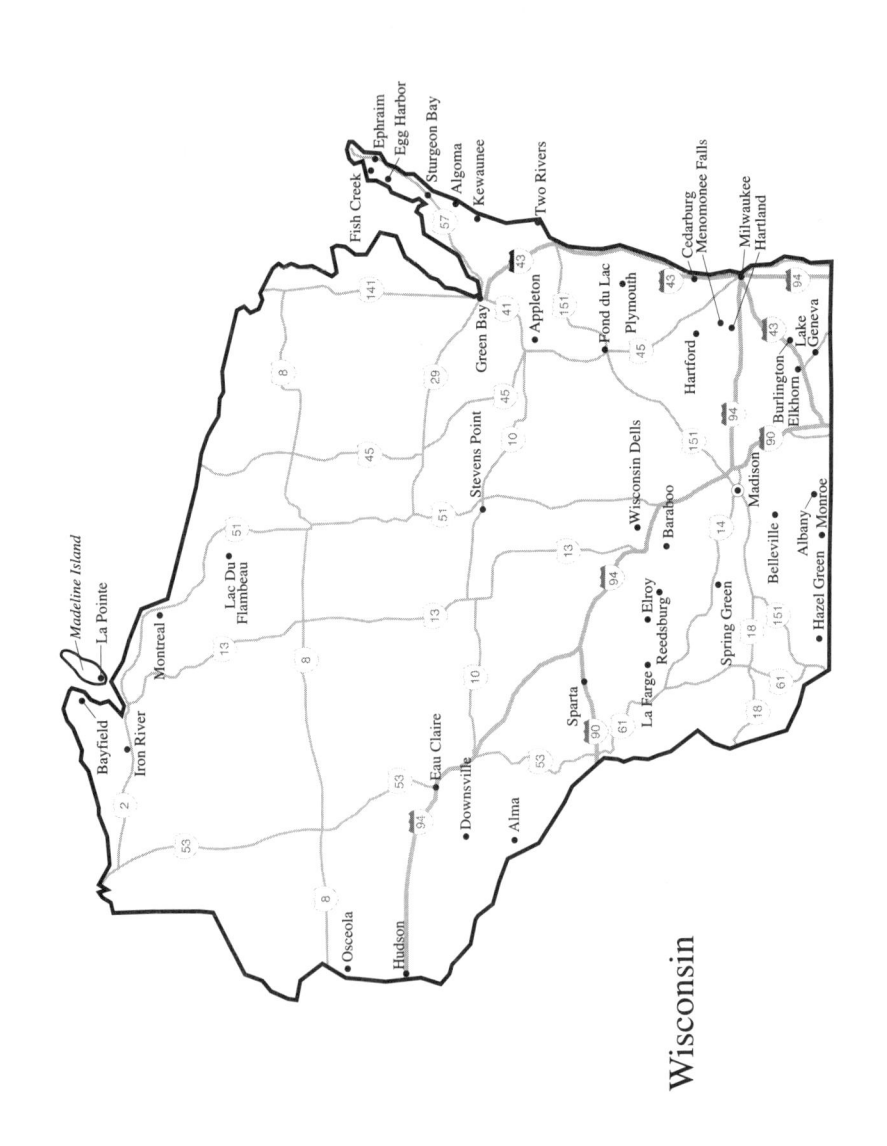

Wisconsin

Wisconsin

ALBANY

Albany Guest House
405 South Mill Street, 53502
(608) 862-3636

Park amongst the blooming flowers; follow the brick path to the restored 1908 block house. Refinished floors support oriental carpets, king- and queen-size beds. Light the master bedroom fireplace or stroll the two acres of lawn and gardens. This great reunion or retreat site offers reduced whole-house rates November through May. Bike the Sugar River Trail or explore south central Wisconsin's Swiss communities.

Hosts: Bob and Sally Braem
Rooms: 6 (4 PB; 2 SB) $60-80
Full Breakfast
Credit Cards: A, B
Notes: 2, 5, 7, 8, 9, 10, 12, 13

ALGOMA

Amberwood Inn
N7136 Highway 42 Lakeshore Drive, 54201
(920) 487-3471

Lake Michigan beachfront. Private wooded acreage on the shores of Lake Michigan, less than five miles from Door County. Large luxury suites, each with private bath, fireplace, and double French doors with private decks opening to the beach. Whirlpool tub, wet bars, refrigerators, Finnish sauna, and hot tub. Sleep to the sound of the waves; awaken to a sunrise over the water. Smoking in designated areas only. Inquire about accommodations for children.

Hosts: Mark and Karen Rittle
Rooms: 5 (PB) $75-105
Full Breakfast
Credit Cards: A, B
Notes: 2, 5, 9, 10, 11, 12, 15

ALMA

The Gallery House
215 North Main Street, 54610
(608) 685-4975

This Civil War mercantile building is nestled below the bluffs on the Mississippi River. The inn offers a return to simple, romantic elegance. The guest rooms have both air conditioning and ceiling fans. The common areas include the front deck, a side deck, and a tranquil fish pond in the side yard. The large and varied original art collection and Jan's gourmet breakfast, served by candlelight, are featured.

Hosts: Jan and Joe Hopkins
Rooms: 3 (PB) $70-90
Full Breakfast
Credit Cards: A, B
Notes: 2, 5, 7, 9, 10, 11, 12, 13

The Gallery House

NOTES: Credit cards accepted: A MasterCard; B Visa; C American Express; D Discover; E Diner's Club; F Other; 2 Personal checks accepted; 3 Lunch available; 4 Dinner available; 5 Open all year; 6 Pets welcome; 7 No smoking; 8 Children welcome; 9 Social drinking allowed; 10 Tennis nearby; 11 Swimming nearby; 12 Golf nearby; 13 Skiing nearby; 14 May be booked through a travel agent; 15 Handicapped accessible.

Laue House Inn
P.O. Box 176, 54610
(608) 685-4923

The comfortable, cozy, and affordable Laue House Inn is the best remaining example of domestic Italianate architecture in Buffalo County. Placed in the National Register of Historic Places in 1979. Step back in time and enjoy the moderately priced rooms of one of Alma's oldest and most elegant houses. There are six guest rooms with TVs and air conditioning. Player piano in the lounge to sing along with and coffee bar for chatting by the fireplace.

Rooms: 6 (SB) $25-38
Continental Breakfast
Credit Cards: None
Notes: 2, 6, 7, 8, 9, 10, 11, 12

APPLETON

The Gathering Place
808 West Front Street, 54914-5465
(920) 731-4418; e-mail: gatherpl@execpc.com
www.execpc.com/~gatherpl/

Architecturally designed and built in 1939, this charming English country home is on the quiet and historic Front Street. Surrounding area has three parks, scenic river views, and first hydroelectrically powered home in the world. Details abound in this cozy, comfortable home. Come to be pampered and enjoy a bountiful breakfast. Scones are a favorite.

Hosts: Madelyn and Dennis Olson
Rooms: 3 (1 PB; 2 SB) $65-95
Full Breakfast
Credit Cards: None
Notes: 2, 5, 7, 10, 11, 12, 14

The Solie Home
914 East Hancock Street, 54911
(888) 739-7966; FAX (414) 734-6661

An early 1900 stucco home tastefully redecorated keeping within the integrity of its time. Of particular interest to visitors are the sculptured plaster walls and woodwork in the living and dining rooms. The home is on a quiet street in a quaint residential neighborhood. Lovely full breakfast includes fresh fruits, a delicious entrée, and always Carole's freshly baked coffee cakes and muffins. Relax and enjoy good-natured, gracious hospitality. Children over 12 welcome.

Hosts: Carole and Riley Solie
Rooms: 3 (SB) $65-105
Full Breakfast
Credit Cards: None
Notes: 2, 5, 7, 10, 11, 12, 13

BARABOO

The Gollmar Guest House Bed and Breakfast
422 Third Street, 53913
(608) 356-9432

Elegant 1889 Victorian circus mansion. Original furniture, antiques, chandeliers, handpainted murals, and beveled glass. Oak and maple floors. Charming guest parlor library. Romantic guest rooms, queen-size beds, and private baths. Full outdoor patio, picnic areas on grounds. Central air conditioning. Four blocks from downtown Baraboo and Circus World Museum, 5 minutes from the International Crane Foundation and Devils Lake State Park, and 10 minutes from the Delton-Dells area. Children over seven are welcome.

Host: Tom Luck
Rooms: 3 (PB) $75
Full Breakfast
Credit Cards: A, B
Notes: 2, 5, 7, 9, 10, 11, 12, 13

Pinehaven Bed and Breakfast
E13083 Highway 33, 53913
(608) 356-3489

This chalet-style inn overlooks a scenic valley and small private lake. Each distinctly different guest room has a queen-size bed or twin beds; some have wicker furniture or antiques. The common room

NOTES: Credit cards accepted: A MasterCard; B Visa; C American Express; D Discover; E Diner's Club; F Other; 2 Personal checks accepted; 3 Lunch available; 4 Dinner available; 5 Open all year; 6 Pets welcome;

has a fireplace, TV/VCR, game table, and baby grand piano. Take a stroll in this inviting setting. Ask about the private guest cottage. Area activities include Devils Lake State Park, Circus World Museum, the Wisconsin Dells, International Crane Foundation, and ski resorts. Excellent restaurants nearby. Inquire about accommodations for children.

Hosts: Lyle and Marge Getschman
Rooms: 4 (PB) $79-135
Full Breakfast
Credit Cards: A, B
Notes: 2, 5, 7, 9, 11, 12, 13

BAYFIELD

Old Rittenhouse Inn

311 Rittenhouse Avenue, P.O. Box 584, 54814
(715) 779-5111

In the quaint Lake Superior fishing village of Bayfield, this Victorian inn features three historic homes, all resplendent with antique furnishings, real wood-burning fireplaces, and expansive views of the town and lake. Guests are invited to the main home, a magnificent Queen Anne Victorian mansion, for complimentary breakfasts or the optional gourmet six-course dinners. Featured in magazines from *Gourmet* to *National Geographic*.

Hosts: Mary and Jerry Phillips
Rooms: 21 ($119-249)
Full Breakfast
Credit Cards: A, B
Notes: 2, 3, 4, 5, 7, 9, 10, 14, 15

BELLEVILLE

Abendruh Bed and Breakfast Swiss Style

7019 Gehin Road, 53508
(608) 424-3808

Experience bed and breakfast Swiss style. This highly acclaimed Wisconsin bed and breakfast offers true Swiss charm and hospitality. The serenity of this peaceful retreat

is one of many treasures that keep guests coming back. Spacious guest rooms adorned with beautiful family heirlooms. Sitting room with high cathedral ceiling and cozy fireplace. An Abendruh breakfast is a perfect way to start a new day or end a peaceful stay.

Host: Mathilde Jaggi
Rooms: 2 (PB) $50-70
Full Breakfast
Credit Cards: None
Notes: 2, 5, 7, 10, 11, 12, 13, 14

BURLINGTON

The Hillcrest Inn and Carriage House

540 Storle Avenue, 53105
(414) 763-4706; FAX (414) 763-7871

On four wooded acres, this stately 1908 Edwardian home offers accommodations which are romantic, luxurious, and private. Walk the paths through English flower gardens or sit on the porch to enjoy the magnificent view of the countryside and waterways. Rooms are available in the main house and in the elegant carriage house. Period antiques, lovely decor, and queen-size beds in each room, with fireplaces, and double whirlpools in selected rooms. Only minutes from Lake Geneva.

Hosts: Mike and Gayle Hohner
Rooms: 6 (4 PB; 2 SB) $65-160
Full Breakfast
Credit Cards: A, B
Notes: 2, 5, 7, 10, 11, 12, 13

CEDARBURG

Stagecoach Inn Bed and Breakfast

W61 N520 Washington Avenue, 53012
(888) 375-0208; FAX (414) 375-6170
www.stagecoach-inn-wi.com

The inn, listed in the national register, is housed in a restored 1853 stone building in downtown Cedarburg. The rooms are

---

7 No smoking; 8 Children welcome; 9 Social drinking allowed; 10 Tennis nearby; 11 Swimming nearby; 12 Golf nearby; 13 Skiing nearby; 14 May be booked through a travel agent; 15 Handicapped accessible.

Stagecoach Inn

furnished with antiques. Suites include whirlpools and fireplaces. Guests enjoy a complimentary wine social in the pub on the first floor across from a chocolate shop. The inn is conveniently within the historic district; walking distance to parks, antique shops, winery, and a variety of excellent restaurants. A truly memorable getaway. A Continental plus breakfast is served.

Hosts: Liz and Brook Brown
Rooms: 12 (PB) $75-130
Continental Breakfast
Credit Cards: A, B, C, D, E
Notes: 2, 5, 7, 9, 10, 11, 12, 13, 14

DOWNSVILLE

The Creamery Restaurant and Inn

State Highway C, P.O. Box 22, 54735
(715) 664-8354

This remodeled turn-of-the-century creamery set in the rolling hills of western Wisconsin contains four large guest quarters with cherry woodwork, handmade tiles, pottery lamps, and concealed TVs. The sweeping views of the Red Cedar River Valley and surrounding hills, along with a reputation for exceptional cuisine and fine wines, has made this family-run inn well known from Chicago to Minneapolis. Dunn County pottery and gift shops adjacent to the inn. Smoking is not permitted in rooms. Eight new rooms and corporate meeting center opening summer 1998.

Hosts: Jane Thomas Deflorin; Richard, John, and David Thomas
Rooms: 4 (PB) $100-130
Continental Breakfast
Credit Cards: A, B, C
Notes: 2, 3, 4, 5, 8, 9, 12, 13

EAU CLAIRE

Otter Creek Inn

2536 Highway 12, 54701
(715) 832-2945

Be pampered! Each antique-filled guest room has a double whirlpool, private bath, telephone, air conditioner, and cable TV. The breakfast menu allows a choice of entrées and breakfast in bed. This spacious inn (more than 6,000 square feet) is a three-story English Tudor with country Victorian decor. Nestled on a wooded acre adjacent to, but high above, the Otter Creek, the inn is less than one mile from numerous restaurants and shops. In-ground pool. AAA-rated.

Hosts: Randy and Shelley Hansen
Rooms: 6 (PB) $79-159
Full Breakfast
Credit Cards: A, B, C, D, E, F
Notes: 2, 5, 7, 9, 10, 11, 12, 13

Otter Creek Inn

EGG HARBOR (DOOR COUNTY)

The Wildflower

7821 Church Street, P.O. Box 34, 54209
(920) 868-9030

Charming and intimate—this new home has blended contemporary amenities with antique

NOTES: Credit cards accepted: A MasterCard; B Visa; C American Express; D Discover; E Diner's Club; F Other; 2 Personal checks accepted; 3 Lunch available; 4 Dinner available; 5 Open all year; 6 Pets welcome;

decor. Fireplaces illuminate queen- or king-size beds. Romantic candlelit double whirlpool or refreshing shower-for-two. Enjoy cool bay breezes from own private balcony or stroll the wildflower path to village activities. Heart-smart breakfast basket delivered to guests' door. Hors d'oeuvres served at 5:00 P.M. Gift shoppe on lower level featuring antiques, collectibles, and home decor.

Host: Judy LaMacchia
Rooms: 3 (PB) $85-130
Continental Breakfast
Credit Cards: A, B, D
Notes: 2, 5, 9, 11, 12, 13, 15

ELKHORN

Ye Olde Manor House Bed and Breakfast

N 7622 State Road 12/67, 53121
(414) 742-2450

Country manor house, circa 1905, on three secluded acres overlooking Lauderdale Lakes. Manor House Suite has private bath and sleeps up to five persons. The hosts invite guests to relax and socialize in the guest living room or on the sun porch. Sumptuous breakfast of home-baked goodies. Special diets are honored. Enjoy hiking or mountain biking in Kettle Moraine Forest, four miles away. Visit Old World Wisconsin (nine miles), a living ethnic museum, or go cross-country or downhill skiing in season. Inquire about accommodations for children.

Hosts: Babette and Marvin Henschel
Rooms: 4 (2 PB; 2 SB) $50-90
Full Breakfast
Credit Cards: A, B, C
Notes: 2, 5, 7, 9, 11, 12, 13, 14

ELROY

East View Bed and Breakfast

33620 County P Road, 53929
(608) 463-7564
www.centuryinter.net/outspokin/eastview.html

The bed and breakfast is about 1,100 feet above sea level which gives it a fantastic view in all directions. About four miles from the start of Elroy-Sparts, "400," and Omaha Bike Trails, little over 35 minutes from the Wisconsin Dells, Wildcat Mountain, Amish community, canoeing on the Kickapoo River, fishing on the Wisconsin River.

Hosts: Dom and Bev Puechner
Rooms: 3 (PB) $65-75
Full Breakfast
Credit Cards: A, B, C
Notes: 2, 5, 7, 8, 12, 13, 14

EPHRAIM

Eagle Harbor Inn

9914 Water Street, P.O. Box 588, 54211
(414) 854-2121; (800) 324-5427

On the Main Street of historic Ephraim in Door County, Eagle Harbor is a gracious, antique-filled country inn. This bed and breakfast is across from the lake and close to the boat ramp, golf course, park, beach, and cross-country ski trails, offering delightful full breakfasts. Beautiful new indoor pool and fitness spa and gathering room for meetings and weddings. Luxurious one- and two-bedroom whirlpool suites with two-way fireplace and kitchen.

Hosts: Nedd and Natalie Neddersen
Rooms: 9 (PB) $79-139
Full Breakfast
Credit Cards: A, B
Notes: 2, 5, 7, 8, 9, 10, 11, 12, 13, 14, 15

Hillside Hotel

9980 Highway 42, P.O. Box 17, 54211
(414) 854-2417; (800) 423-7023

This beautifully restored 1890s country-Victorian inn overlooks Eagle Harbor on Green Bay. Special to this inn are the full, delightful breakfasts and afternoon teas; feather beds; a spectacular view from the 100-foot veranda and most guest rooms; antique furnishings; and a large, private beach. The hosts also have two deluxe housekeeping cottages available for guests. Near galleries, shops, water sports, and cultural events for visitors to enjoy.

---

7 No smoking; 8 Children welcome; 9 Social drinking allowed; 10 Tennis nearby; 11 Swimming nearby; 12 Golf nearby; 13 Skiing nearby; 14 May be booked through a travel agent; 15 Handicapped accessible.

Hillside is listed in the National Register of Historic Places.

Rooms: 12 (SB) $73-94
Full Breakfast
Credit Cards: A, B, D
Notes: 2, 5, 7, 8, 9, 10, 11, 12, 13, 14

FISH CREEK

Thorp House Inn and Cottages
4135 Bluff Lane, P.O. Box 490, 54212-0490
(920) 868-2444

Find history and charm with a view of the bay on a quiet, wooded street in the heart of Fish Creek. Gracious antique-filled guest rooms feature private baths (one with whirlpool), air conditioning, guest library, fireplaced parlor, and delicious home-baked breakfasts. Cottages feature wood-burning fireplaces, country antiques, kitchens, decks, and full baths (some with whirlpools). "Inspiration for Lavyrle Spencer's best-selling *Bittersweet*"— *McCall's* magazine. Write or call for detailed brochure. Smoking is not permitted in the inn. Children are welcome in cottages.

Hosts: Christine and Sverre Falck-Pedersen
Rooms: 4 (PB) $75-145
Cottages: 6 (PB)
Continental Breakfast
Credit Cards: None
Notes: 2, 5, 7, 9, 10, 11, 12, 13

Thorp House Inn and Cottages

FOND DU LAC

Dixon House

Dixon House
W 7190 Forest Avenue, 54937
(920) 923-3340

Century-old farmhouse on 80 acres, two miles west of Fond du Lac off Highway 23. Two upstairs bedrooms with air conditioning, shared full bath with tub and shower. Laundry facilities. Dining room, kitchen, and air porches downstairs. Full breakfast is served on weekends; Continental breakfast is served on weekdays. Smoking permitted outside only. Trained pets are welcomed. Gift certificates are available.

Hosts: Ron and Barbara Kuhls
Rooms: 2 (2 SB) $54-84
Full and Continental Breakfasts
Credit Cards: None
Notes: 2, 5, 7, 8, 12

GREEN BAY

The Astor House
637 South Monroe Avenue, 54301
(920) 432-3585; (888) 303-6370
FAX (920) 436-3145
e-mail: astor@execpc.com
www.astorhouse.com

Rooms in five decorative motifs indulge guests: restful Victorian London room; country French Marseilles garden; expansive third-floor Hong Kong retreat; the Gothic elegance of Vienna balconies; and desert-palette of Laredo. Private baths,

NOTES: Credit cards accepted: A MasterCard; B Visa; C American Express; D Discover; E Diner's Club; F Other; 2 Personal checks accepted; 3 Lunch available; 4 Dinner available; 5 Open all year; 6 Pets welcome;

whirlpools, fireplaces, refrigerators, cable TV, telephone, stereos, videos, and CDs all provide first-class comfort. Outstanding baked goods, fruit, and gourmet coffee greet the guests each morning. The ideal choice for a business or vacation trip.

Host: Doug Landwehr
Rooms: 5 (PB) $109-149
Continental Breakfast
Credit Cards: A, B, C, D, E
Notes: 2, 5, 7, 9, 12, 14

HARTFORD

Jordan House

81 South Main Street, 53027
(414) 673-5643

This warm and comfortable Victorian home, furnished with beautiful period antiques, is only 40 miles from Milwaukee. Near the attractions of majestic Holy Hill Shrine, Horicon Wildlife Refuge, and Pike Lake State Park. Walk to the state's largest antique auto museum, which features Kissel automobiles, or browse through the many antique shops and do some downtown shopping.

Rooms: 4 (1 PB; 3 SB) $55-65
Full Breakfast
Credit Cards: A, B
Notes: 2, 5, 8, 10, 11, 12, 13

HARTLAND

Monches Mill House

W301 N9430 Highway E, 53029
(414) 966-7546 (answering machine)

Circa 1842. On the bank of the Oconomowoc River, in a tranquil pastoral setting, is this historic house furnished with antiques. Tennis, canoeing, hiking on the Ice Age Trail, biking in the Kettle Moraine, Ping-Pong in the barn, and a Jacuzzi in the solar house. Breakfast can be served on the porch, deck, patio, or in front of the fireplace. In winter, enjoy skating on the pond or cross-country skiing on property or on groomed trails nearby. Dogs and children welcome. Reservations only. Lunch is available during the summer.

Hosts: Elaine and Harvey Taylor
Rooms: 4 (1 PB; 3 SB) $50-75
Continental Breakfast
Credit Cards: None
Notes: 2, 5, 6, 8, 9, 10, 11, 12, 13, 15

HAZEL GREEN

De Winters of Hazel Green

2205 Main Street, 53811
(608) 854-2768

De Winters of Hazel Green is housed in a Federal and Greek Revival-style brick building built 180 years ago for John Faherty's home and store. By the end of the century, the building was a hotel, hosting up to 45 people a night. The property was purchased in 1946 by Edward Simison. His son, Don, started renovation of the building in 1984. Don has furnished the house and store with heirlooms from his family. Come enjoy De Winters of Hazel Green and awaken to a home-cooked full breakfast.

Rooms: 3 (1 PB; 2 SB) $45-75
Full Breakfast
Credit Cards: None
Notes: 2, 11, 12, 13

Wisconsin House Stage Coach Inn

2105 Main Street, 53811-0071
(608) 854-2233

The inn is a historic, country-furnished bed and breakfast. Built in 1846 as a stagecoach inn, it now offers six guest rooms and two guest suites. Just 10 minutes from Galena, 12 minutes from Dubuque, and 15 minutes from Platteville, the inn is convenient to all the attractions of the tri-state area.

Hosts: Ken and Pat Disch
Rooms: 8 (6 PB; 2 SB) $55-115
Full Breakfast
Credit Cards: A, B, D
Notes: 2, 4, 5, 7, 8, 9, 11, 12, 13, 14

---

7 No smoking; 8 Children welcome; 9 Social drinking allowed; 10 Tennis nearby; 11 Swimming nearby; 12 Golf nearby; 13 Skiing nearby; 14 May be booked through a travel agent; 15 Handicapped accessible.

WI

Jefferson-Day House
1109 Third Street, 54016
(715) 386-7111

This 1857 home offers antique collections, air-conditioned rooms, double whirlpools, gas fireplaces, and four-course fireside breakfasts. The pleasing decor and friendly atmosphere will relax guests, while the nearby St. Croix River, Octagon House museum, and Phipps Center for the Arts will bring enjoyment. Thirty minutes from Minneapolis, St. Paul, and the Mall of America. Children over 12 inquire.

Hosts: Tom and Sue Tyler
Rooms: 5 (PB) $99-179
Full Breakfast
Credit Cards: A, B, C, D, E
Notes: 2, 5, 6, 7, 9, 10, 11, 12, 13, 14

Jefferson-Day House

IRON RIVER

Iron River Trout Haus
P.O. Box 662, 54847
(888) 262-1453; FAX (715) 372-5511
e-mail: javatrt@win.bright.net
www.trouthaus.com

On 40 beautiful wooded acres, the Iron River Trout Haus is a completely renovated 1891 farmhouse, decorated with artifacts from the host's expeditions around the world. Guests have a choice of four themed rooms based on natural and historic aspects of the area. The distinction is the trout ponds where guests can catch trout for breakfast with a two-night stay. Come for the beauty. Savor the gourmet breakfast. Stay for the service.

Hosts: Ron and Cindy Johnson
Rooms: 4 (2 PB: 2 SB) $55-65
Full Breakfast
Credit Cards: A, B
Notes: 2, 5, 7, 11, 12, 13

KEWAUNEE

The "Gables" Bed and Breakfast Inn
821 Dodge Street, 54216
(920) 388-0220

Relax and be pampered in the 22-room Queen Anne Victorian in the National Register of Historic Places. Five guest rooms. Two with half baths. Serving a gourmet breakfast featuring Wisconsin foods. Hosts act as ambassadors to whole area. Three blocks from Lake Michigan (eight-mile beach) and only 20 minutes to Door County. Wonderful, quiet, tree-lined streets, and lots more to offer the romantic getaway. Gift certificates available.

Hosts: Earl and Penny Dunbar
Rooms: 5 (1 PB; 4 SB) $60-75
Full Breakfast
Credit Cards: None
Notes: 2, 5, 7, 9, 10, 11, 12, 13

LAC DU FLAMBEAU

Ty-Bach
3104 Simpson Lane, 54538
(715) 588-7851

For a relaxing getaway anytime of the year, share this modern home on the shore of a tranquil northwoods lake with 160 acres of woods to explore. Guest quarters include a large living area and a deck overlooking Golden Pond. Visit the area attractions: the cranberry marshes, the Native American museum, powwows,

NOTES: Credit cards accepted: A MasterCard; B Visa; C American Express; D Discover; E Diner's Club; F Other; 2 Personal checks accepted; 3 Lunch available; 4 Dinner available; 5 Open all year; 6 Pets welcome;

Ty-Bach

professional theater, wilderness cruises, and more. Golf is 12 miles away. Guests are pampered with delicious country breakfasts served at flexible times. Outdoor spa. Closed March and April. Inquire about pets being welcome.

Hosts: Kermit and Janet Bekkum
Rooms: 2 (PB) $60-70
Full Breakfast
Credit Cards: None
Notes: 2, 7, 9, 10, 11, 12, 13

LA FARGE

Trillium

Route 2, Box 121, 54639
(608) 625-4492

One's own private cottage on this farm amid 85 acres of fields and woods near a tree-lined brook. Experience Wisconsin in a thriving Amish farm community just 35 miles southeast of La Crosse. Children under 12 stay free.

Host: Rosanne Boyett
Cottage: 1 (PB) $75-85
Full Breakfast
Credit Cards: None
Notes: 2, 5, 7, 8, 9, 10, 11, 12, 13

LAKE GENEVA

Eleven Gables Inn on the Lakes

493 Wrigley Drive, 53147
(414) 248-8393; www.lkgeneva.com

Nestled in evergreens amid giant oaks in the Edgewater historic district, this quaint lakeside carpenter Gothic inn offers privacy in a prime area. The romantic bedrooms, bridal chamber, and unique country cottages all have fireplaces, baths, TVs, wet bars, kitchenettes or cocktail refrigerators. Some of the accommodations have charming lattice courtyards, balconies, and private entrances. A private pier provides exclusive water activities for guests. Bike rentals are available. This charming "Newport of the Midwest" community provides visitors with fine dining, boutiques, and entertainment year-round. Call about rates and special packages.

Host: A. Milliette
Rooms: 12 (PB)
Full Breakfast weekends
Continental Breakfast midweek
Credit Cards: A, B, C, D, E
Notes: 5, 8, 9, 10, 11, 12, 13, 14, 15

T. C. Smith Inn Historic Bed and Breakfast

865 Main Street, 53147
(414) 248-1097; (800) 423-0233
wwte.com/tcinn.htm

Experience classic elegance and recapture the majesty of 19th-century ambiance. Listed in the National Register of Historic Places. Downtown lake-view inn, complete with oriental carpets, period antiques, and European paintings. Eight spacious guest chambers with private baths, most with whirlpools and fireplaces. Delicious buffet breakfast served. Magnificent honeymoon suites with Grecian-style marble and walnut 6-by-10-foot lighted whirlpool spa. A garden, a fountain, and neoclassical statues grace the large courtyard surrounding the 1845 historical mansion. Veranda, rooftop, balcony, gazebo overlook the restored European formal gardens.

Hosts: The Marks Family
Rooms: 8 (PB) $95-395
Full Breakfast
Credit Cards: A, B, C, D, E
Notes: 2, 5, 6, 7, 8, 9, 10, 11, 12, 13, 14

---

7 No smoking; 8 Children welcome; 9 Social drinking allowed; 10 Tennis nearby; 11 Swimming nearby; 12 Golf nearby; 13 Skiing nearby; 14 May be booked through a travel agent; 15 Handicapped accessible.

LA POINTE

Wood's Manor
P.O. Box 7, 54850
(800) 966-3756; FAX (715) 747-3110
e-mail: tundra@islandelegance.com

Historical manor house on Madeline Island in Lake Superior. Seven guest rooms in the manor. Three rooms in adjacent carriage house and northwoods-styled "lodge." Honeymoon suite available. Breathtaking view, private baths, hot tubs, sauna, canoes, and bicycles. Breakfast included. Some pets allowed, depending on room chosen and animal.

Hosts: Joe Oberzut and Lisa Byrne
Rooms: 10 (PB) $119-229
Continental Breakfast
Credit Cards: A, B
Notes: 2, 7, 8, 9, 10, 11, 12, 15

Wood's Manor

MADISON

Annie's Bed and Breakfast
2117 Sheridan Drive, 53704
(608) 244-2224 (phone/FAX)
www.bbinternet.com/annies

Since 1985, when guests want the world to go away, they come to Annie's Bed and Breakfast. This quiet little inn on Warner Park offers a beautiful view and deluxe accommodations. Enjoy the romantic gazebo surrounded by butterfly gardens or the lily pond by the terrace for morning coffee, followed by a sumptuous breakfast. Guests have a whole floor of space, including two bedrooms with a connecting bath, a whirlpool room, pine-paneled library with a beautiful

Annie's

fireplace, and dining room with a large nature aquarium. Six minutes to downtown and campus. Children over 12 welcome.

Hosts: Anne and Larry Stuart
Suite: $128-179
Full Breakfast
Credit Cards: A, B, C
Notes: 2, 5, 7, 9, 10, 11, 12, 13

Arbor House
An Environmental Inn
3402 Monroe Street, 53711
(608) 238-2981

The inn is across the street from the University Arboretum with its 1,200 acres ideal for biking, walking, and bird watching. While preserving the charm of this nationally registered historic home, the award-winning inn is evolving into a model for urban ecology. Whirlpools and TVs in most guest rooms. Full gourmet breakfast served weekends; Continental plus breakfast on weekdays. Guests are treated to a Gehl's iced cappuccino welcoming beverage upon arrival, as well as

Arbor House

NOTES: Credit cards accepted: A MasterCard; B Visa; C American Express; D Discover; E Diner's Club; F Other; 2 Personal checks accepted; 3 Lunch available; 4 Dinner available; 5 Open all year; 6 Pets welcome;

a canoeing pass, use of mountain bikes, and Aveda personal care products. Corporate rate and meeting space are available.

Hosts: John and Cathie Imes
Rooms: 8 (PB) $84-195
Credit Cards: A, B, C
Notes: 2, 5, 7, 8, 9, 10, 11, 12, 13, 15

Collins House Bed and Breakfast
704 East Gorham, 53703
(608) 255-4230

The Collins House captures the essence of Madison, from its restored Prairie-style architecture to its lakefront location and capitol-university proximity. Experience this midwestern, down-to-earth ambiance while enjoying a host of indulgences: famous full breakfasts (such as oatmeal pancakes with brown sugar pecan sauce and sautéed apples; creamy scrambled eggs with asparagus and shiitake mushrooms), fresh homemade pastries and signature chocolate truffles from the bakery, whirlpools, and lake sunset. The staff are eager to share their love of Madison and make every stay memorable. Inquire about accommodations for pets.

Hosts: Barb and Mike Pratzel
Rooms: 5 (PB) $85-140
Full Breakfast
Credit Cards: A, B, D
Notes: 2, 5, 7, 8, 9, 10, 11, 13

Mansion Hill Inn
424 North Pinckney Street, 53703
(608) 255-3999; (800) 798-9070
FAX (608) 255-2217

Eleven luxurious guest rooms, each with a sumptuous bath. Whirlpool tubs, stereo with headphones, hand-carved marble fireplaces, minibars, and elegant Victorian furnishings help to make this restored mansion Madison's only four-diamond inn. Private wine cellar, VCRs, and access to private dining and an athletic club are available upon request. Turndown service. Evening refreshments are available in the parlor. The ideal spot for a perfect honeymoon. Listed in the National Register of Historic Places.

Host: Janna Wojtal
Rooms: 11 (PB) $140-300
Continental Breakfast
Credit Cards: A, B, C
Notes: 2, 5, 7, 9, 12, 14

MENOMONEE FALLS

Dorshel's Bed and Breakfast Guest House
W140 N7616 Lilly Road, 53051-4414
(414) 255-7866

Contemporary home decorated with beautiful antiques in a lovely, wooded residential area. Enjoy breakfast on a screened porch or in the formal dining room. Play a game of pool or watch the wildlife feast at special feeders. Two fireplaces offer cozy warmth. Only 20 minutes from Milwaukee. Full Continental breakfast always includes Wisconsin's finest cheese, fresh fruits of the season, and special breads and pastries.

Hosts: Dorothy and Sheldon Waggoner
Rooms: 3 (2 PB; 1 SB) $50-70
Continental Breakfast
Credit Cards: None
Notes: 2, 5, 11, 12, 13

MILWAUKEE

County Clare: An Irish Inn and Pub
1234 Astor Street, 53202
(414) 27-CLARE (25273)

Built in the Georgian style (common to Irish guest houses), County Clare features 31 rooms with four-poster beds, remote control TVs, and Irish artwork. The spacious private baths showcase double whirlpools and showers. County Clare's pub and restaurant features stained and beveled glass, handsome maple millwork, and Irish artwork; soups, salads, sandwiches, and daily Irish lunch and dining specials are served.

---

7 No smoking; 8 Children welcome; 9 Social drinking allowed; 10 Tennis nearby; 11 Swimming nearby; 12 Golf nearby; 13 Skiing nearby; 14 May be booked through a travel agent; 15 Handicapped accessible.

County Clare

Parking is available to inn guests. Continental plus breakfast served.

Host: Dennis James
Rooms: 31 (PB) $79-129
Continental Breakfast
Credit Cards: A, B, C, D, E
Notes: 2, 3, 4, 5, 10, 11, 12, 14, 15

The Crane House

346 East Wilson Street, 53207
(414) 483-1512

Beautiful 1896 Victorian home in historic Bay View district. Less than 10 minutes from downtown and airport. Furnished with heirlooms and mix of contemporary and antique pieces. Lush perennial garden. Full breakfast is served. Off-street parking is available. Central air conditioning. Please write or call for brochure.

Hosts: Paula Tirrito and Steven Skavroneck
Rooms: 4 (S2B) $58-70
Full Breakfast
Credit Cards: A, B, D
Notes: 2, 5, 8, 9, 10, 11, 12

MONROE

Victorian Garden Bed and Breakfast

1720 16th Street, 53566-2643
(608) 328-1720; e-mail: vicgard@utelco.tds.net
www.apu.com/vicgard

This eclectic Victorian/Queen Anne home is waiting to greet guests with its lace-covered windows, wraparound porches, gardens, antiques, family heirlooms, queen-size beds, and gracious hospitality. Open to guests are the sitting room with baby grand piano, formal parlor, informal parlor with TV, dining room, wraparound porches, and gardens. A full breakfast of fruit, homemade cereal, muffins, and main dish, which may include eggs, meats, and cheese, is served at 8:30 A.M. in the formal dining room. Bedrooms have 100 percent cotton linens and private baths. A warm, friendly atmosphere will greet each guest.

Hosts: Jane and Pete Kessenich
Rooms: 4 (3 PB; 1 SB) $45-85
Full Breakfast
Credit Cards: A, B, D
Notes: 2, 5, 7, 9

MONTREAL

The Inn Bed and Breakfast

104 Wisconsin Avenue, 54550
(715) 561-5180

Built in 1913 as the office for Montreal Mining Company, the inn is a handsome four-square structure in the middle of Montreal, an iron mining company-owned town in the National Register of Historic Places. The Canadian influence is apparent in street names: Ottawa, Ontario, Toronto. Minutes from Lake Superior circle tour route, the inn features family antiques, stenciling, crocheted and quilted spreads, a Finnish sauna, a fireplace room, and full breakfast.

NOTES: Credit cards accepted: A MasterCard; B Visa; C American Express; D Discover; E Diner's Club; F Other; 2 Personal checks accepted; 3 Lunch available; 4 Dinner available; 5 Open all year; 6 Pets welcome;

The Inn

Rooms: 4 (PB) $50-70
Full Breakfast
Credit Cards: None
Notes: 2, 5, 7, 8, 9, 10, 11, 12, 13

OSCEOLA

Pleasant Lake Bed and Breakfast

2238 60th Avenue, 54020-4509
(715) 294-2545; (800) 294-2545
e-mail: pllakebb@centuryinter.net

Enjoy a romantic getaway in one of the history-filled rooms on beautiful Pleasant Lake. While there, guests may take a leisurely walk in the woods, watch the birds and other wildlife, enjoy the lake in the canoe or paddleboat, sit around the bonfire, and watch the moon and stars reflecting on the lake. Then relax in one of the whirlpools and enjoy a fireplace or curl up with a book in guests' private sunroom. Limited handicapped accessibility.

Pleasant Lake

Hosts: Richard and Charlene Berg
Rooms: 7 (PB) $60-125
Full Breakfast
Credit Cards: A, B
Notes: 2, 5, 7, 8, 9, 12, 13

PLYMOUTH

52 Stafford An Irish Guest House

52 Stafford Street, 53073
(414) 893-0552; (800) 421-4667

Listed in the National Register of Historic Places, this inn has 19 rooms, 17 of which have whirlpool baths and cable TVs. 52 Stafford features one of the most beautiful pubs in America, serving lunch daily and dinner seven nights a week. There are 35,000 acres of public recreation land nearby; cross-country skiing, hiking, biking, sports fishing, boating, swimming, and golf. Enjoy crystal-clear lakes and beautiful fall colors. Continental breakfast is served weekdays. Full breakfast is served weekends.

Hosts: Rip and Christine O'Dwanny
Rooms: 19 (PB) $79.50-119.50
Full and Continental Breakfast
Credit Cards: A, B, C, D, E, F
Notes: 2, 3, 4, 5, 6, 8, 9, 10, 11, 12, 13, 14

REEDSBURG

Parkview Bed and Breakfast

211 North Park Street, 53959
(608) 524-4333; e-mail: parkview@jvlnet.com
www.jvlnet.com/~parkview

In Reedsburg's historic district, this 1895 Queen Anne Victorian home has fish ponds, a windmill, and playhouse enhancing the grounds. Across from City Park and one block from downtown. Discover the original woodwork and hardware, tray ceilings, suitor's window, and built-in buffet inside this cozy home. Wisconsin

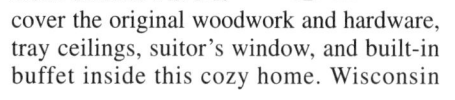

---

7 No smoking; 8 Children welcome; 9 Social drinking allowed; 10 Tennis nearby; 11 Swimming nearby; 12 Golf nearby; 13 Skiing nearby; 14 May be booked through a travel agent; 15 Handicapped accessible.

Dells, Baraboo, Spring Green, and bike trails are nearby. Inquire about accommodations for children.

Hosts: Tom and Donna Hofmann
Rooms: 4 (2 PB; 2 SB) $65-80
Full Breakfast
Credit Cards: A, B, C
Notes: 2, 5, 7, 9, 10, 11, 12, 13, 14

SPARTA

The Franklin Victorian Bed and Breakfast
220 East Franklin Street, 54656
(608) 269-3894; (800) 845-8767

This turn-of-the-century home welcomes guests to bygone elegance with small-town quiet and comfort. The four spacious bedrooms, two with a shared bath and two with private baths, provide a perfect setting for ultimate relaxation. Enjoy a full home-cooked breakfast served before starting the day of hiking, biking, skiing, canoeing, antiquing, or exploring this beautiful area. Canoe rental and shuttle service for bikers and canoeists available. Children over 10 welcome.

Hosts: Lloyd and Jane Larson
Rooms: 4 (2 PB; 2 SB) $75-95
Full Breakfast
Credit Cards: A, B
Notes: 2, 5, 7, 9, 11, 12, 13, 14

Just-N-Trails Country Inn/Nordic Ski Center
Route 1, Box 274, 54656
(608) 269-4522; (800) 488-4521
FAX (608) 269-3280

A country inn specializing in recreation, relaxation, and romance. Separate buildings: Paul Bunyan log cabin with two bedrooms, *Little House on the Praire* log cabin, and the Granary, a wood-frame cottage, each with a whirlpool and fireplace; dinners by reservation. Two suites in 1920 farmhouse on farm. Ralph Lauren linens. Four-course breakfasts. Near famous Elroy-Sparta Bike Trail. Cross-country skiing, snowshoeing, and snowtubing on premises. Ski lessons and ski rentals.

Hosts: Donna and Don Justin
Rooms: 7 (PB) $80-300
Full Breakfast
Credit Cards: A, B, C, D
Notes: 2, 4, 5, 6, 7, 8, 10, 11, 12, 13, 14

SPRING GREEN

Bettinger House Bed and Breakfast
Highway 23, Plain, 53577
(608) 546-2951

This 1904 brick home, once owned by the host's midwife grandmother, is near the world-famous House on the Rock, Frank Lloyd Wright's Taliesin, and the American Players Theatre. A home-cooked full breakfast is served every morning.

Hosts: Marie and Jim Neider
Rooms: 5 (2 PB; 3 SB) $55-70
Full Breakfast
Credit Cards: None
Notes: 2, 5, 7, 8, 9, 10, 11, 12, 14

STEVENS POINT

Dreams of Yesteryear Bed and Breakfast
1100 Brawley Street, 54481
(715) 341-4525

Designed by J. H. Jeffers, this bed and breakfast was built in 1901 and is lavish in Victorian detail. Period furniture is evident throughout. The hosts love to visit with guests and talk about this elegant home and its furnishings. The home is listed in the National Register of Historic Places, and its restoration was featured in *Victorian Homes* magazine. Children over 12 welcome.

Hosts: Bonnie and Bill Maher
Rooms: 6 (PB) $55-135
Full Breakfast
Credit Cards: A, B, C, D
Notes: 2, 5, 7, 9, 10, 11, 12, 13, 14

NOTES: Credit cards accepted: A MasterCard; B Visa; C American Express; D Discover; E Diner's Club; F Other; 2 Personal checks accepted; 3 Lunch available; 4 Dinner available; 5 Open all year; 6 Pets welcome;

STURGEON BAY

Inn at Cedar Crossing
336 Louisiana Street, 54235
(920) 743-4200 (lodging); (920) 743-4249 (dining)

Warm hospitality, elegant antique-filled guest rooms, and creative regional cuisine are a tradition at this most intimate Door County inn, listed in the National Register of Historic Places. Luxurious whirlpool tubs, cozy fireplaces, and evening refreshments await pampered travelers. Exquisite dining (breakfast, lunch, and dinner) features fresh regional ingredients, scratch bakery, fine wines, and libations. A hearty Continental breakfast is included in rates. Set in the beauty and culture of Wisconsin's Door Peninsula. Inquire about accommodations for children. Dining room is handicapped accessible.

Host: Terry Smith
Rooms: 9 (PB) $95-155
Continental Breakfast
Credit Cards: A, B, D
Notes: 2, 3, 4, 5, 7, 9, 10, 11, 12, 13, 14

The Scofield House Bed and Breakfast
908 Michigan Street, P.O. Box 761, 54235
(920) 743-7727; (888) 463-0204
e-mail: scofhse@mail.wiscnet.net
www.scofieldhouse.com

Described as "Door County's most elegant bed and breakfast." Victorian Queen Anne, circa 1902. Very ornate interior with inlaid floors and ornamented woodwork. Six guest rooms, each with private bath, double whirlpool, fireplace, cable TV, VCR, stereo, movie library. High Victorian decor throughout with fine antiques. Air conditioned. Full breakfast and afternoon sweet treats and teas. Color brochure. Mobil three-star and AAA three-diamond. Featured in *Chicago Tribune*, *Country Inns*, and *Midwest Living*, *Wisconsin Trails*.

Hosts: Bill and Fran Cecil
Rooms: 6 (PB) $93-196

The Scofield House

Full Breakfast
Credit Cards: None
Notes: 2, 5, 7, 9, 10, 11, 12, 13

White Lace Inn
16 North Fifth Avenue, 54235
(414) 743-1105

The White Lace Inn is a romantic getaway featuring four restored turn-of-the-century homes surrounding lovely gardens and a gazebo. The 18 wonderfully inviting guest rooms and suites are furnished with antiques, four-poster and Victorian beds, in-room fireplaces in some rooms, and double whirlpool tubs in others. Readers' choice of *Midwest Living* magazine readers and *Wisconsin Trails*. Inquire about accommodations for children.

White Lace Inn

---

7 No smoking; 8 Children welcome; 9 Social drinking allowed; 10 Tennis nearby; 11 Swimming nearby; 12 Golf nearby; 13 Skiing nearby; 14 May be booked through a travel agent; 15 Handicapped accessible.

Hosts: Bonnie and Dennis Statz
Rooms: 18 (PB) $99-199
Continental Breakfast
Credit Cards: A, B, C, D
Notes: 2, 5, 7, 9, 10, 11, 12, 13, 15

TWO RIVERS

Red Forest Bed and Breakfast
1421 25th Street, 54241
(920) 793-1794; (888) 250-2272

The Red Forest Bed and Breakfast is on Wisconsin's east coast. Minutes from Manitowoc, Wisconsin's port city of the Lake Michigan car ferry. Also midway from Chicago and the Door County Peninsula. The hosts invite guests to step back in time to 1907 and enjoy the gracious three-story, Shingle-style home, highlighted with stained-glass windows and heirloom antiques. Inquire about accommodations for children.

Hosts: Kay and Alan Rodewald
Rooms: 4 (2 PB; 2 SB) $65-85
Full Breakfast
Credit Cards: A, B, C, D
Notes: 2, 5, 7, 9, 10, 11, 12, 13, 14

Red Forest

WISCONSIN DELLS

The Buckley House
P.O. Box 598, 53965
(608) 586-5752; (888) 689-4875
FAX (608) 586-4744

An early 1900s country Victorian home, with an inviting wraparound porch, nestled

The Buckley House

on six acres with a pond and a breathtaking view. Truly a Currier and Ives setting. Enjoy antiques, in-room whirlpools, queen-size brass beds, quilts. Outdoors: fresh air, flower gardens, bright stars, and moonlight. Hiking, biking, skiing, snowmobiling, antiquing, and auctions. A quiet, peaceful retreat, yet only minutes from Wisconsin Dells, with waterparks, riverboat tours, museums, and top-name entertainment. Inquire about accommodations for children.

Hosts: Michael and Kathie Lake
Rooms: 3 (PB) $60-175
Full Breakfast
Credit Cards: A, B
Notes: 2, 5, 7, 11, 12, 13

Thunder Valley Inn
W15344 Waubeek Road, 53965
(608) 254-4145

Scandinavian hospitality in a country setting. Homemade breads, rolls, and jams will delight the guests. Real old-fashioned comfort. Summer evening family fiddling, and Chautauquas. Stroll the farmstead, pet the animals, or relax with a good book and cider or Norsk coffee. Near the famous Wisconsin Dells. Rated one of 10 Midwest best. Children welcome.

Hosts: Anita, Kari, and Sigrid Nelson
Rooms: 6 (PB) $45-80
Full Breakfast
Credit Cards: A, B
Notes: 2, 5, 7, 8, 9, 10, 11, 12, 13

NOTES: Credit cards accepted: A MasterCard; B Visa; C American Express; D Discover; E Diner's Club; F Other; 2 Personal checks accepted; 3 Lunch available; 4 Dinner available; 5 Open all year; 6 Pets welcome;

Terrace Hill
Bed and Breakfast
922 River Road, 53965
(608) 253-9363

Terrace Hill Bed and Breakfast is at the gateway of scenic River Road. Six miles of natural beauty which begins at the doorstep, just one and one-half blocks from the hustle and bustle of downtown Wisconsin Dells. Relax and enjoy the century-old Victorian home with its Old World charm. Serenely quiet location. Private baths, whirlpool, air conditioning, private parking, and full breakfasts. Serendipity.

Hosts: Lynn and Lenard Novak
Rooms: 5 (PB) $55-140
Full Breakfast
Credit Cards: A, B, C, D
Notes: 2, 5, 7, 8, 11, 12, 13

The White Rose
Bed and Breakfast Inn
910 River Road, 53965
(608) 254-4431; (800) 482-4724
e-mail: whiterose@jvlnet.com

As a romantic retreat or family fun getaway, guests' comfort and relaxation is the inn's pleasure. The White Rose Bed and Breakfast Inn invites guests to visit its gardens, relax in the parlor, or experience rich indulgence at the Secret Garden Café, at the lower level of the Victorian bed and breakfast, offering the famous international cuisine of the Cheese Factory Restaurant. Doubles, queen-size, and suites available, all with private baths. Heated outdoor pool.

Rooms: 6 (PB) $65-115
Credit Cards: A, B, C
Notes: 2, 3, 4, 5, 7, 8, 9, 11, 12, 13, 14, 15

---

7 No smoking; 8 Children welcome; 9 Social drinking allowed; 10 Tennis nearby; 11 Swimming nearby; 12 Golf nearby; 13 Skiing nearby; 14 May be booked through a travel agent; 15 Handicapped accessible.

Canada

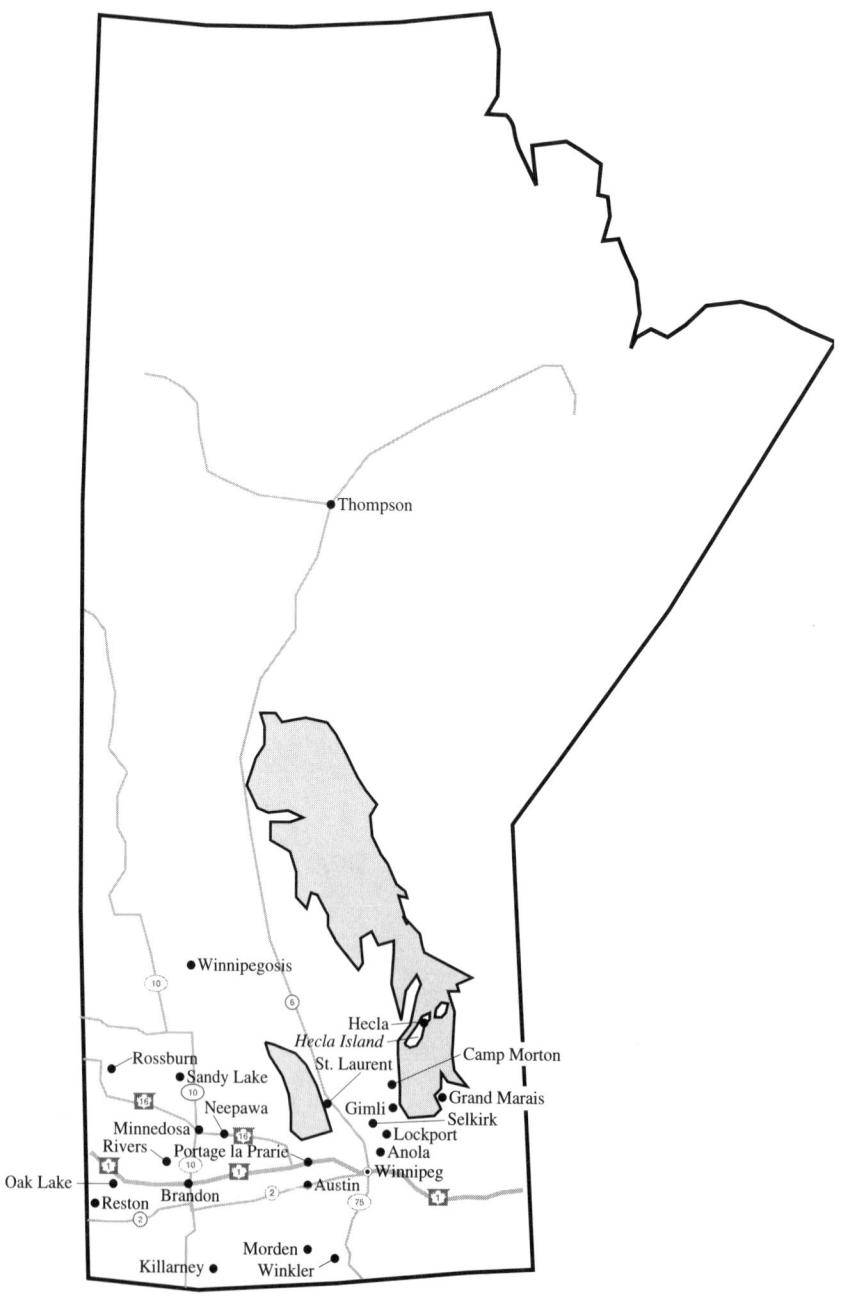

Manitoba

Manitoba

ANOLA

Bed and Breakfast of Manitoba

434 Roberta Avenue, Winnipeg, R2K 0K6
(204) 661-0300; FAX (204) 663-8114
e-mail: paulac@escape.ca
www.bedandbreakfast.mb.ca

Deer Run. Share in the comforts of rural life in tranquil surroundings close to Winnipeg. Breakfast served with country fare by gracious hosts. Wildlife in the area. Trout pond. Vegetable, berry, and floral gardens. Only 27 kilometers from the city of Winnipeg. $35.

AUSTIN

Bed and Breakfast of Manitoba

434 Roberta Avenue, Winnipeg, R2K 0K6
(204) 661-0300; FAX (204) 663-8114
e-mail: paulac@escape.ca
www.bedandbreakfast.mb.ca

The Oak Tree Bed and Breakfast. Relax. Visit this modern rural home and beautiful shaded yard; enjoy nature and its abundant wildlife and birds. Attractions nearby include Manitoba Agricultural Museum, Spruce Woods Provincial Park, five golf courses, cross-country skiing, and snowshoeing. Full breakfast. $50 Canadian.

BRANDON

Bed and Breakfast of Manitoba

434 Roberta Avenue, Winnipeg, R2K 0K6
(204) 661-0300; FAX (204) 663-8114
e-mail: paulac@escape.ca
www.bedandbreakfast.mb.ca

Casa Maley. For a unique, comfortable family atmosphere and a display of genuine hospitality, come and stay at the Casa Maley! This European-style three-story Tudor house, built in 1912 with red brick exterior, has a fairy-tale, gingerbread-house appearance. For breakfast guests have a choice of the host's specialties: exquisite and mouth-watering French toast, super-delicious omelet, sizzling bacon and eggs, big fluffy pancakes, an exotic fruit salad; and the blended oatmeal porridge is a dream come true. No smoking. $45 Canadian.

White House Bed and Breakfast. This bed and breakfast is on the north side of the Trans-Canada Highway next to Chalet Motel and Restaurant. Private parking. Greens on premises and a nine-hole golf course next door. Airport and bus pickup free. $40-55 Canadian.

CAMP MORTON

Bed and Breakfast of Manitoba

434 Roberta Avenue, Winnipeg, R2K 0K6
(204) 661-0300; FAX (204) 663-8114
e-mail: paulac@escape.ca
www.bedandbreakfast.mb.ca

Ash Grove Bed and Breakfast. Eight kilometers north of Gimli; 14-room house on two acres of parklike lawns and gardens. Mere minutes away from beaches, hiking/biking trails, golf courses. Continental breakfast. Children and dogs welcome. Open Thursday through Monday, May through September. $50-55.

NOTES: Credit cards accepted: A MasterCard; B Visa; C American Express; D Discover; E Diner's Club; F Other; 2 Personal checks accepted; 3 Lunch available; 4 Dinner available; 5 Open all year; 6 Pets welcome; 7 No smoking; 8 Children welcome; 9 Social drinking allowed; 10 Tennis nearby; 11 Swimming nearby; 12 Golf nearby; 13 Skiing nearby; 14 May be booked through a travel agent; 15 Handicapped accessible.

GRAND MARAIS

Bed and Breakfast of Manitoba
434 Roberta Avenue, Winnipeg, R2K 0K6
(204) 661-0300; FAX (204) 663-8114
e-mail: paulac@escape.ca
www.bedandbreakfast.mb.ca

Inn Among the Oaks. In cottage country, welcome to this rustic two-story home, built of cedar and local pine, hidden amongst the oaks and saskatoon bushes. Enjoy the secluded yard, swim in the outdoor pool, or take a relaxing soak in the indoor hot tub. Spacious, comfortable bedrooms. Tasty breakfasts in the airy sunlit dining room. Enjoy Lake Winnipeg's beautiful sandy beaches and marshes rich in opportunity for eco-tourism. Beautiful cross-country ski trails and snowmobiling in winter. German, some French spoken. $45 Canadian.

HECLA ISLAND

Solmandson Gesta Hús
Hecla Provincial Park, P.O. Box 76, R0C 2R0
(204) 279-2088
e-mail: holtz@mb.sympatico.ca
www.heclatourism.mb.ca

The guest house is within Hecla Provincial Park on 43 acres of private property. Enjoy luxurious European-style hospitality in a newly renovated and completely modern, comfortable home in an original Icelandic settlement. Relax on the veranda and enjoy the beautiful view of Lake Winnipeg. Enjoy the tranquil and peaceful atmosphere while petting the dogs and cats or feeding the ducks. The host is a commercial fisherman, so feast on the catch of the day along with garden-fresh vegetables for the evening meal.

Hosts: Dave and Sharon Holtz
Rooms: 4 (1 PB; 3 SB) $45-75
Full Breakfast
Credit Cards: A, B
Notes: 2, 4, 5, 6, 7, 8, 9, 10, 11, 12, 13, 14

KILLARNEY

Bed and Breakfast of Manitoba
434 Roberta Avenue, Winnipeg, R2K 0K6
(204) 661-0300; FAX (204) 663-8114
e-mail: paulac@escape.ca
www.bedandbreakfast.mb.ca

Country Comfort Bed and Breakfast. Quiet country location off Highway 3 between Killarney and Boissevain. Offers private entrance, featuring two bedrooms with facilities for up to 10 persons. Includes living and recreational facilities. Excellent lodging for hunters; includes freezer, refrigerator, and microwave. Children welcome. Close proximity to International Peace Garden, Boissevain art murals, Bottineau Ski Park, golf courses, many parks and lakes for water sports, fishing, skating, tobogganing, snowmobiling, cross-country skiing. Excellent hunting in area (birds and deer). Advance reservations appreciated. $50.

LOCKPORT

St. Andrews Bed and Breakfast
588 McPhillips Road, R1A 3M3
(204) 757-4533

Enjoy this peaceful country home, beautifully landscaped yard, relaxing on the patio. One guest room with comfortable twin beds, cozy sitting area, TV and radio, and many thoughtful extras. A full breakfast is served in the dining room. The home is a bungalow with central air and fireplace. Four miles north of St. Andrews airport on Highway 230 (McPhillips Road). Winnipeg city center is 30 minutes away. It only takes 15 minutes to reach Garden City area, minutes from golfing, fishing, shopping, sightseeing, historic sites, and attractions.

Hosts: Wm. (Nick) and Janice Shott
Room: 1 (PB) $75
Full Breakfast
Credit Cards: A, B
Notes: 3, 7, 11, 12

NOTES: Credit cards accepted: A MasterCard; B Visa; C American Express; D Discover; E Diner's Club; F Other; 2 Personal checks accepted; 3 Lunch available; 4 Dinner available; 5 Open all year; 6 Pets welcome;

MINNEDOSA

Bed and Breakfast of Manitoba

434 Roberta Avenue, Winnipeg, R2K 0K6
(204) 661-0300; FAX (204) 663-8114
e-mail: paulac@escape.ca
www.bedandbreakfast.mb.ca

The Castle. Restored two-turret 1901 Queen Anne two and one-half story Heritage site on river. In town, very quiet. Near lake resort, golf, skiing. Private large honeymoon suite with soaking tub and balcony. Leaded glass Music Room with fireplace, antiques, oriental carpets, and conservatory. Bicycles available. Group retreats and workshops in one of the most beautiful towns in Manitoba. $50-60.

Fairmount Bed and Breakfast. Fairmount is a 1914 farmhouse sitting on the edge of a slough (prairie waterway) in Minnedosa's beautiful pothole country. A wonderful place to see both woodland and wetland birds. Unwind while watching sheep graze on the pastures by the water, or spend some time hiking and skiing at Riding Mountain National Park, only 25 minutes up Highway 10. It specializes in country cooking, using products from own and surrounding farms. Spanish spoken. $50.

The Garden Path. The two and one-half-story brick home was constructed in 1903, and sits on a large lot with mature landscaping and gardens. Three guest rooms available on the second floor. The main floor features breakfast on the casual sun porch or in the formal dining room. Bay windows, hardwood floors, fireplace, piano, books, games table, craft, plants, and antiques highlight the living room. $45 Canadian.

Rosebriar Bed and Breakfast. Ideally in southern Manitoba, offering modern convenience served with old-fashioned hospitality. The guest area features two spacious bedrooms, bath, and cozy sitting room—complete with TV/VCR, refrigerator, and wood-burning fireplace. Breakfast includes delicious homemade breads and jams. Enjoy numerous activities winter and summer for sports enthusiasts; also artists' displays, craft shows, auctions, beautiful gardens, and miles of hiking trails.

The Castle Bed and Breakfast

149 Second Avenue SW, P.O. Box 1705, R0J 1E0
(204) 864-2830 (phone/FAX)

The only bed and breakfast in a castle on the Yellowhead Highway. A prime example of Queen Anne style, the castle has been restored and was designated a municipal Heritage site. The castle has 6,000 square feet of living space and a small home neatly attached by a tunnel passageway. It was built in 1901 for Judge Myers. Stay in a charming town in a completely modernized landmark house having a river flowing past the three- to four-acre grounds. Features large honeymoon suite, contemporary art collection, antiques, oriental carpets, and conservatory. Hosts are both artists.

Host: Richard Yates
Rooms: 4 (PB) $55-90
Full Breakfast
Credit Cards: A
Notes: 2, 5, 6, 8, 9, 10, 11, 12, 13

MORDEN

Bed and Breakfast of Manitoba

434 Roberta Avenue, Winnipeg, R2K 0K6
(204) 661-0300; FAX (204) 663-8114
e-mail: paulac@escape.ca
www.bedandbreakfast.mb.ca

Rosebriar Bed and Breakfast. In southern Manitoba, offering modern convenience with old-fashioned hospitality. The guest area features two spacious bedrooms, bath, and cozy sitting room with TV/VCR, refrigerator, and wood-burning fireplace. Breakfast includes

---

7 No smoking; 8 Children welcome; 9 Social drinking allowed; 10 Tennis nearby; 11 Swimming nearby; 12 Golf nearby; 13 Skiing nearby; 14 May be booked through a travel agent; 15 Handicapped accessible.

delicious homemade breads and jams. Enjoy numerous activities such as golfing, fishing, skiing, artists' displays, craft shows, auctions, beautiful gardens, and miles of hiking and snowmobile trails. Visa accepted. Cash discounts. $45-60.

NEEPAWA

Bed and Breakfast of Manitoba

434 Roberta Avenue, Winnipeg, R2K 0K6
(204) 661-0300; FAX (204) 663-8114
e-mail: paulac@escape.ca
www.bedandbreakfast.mb.ca

The Garden Path Bed and Breakfast. Enjoy Manitoba's most beautiful town while staying at this two and one-half story brick Heritage home. Mature landscaped gardens on peaceful, spacious grounds. Close to all town attractions and facilities. House features include fireplace, antiques, crafts, piano, bay windows, hardwood floors. Three attractively decorated guest rooms on second floor. Full buffet breakfast. Warm hospitality, inviting atmosphere create a unique experience. Baseball, cat, and gardening languages spoken. Multiple bookings 10 percent discount. MasterCard and Visa accepted. $49-59.

OAK LAKE

Prairie View Bed and Breakfast

Box 186, R0M 1P0
(204) 855-2149

Enjoy this newly renovated country home. Just off Highway 1 on the east side of a small town with lots to offer. Check out the craft shops and art gallery, go for a round of golf, or just sit on the deck and relax listening to the birds. Watch TV or sit by the fireplace in the cozy sitting room. Ten minutes from Oak Lake Beach Bird Sanctuary and the scenic Assiniboine Valley; 35 minutes from Brandon.

Hosts: Erwin and Lillian Enns
Rooms: 4 (2 PB; 2 SB) $30-35

Full and Continental Breakfast
Credit Cards: None
Notes: 2, 5, 7, 8, 9, 11, 12

PORTAGE LA PRAIRIE

Bed and Breakfast of Manitoba

434 Roberta Avenue, Winnipeg, R2K 0K6
(204) 661-0300; FAX (204) 663-8114
e-mail: paulac@escape.ca
www.bedandbreakfast.mb.ca

Echo Bay Bed and Breakfast. Come and enjoy a quiet country setting in a small town by Lake Manitoba. Close to the beach, golf course, restaurants, skating rink, bowling alley, bingo. In the heart of goose country for hunters; close to the well-known All Canada Goose Shoot. Private Continental breakfast; other meals available by arrangement. Weekly rates available. $30-40 Canadian.

Evergreen Gate. Enjoy sunny breakfasts in the beauty of private parklike surroundings. The large deck, airy screened porch, lounge, and kitchenette are at guests' disposal. Only one-half hour north of Winnipeg on scenic River Road. Ideal for walking, cycling (bicycles available), and visiting historic Selkirk, Lower Fort Garry, and Oak Hammock Marsh. *On parle français.* $40-50 Canadian.

RESTON

Bed and Breakfast of Manitoba

434 Roberta Avenue, Winnipeg, R2K 0K6
(204) 661-0300; FAX (204) 663-8114
e-mail: paulac@escape.ca
www.bedandbreakfast.mb.ca

Sundial Bed and Breakfast. A dream bed and breakfast—a Heritage home in a friendly small town in southwestern Manitoba on Highway 2. The town offers a craft shop, nine-hole golf course, RV park, and great restaurants. Red brick, two and one-half-story house with private yard with

NOTES: Credit cards accepted: A MasterCard; B Visa; C American Express; D Discover; E Diner's Club; F Other; 2 Personal checks accepted; 3 Lunch available; 4 Dinner available; 5 Open all year; 6 Pets welcome;

trees, second-floor balcony for guests, TV, VCR, and bicycles for the use of more active visitors. Varied breakfast menu served at guests' convenience. $40.

RIVERS

Cozy River Inn
Box 838, R0K 1X0
(204) 328-4457 (phone/FAX)

Enjoy a taste of country living close to town at this guest house one kilometer east of Rivers on Highway 25. Two individual theme rooms with full baths and entrances in a well-treed yard. Continental breakfast includes homemade muffins, bread, jam, and fruit. Smoke-free environment. Lake Wahtopanah provides excellent summer and winter activities; great hunting area. Several fine restaurants, golf course, tennis courts. Close to Brandon. Call ahead for reservations. Open year-round.

Hosts: Lynn and Jake Kroeger
Rooms: 2 (PB) $60
Continental Breakfast
Credit Cards: B
Notes: 2, 5, 7, 8, 9, 10, 11, 12, 13

ROSSBURN

Maple Grove Bed and Breakfast
Box 471, R0J 1V0
(204) 859-3064 (phone/FAX) (204) 859-2221

Trees, birds, wildlife, grain fields, and conservation area surround this Victorian country home, built in 1910. Enjoy the quiet, relaxing surroundings, sunsets, and wild berries in season. Full breakfast is included. Evening meals are available with advance notice and extra charge. Complimentary tea and coffee. Smoking permitted on the veranda only. Only 11 kilometers to Rossburo, 11 kilometers to Arrow Lake, and 25 kilometers to Rossman Lake for fishing, golfing, boat launch, and ice fishing. Cross-country skiing and snowmobiling in the area. Riding Mountain National Park only 45 minutes away. Open year-round.

Maple Grove

Hosts: Kathy and Bert Swann
Rooms: 3 (3 SB) $40
Full and Continental Breakfast
Credit Cards: None
Notes: 4, 5, 7, 8, 11, 12, 13

ST. LAURENT

Bed and Breakfast of Manitoba
434 Roberta Avenue, Winnipeg, R2K 0K6
(204) 661-0300; FAX (204) 663-8114
e-mail: paulac@escape.ca
www.bedandbreakfast.mb.ca

Echo Bay Bed and Breakfast. Come and enjoy a quiet country setting in a small town by Lake Manitoba. Close to beach, golf courses, and restaurants. Private quarters. Continental breakfast included. In the heart of goose country, offering hunting lodge accommodations for the month of October (all meals served for additional charge by arrangement). Accommodation includes two bedrooms, living room, large private deck. Just off Highway 6, only 45 minutes from Winnipeg's north perimeter. $40.

SANDY LAKE

Bed and Breakfast of Manitoba
434 Roberta Avenue, Winnipeg, R2K 0K6
(204) 661-0300; FAX (204) 663-8114
e-mail: paulac@escape.ca
www.bedandbreakfast.mb.ca

Appleyard's Bed and Breakfast. Rustic lake-front cabin with upper and lower

---

7 No smoking; 8 Children welcome; 9 Social drinking allowed; 10 Tennis nearby; 11 Swimming nearby; 12 Golf nearby; 13 Skiing nearby; 14 May be booked through a travel agent; 15 Handicapped accessible.

decks. Fire-pit and lakeside seats. Adjacent to the village, golf course, and restaurants. Only 15 minutes from Riding Mountain National Park, Clear Lake/Wassagaming. Only one hour to Dauphin (Country Fest and Ukranian Festival). The region is rich in recreational and cultural activities. Climate-controlled rooms with homemade quilts on beds. Crib available. Home-cooked breakfasts. $45-50.

SELKIRK

Bed and Breakfast of Manitoba

434 Roberta Avenue, Winnipeg, R2K 0K6
(204) 661-0300; FAX (204) 663-8114
e-mail: paulac@escape.ca
www.bedandbreakfast.mb.ca

Evergreen Gate Bed and Breakfast. As a peaceful getaway destination or a base for exploring the interlake, Evergreen Gate awaits guests in private parklike surroundings only one-half hour north of Winnipeg. High above the scenic Red River, this unique home is ideally positioned for walking, cycling, pelican watching, and visiting Lower Fort Garry, Oak Hammock Marsh, Selkirk, and the Lake Winnipeg beaches. A large deck, screened porch, lounge, and kitchenette complement the quiet, comfortable guest bedrooms. Babysitting available. French spoken. $45-55.

THOMPSON

Bed and Breakfast of Manitoba

434 Roberta Avenue, Winnipeg, R2K 0K6
(204) 661-0300; FAX (204) 663-8114
e-mail: paulac@escape.ca
www.bedandbreakfast.mb.ca

Shinook's Bed and Breakfast. Guests will receive a warm, friendly welcome whether vacation traveling or on business. The hosts have many interests and stories to share with guests. A full scrumptious breakfast is served in the country-style kitchen. Tea and a snack are served each evening at no extra cost. A spacious room with four single beds, two private bathrooms. A private den with TV/VCR. Good old northern hospitality with great home cooking. $45.

WINKLER

Perfect Peace Bed and Breakfast

6 Crocus Bay, R6W 1E3
(204) 325-9953

Attractive home, private lawn-bowling greens, quiet area, easy access to four different golf courses, several parks, and experimental station where one may view beautiful flowers and scenery, ideal for photographers. Relax beside the backyard fish pond or in the family room with TV.

Hosts: Henry and Margaret Unger
Rooms: 2 (PB) $35-40
Full Breakfast
Credit Cards: None
Notes: 2, 3, 5, 7, 8, 10, 11, 12, 13

WINNIPEG

Bed and Breakfast of Manitoba

434 Roberta Avenue, Winnipeg, R2K 0K6
(204) 661-0300; FAX (204) 663-8114
e-mail: paulac@escape.ca
www.bedandbreakfast.mb.ca

Andrews. Beautiful river property in older treed neighborhood. Close to bus, restaurants, and attractions. Enjoy bedroom suite with private bath and private TV lounge. Cruise the river in hosts' canoe, enjoy the flowers, or relax in the gazebo. Bike, exercise equipment available. Home-baked breakfasts. Close to airport, bus depot, VIA Rail, Trans-Canada Highway city route. Discounts for long stays. $50 Canadian.

Anne's Garden. Enjoy home-baked breakfast, tea, coffee, and snacks anytime in

NOTES: Credit cards accepted: A MasterCard; B Visa; C American Express; D Discover; E Diner's Club; F Other; 2 Personal checks accepted; 3 Lunch available; 4 Dinner available; 5 Open all year; 6 Pets welcome;

living room or patio overlooking beautifully treed yard. Quiet surroundings for bird watching, reading, or relaxing. Close to University of Manitoba, The Forks, golf course, and Fort Whyte Nature Centre. English, German, and Spanish spoken. Near Pembina Highway. $30-45 Canadian.

Bannerman East. Enjoy this lovely Georgian home, evening tea, and quiet walks in St. Johns Park or along the Red River. Close to Seven Oaks House, the planetarium, concert hall, and Rainbow Stage. $48 Canadian.

Bright Oakes. Spacious home on one-half acre of parklike grounds near the Red River. Close to St. Vital Park, University of Manitoba, good restaurants, and St. Vital Shopping Center. Easy access to the mint, St. Boniface Hospital, and downtown. English, French, and Polish spoken. $45 Canadian.

Butterfly Bed and Breakfast. Nestled among beautiful elm trees in a quiet neighborhood just a 15-minute walk from downtown, two-minute walk to Portage Avenue, and the major bus routes. River walk to The Forks nearby. Full breakfast is included. Diverse cultures appreciated. Discounts for longer stays. $52.

Fraser's Grove Bed and Breakfast. Convenient to public transit. Close to golf, parks, shopping, and downtown. Finest accommodations with truly knowledgeable, warm, friendly hospitality. The best brownie cake anywhere! $50 Canadian.

Mary Jane's Place. Enjoy a relaxed atmosphere in this unique three-story home with beautiful oak interior. Excellent transit service, near downtown, will pick up at the airport. Quick access to The Forks Market, zoo, hospital, and Dalnavert Museum. $35-55 Canadian.

Meadow Lake Bed and Breakfast. Wonderfully quiet and relaxing suburban location, yet so close to downtown. There are a lake and a meadow for year-round walks and winter toboganing. Comfortable great room with fireplace, TV/VCR, wide selection of movies and books for guests' use. Close to Club Regent Casino, golf course, fitness center, restaurants, and major shopping center. Main-floor accommodations. Breakfast includes a selection of homemade breads and jams, waffles, and crêpes. Transportation and tours can be arranged. German and some Spanish spoken. $35-50 Canadian.

Niagara House. A 1926 vintage home in River Heights. Close to airport; direct bus routes to downtown and Polo Park shopping center; easy access to perimeter and Trans-Canada Highway. Assiniboine Park nearby, as well as local shops, recreational facilities, and playground. Enjoy a relaxing stay in an atmosphere enhanced by surroundings. Children and pets welcome. Babysitting available. $45 Canadian.

Oakdale Bed and Breakfast. A charming mix of contemporary home with antique furnishings in a quiet residential neighborhood. Large private backyard with deck. Direct bus route to city center; easy access to airport, perimeter, and Trans-Canada Highway. Close to Assiniboine Park and zoo, golf courses, most major shopping centers. Enjoy breakfast in the great room. German spoken. $50 Canadian.

Prairie Comfort. Come for a relaxing stay in this quiet, quaint, cozy home. Guests enjoy use of living room and TV. In Fort Garry near Pembina Highway. Quick access to excellent city transit service to downtown and University of Manitoba. Near golf course, Crescent Park, and Fort Whyte Nature Centre. $30-45 Canadian.

7 No smoking; 8 Children welcome; 9 Social drinking allowed; 10 Tennis nearby; 11 Swimming nearby; 12 Golf nearby; 13 Skiing nearby; 14 May be booked through a travel agent; 15 Handicapped accessible.

Ravelston Manor. Old World hospitality with the comforts and amenities of today. A comfy bedroom awaits guests on the main floor and the family room on the lower level is reserved for guests, complete with regulation-size pool table, fireplace, and hot tub. Outdoors, enjoy the large deck and heated pool. Homemade bread and jams accompany the choice of breakfast items. $50 Canadian.

Shar-A-Cuppa Bed and Breakfast. Relax in the cozy bilevel home with two guest rooms, three-piece bath, and private family room with fireplace on the lower level. There is also a deck off the dining area and a patio by the garden. $40 Canadian.

Southern Rose Guest House. Experience the charm of decades past with a touch of southern hospitality. Enjoy morning breakfast in the formal dining room or on the wraparound cedar sun deck. Getaway to yesterday! Red brick exterior, warm woods, burnished brass-trimmed leaded glass, flickering fireplace, and live greenery. The yard provides a retreat to read, converse, or enjoy the afternoon sun. Play horseshoes, volleyball, or relax in redwood hot tub. Close to Polo Park shopping mall, The Forks, casino, good restaurants, zoo, airport, Winnipeg Convention Centre, and bicycle route. Just off express bus route. $35-48 Canadian.

Ellie's Bed and Breakfast

77 Middle Gate, R3C 2C5
(204) 772-5832; fax (204) 783-1462

Enjoy a stay in historic Armstrong's Point. A peaceful and picturesque cul-de-sac in the heart of Winnipeg. Hosts are well traveled and love to cook. Superb omelets plus, bread, scones, muffins, and cinnamon buns, jams, and jellies all homemade. "Make us your home away from home." Near bus service and all major attractions. Take the river walk to The Forks Market. Will pick up guests for additional charge, air, bus, or train.

Hosts: Peter and Eugenia Ellie
Rooms: 3 (3 SB) $50-60
Full Breakfast
Credit Cards: None
Notes: 2, 3, 4, 7, 8, 9

Mary Jane's Place

144 Yale Avenue, R3M 0L7
(204) 453-8104

Enjoy stay in a relaxed atmosphere in a unique three-story brick home nestled in the heart of Winnipeg's historic area of Crescentwood. Enjoy a leisurely walk in the neighborhood and view historic housing, the Assinaboine River, Little Italy, and Wellington Crescent's walking and jogging trail. The home has an oak interior, beautiful fireplaces, stained- and beveled-glass accents. Close to the airport, downtown, and all attractions. Easy to find from all directions. Hosts cater to guests' breakfast needs. Close to three bus routes. During special events rates will be slightly higher.

Hosts: Jack and Mary Jane
Rooms: 4 (1 PB; 3 SB) $45-55 Canadian
Full Breakfast
Credit Cards: None
Notes: 5, 7, 9, 10, 11, 12

Twin Pillars

235 Oakwood Avenue, R3L 1E5
(204) 452-4925 (phone/FAX)
e-mail: tls@escape.ca

Ten minutes from downtown, near all major bus routes; walk to Osborne Village, River Walk, near shops, restaurants, theatre. Enjoy a stay in a beautiful turn-of-the-century home with lovely verandas, across from park. Air conditioned. Continental plus breakfasts. Sightseeing information; babysitting available with prior notification. Linens and towels are washed with hypo-allergenic products. Smoking permitted in designated areas. Kid's pool available for swimming.

NOTES: Credit cards accepted: A MasterCard; B Visa; C American Express; D Discover; E Diner's Club; F Other; 2 Personal checks accepted; 3 Lunch available; 4 Dinner available; 5 Open all year; 6 Pets welcome;

Hosts: Bev Suek and Joe Taylor
Rooms: 4 (4 SB) $45-50
Continental Breakfast
Credit Cards: None
Notes: 2, 5, 6, 8, 9, 10, 12

WINNIPEGOSIS

Lytwyn's Bed and Breakfast

Box 203, R0L 2G0
(204) 656-4765; FAX (204) 656-4785

Come and enjoy complete privacy and space in the large suite. Relax in the hot tub or curl up by the fireplace. Refrigerator, microwave, and coffee maker. Satellite TV, reading material, and movie selection. Rural home near lake and golf course. Excellent area for hunting, snowmobiling, fishing, boating, cross-country skiing, photography, or nature hikes. Large yard for parking RVs, trailers, etc. Come and enjoy Manitoba's beautiful scenery and warm hospitality. German and Ukrainian translators available. Lunch and dinner available at an additional charge.

Hosts: Jim and Sherry Lytwyn
Rooms: 1 (PB) $55
Full and Continental Breakfast
Credit Cards: None
Notes: 2, 5, 9, 11, 12

---

7 No smoking; 8 Children welcome; 9 Social drinking allowed; 10 Tennis nearby; 11 Swimming nearby; 12 Golf nearby; 13 Skiing nearby; 14 May be booked through a travel agent; 15 Handicapped accessible.

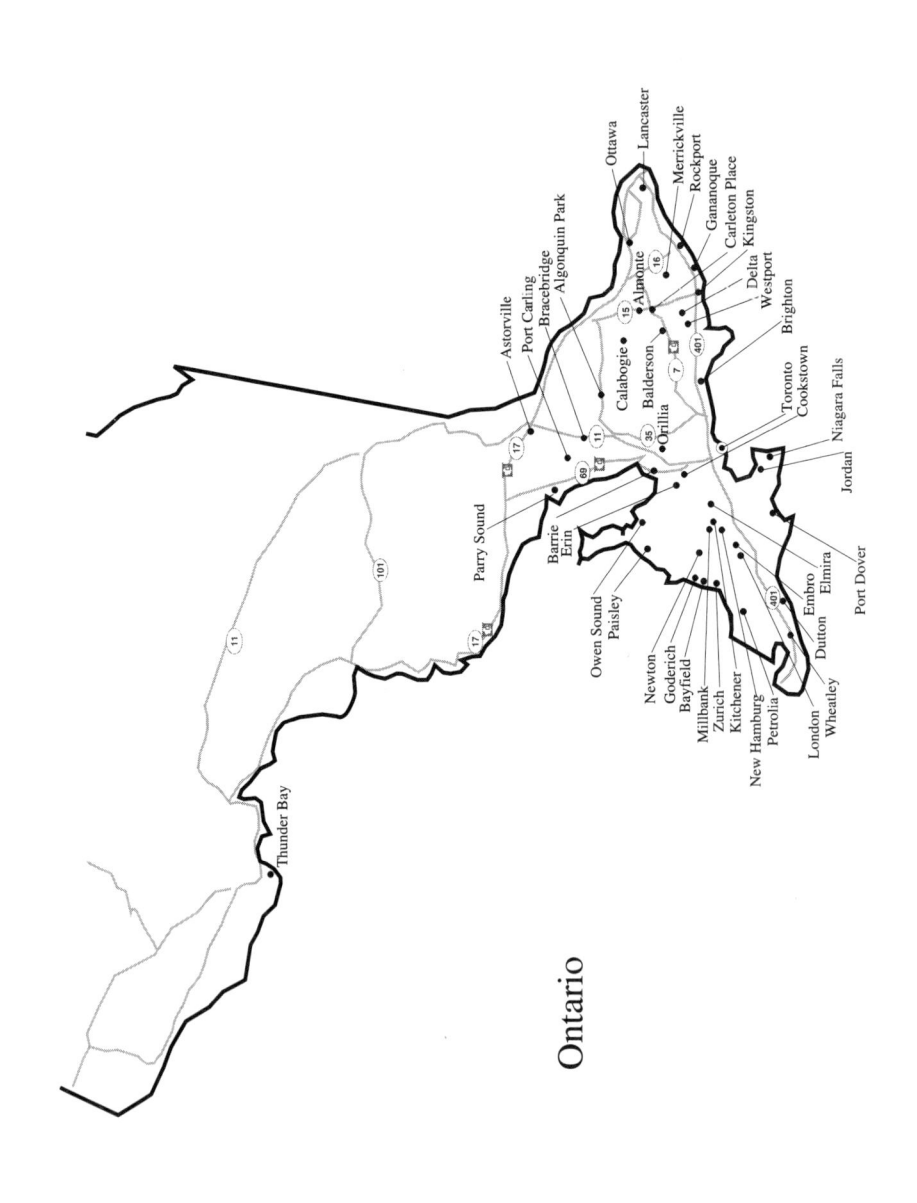

Ontario

Ontario

ALGONQUIN PARK

Arowhon Pines
Algonquin Park, Box 10001, Huntsville, P1H 2G5
(705) 633-5661; (416) 483-4393 (winter)

Rates include three meals per day and use of all recreational facilities: canoes, sailboats, sailboards, hiking trails, tennis courts, sauna, swimming in pristine waters, and games room. Open June through mid-October. Smoking is not permitted in some cabins. BYOB. Breakfast, lunch, and dinner are included in room rates.

Hosts: Eugene and Helen Kates
Rooms: 50 (PB) $120-230
Full Breakfast
Credit Cards: A, B
Notes: 2, 3, 4, 8, 10, 11, 12, 14

ALMONTE

Mount Blow Farm
Rural Route 2, K0A 1A0
(613) 256-3692; FAX (613) 256-8032

Enjoy staying in this restored 150-year-old log farmhouse on this sixth-generation century farm furnished with family antiques. Country-style cooking includes homemade bread, muffins, jams, jellies, honey, and maple syrup. Play the piano, swim in the pool, relax on the veranda, and walk the fields and lanes of the 200-acre farm or ski there in the winter. Watch for white-tailed deer, foxes, and bluebirds. This bed and breakfast is a 45-minute drive from Ottawa, the nation's capital. Visit museums, antique shops, and flea markets nearby. Lunch and dinner available upon request.

Hosts: Eleanor and Laurie Rintoul
Rooms: 3 (SB) $45-60 Canadian
Full Breakfast
Credit Cards: None
Notes: 2, 5, 7, 8, 9, 10, 11, 12, 13

The Squirrels
Box 729, 190 Parkview Drive, K0A 1A0
(613) 256-2995
www.bbcanada.com/29.html

The hosts enjoy swapping travel tales with their guests in a unique air-conditioned home designed in the style of a German chalet. They serve a hearty breakfast in the sunroom overlooking the garden. Two doubles, with one king-size and two twin beds, and one single room. Twenty minutes' drive from the Corel Centre Ottawa obliquely opposite Almonte Community Centre.

Hosts: Pat and Ian Matheson
Rooms: 3 (3 SB) $45
Full Breakfast
Credit Cards: None
Notes: 5, 7, 8, 9, 10, 11, 12, 13

ASTORVILLE

Hummingbird Hill Bed and Breakfast
254 Edmond Road, P0H 1B0
(705) 752-4547; (800) 661-4976
e-mail: mabb@vianet.on.ca
www.bbcanada.com/955.html

Unique geodesic dome cedar home has outdoor hot tub, sauna, screened cedar gazebo, extensive gardens and pond. Bird watching, privacy. Elegant, spacious accommodations, Victorian Room with en suite, Ivy Room with en suite, and the Loft with fireplace

---

NOTES: Credit cards accepted: A MasterCard; B Visa; C American Express; D Discover; E Diner's Club; F Other; 2 Personal checks accepted; 3 Lunch available; 4 Dinner available; 5 Open all year; 6 Pets welcome; 7 No smoking; 8 Children welcome; 9 Social drinking allowed; 10 Tennis nearby; 11 Swimming nearby; 12 Golf nearby; 13 Skiing nearby; 14 May be booked through a travel agent; 15 Handicapped accessible.

Hummingbird Hill

and shared luxury bath. Meals are gourmet, heart smart, low calorie, and vegetarian. Country living at its best.

Hosts: Marianne and Gary Persia
Rooms: 3 (1 PB; 1 SB) $60-65
Full Breakfast
Credit Cards: B
Notes: 2, 3, 4, 5, 6, 7, 8, 9, 10, 11, 12, 13

BALDERSON

Woodrow Farm and Guest Ranch

3062 Concession 8A Drummond, Rural Route 1, K0G 1A0
(613) 267-1493; (800) 582-2311
FAX (613) 267-1766
e-mail: whitedun@capitalnet.com

Just minutes from Perth, quiet country location, century home (1884) on 94 scenic areas. Bed and breakfast, choice of full country style or Continental breakfast. Also available, one to four days, all inclusive horseback riding, fishing, or craft breakaway packages. Three guest rooms, king-size, double, or twin beds, guest dining room and lounge with fireplace, video library. Nature trail running through the farm. Massage therapy available. Ski or snow shoe from the door.

Host: Ann Miller
Rooms: 3 (1 PB; 2 SB) From $60 Canadian
Full or Continental Breakfast
Credit Cards: B, F
Notes: 2, 3, 4, 5, 8, 9, 10, 11, 12, 13, 14

BARRIE

Cozy Corner

2 Morton Cresent, L4N 7T3
(705) 739-0157

A popular location: Georgian Bay, Wasaga Beach on the doorstep, close to the Muskoka Lakes, vacationland to many from the USA and Canada. Site of summer homes of Hollywood celebrities—Kurt Russell, Goldie Hawn, Rodney Dangerfield, and others. Yet only 36 miles north of Toronto. The elegant home offers luxurious and safe accommodation. Deluxe bedding, hair dryers, private TV, and parking. Delicious breakfasts and *joie de vivre* are standard. Brochure available.

Hosts: Charita and Harry Kirby
Rooms: 2 (S1B) $65
Suite: 1 (PB) $110
Full Breakfast
Credit Cards: B
Notes: 4, 5, 7, 9, 10, 11, 12, 13, 14

BAYFIELD

The Little Inn of Bayfield

Main Street, P.O. Box 100, N0M 1G0
(519) 565-2611; (800) 565-1832

Originally a stagecoach stop, the inn has been welcoming guests to this picturesque lakeside village since the 1830s. This designated Heritage inn is replete with fireplaces, en suite whirlpools, sauna, games, and books. Fine dining has long been a tradition, with superb meals and imaginative menus. Guests have a perfect base from which to explore the countryside and attend the Stratford and Blyth Festivals. There is much to do any time of the year. Smoking permitted in designated areas only.

Hosts: Patrick and Gayle Waters
Rooms: 30 (PB) $110-225
Cards: A, B, C, E
Notes: 2, 3, 4, 5, 8, 10, 11, 12, 13, 14, 15

NOTES: Credit cards accepted: A MasterCard; B Visa; C American Express; D Discover; E Diner's Club; F Other; 2 Personal checks accepted; 3 Lunch available; 4 Dinner available; 5 Open all year; 6 Pets welcome;

BRACEBRIDGE

Century House Bed and Breakfast
155 Dill Street, P1L 1E5
(705) 645-9903; e-mail: cnturybb@muskoka.com

Accommodation for "gentle folk" in this charming, air-conditioned, restored century-old home in the province's premier recreational lake district, a two-hour drive north of Toronto. Sandy's breakfasts are creative and generous. Waffles with local maple syrup are a specialty. Century House is close to shopping, beaches, and many craft studios and galleries. Enjoy the sparkling lakes, fall colors, studio tours, and cross-country skiing in the winter. A friendly dog is in residence.

Hosts: Norman Yan and Sandy Yudin
Rooms: 3 (SB) $65-70
Full Breakfast
Credit Cards: B
Notes: 5, 7, 10, 11, 12, 13, 14

Century House

BRIGHTON

Harbour Haven
44 Harbour Street, Rural Route #3, K0K 1H0
(613) 475-1006

Relax by the pool at this contemporary home, in a rural residential setting. On the waterfront by Brighton Bay and within minutes of Presqu'ile Provincial Park. Enjoy separate accommodations featuring fine linens, quilts, and duvets. "Allow us to pamper you as you celebrate a special occasion or enjoy a weekend getaway. You will find warm hospitality awaits you."

Hosts: Linda and Jim Payne
Rooms: 3 (3 SB) $55
Full Breakfast
Credit Cards: None
Notes: 5, 7, 9, 10, 11, 12, 13

CALABOGIE

Julie's on the Lake Bed and Breakfast
Rural Route 2, K0J 1H0
(613) 752-2387
www.bbcanada.447.html

Enjoy the tranquility on the banks of beautiful Calabogie Lake. Thrill to the spectacular sunsets. Three comfortable bedrooms with radio and reading lamps in each. A three-piece bath is shared. Start the morning with an "energizer full breakfast." Good dining in five area restaurants. Just a short walk to a 27-hole golf course. Ten-minute drive to alpine skiing—well-groomed snowmobile trails, and cross-country skiing.

Rooms: 3 (1 PB; 3 SB) $45-55
Full Breakfast
Credit Cards: None
Notes: 2, 5, 7, 8, 9, 10, 11, 12, 13, 15

COOKSTOWN

Victoria House Bed and Breakfast
36 Victoria Street East, L0L 1L0
(705) 458-0040 (phone/FAX)
e-mail: pine@bconnex.net

In the picturesque village of Cookstown with its many antique and craft shops, this comfortable, well-kept home offers two spacious, very private guest rooms with queen-size beds and en suite baths. Enjoy the garden, decks, and living room with fireplace, TV, VCR, and piano. Easy walk

---

7 No smoking; 8 Children welcome; 9 Social drinking allowed; 10 Tennis nearby; 11 Swimming nearby; 12 Golf nearby; 13 Skiing nearby; 14 May be booked through a travel agent; 15 Handicapped accessible.

to quaint Cookstown or a short drive to lakes, cottage country, golf, skiing, outlet mall; approximately one hour to downtown Toronto. Highway 400/89/27.

Hosts: Gisele and Alfred Baues
Rooms: 2 (PB) $65
Full Breakfast
Credit Cards: None
Notes: 2, 6, 7, 9, 12, 13

DELTA

Denaut Mansion Country Inn
5 Mathew Street, K0E 1G0
(613) 928-2588 (phone/FAX)

Restored 1849 stone mansion features art work, pottery, and carpets from around the world. Each room with en suite bath. Imaginatively presented, simply prepared three-course set menu dinners served in the candlelit dining room or enclosed verandah. Licensed. Pool, air conditioning, walking, canoeing, golf antiquing, hosts' own mapped loop cycle routes. Set on 11 wooded acres in a village setting in the Rideau Lakes, one-half hour from I-81 and the Ivy Lea Bridge. Colour brochure. Continental plus breakfast. Cross-country skiing nearby.

Hosts: Deborah and David Peets
Rooms: 5 (PB) $110-135 Canadian
Continental Breakfast
Credit Cards: A, B
Notes: 4, 5, 7, 8, 11, 12, 13

DUTTON

Hollingshead House
235 Main Street, N0l 1J0
(519) 762-2244

An elegantly decorated 10-room home with a historical Heritage in Elgin County. Built by the owner of the Dutton Flour Mill in the late 1800s, it now stands as a proud landmark for this relaxing and rural community. It has recently been restored to its original Victorian splendor, boasting 12-foot-high ceilings, hardwood floors, and a magnificent natural wood staircase framed with beautiful detailed fretwork. Private bath has a Jacuzzi for two.

Hosts: John and Julian
Rooms: 4 (1 PB; 3 SB) $55-85
Full Breakfast
Credit Cards: None
Notes: 2, 4, 5, 7, 8, 9, 11, 12, 13, 14, 15

ELMIRA

The Evergreens
Rural Route 1, N3B 2Z1
(519) 669-2471

Welcome to a quiet bed and breakfast nestled among the evergreens. Enjoy long walks through the forest, swimming in the pool, or cross-country skiing in winter. Two comfortable bedrooms with two guest bathrooms, and breakfast with homemade baking and preserves. In Mennonite country, with Elmira, St. Jacobs, and Elora nearby. North of Elmira, east off Regional Road 21 on Woolrich Road 3. Smoking is not permitted in home. Open year-round.

Hosts: Rodger and Doris Milliken
Rooms: 2 (SB) $50
Full Breakfast
Credit Cards: None
Notes: 2, 5, 6, 7, 8, 9, 11, 12, 13

Teddy Bear Bed and Breakfast Inn
Rural Route 1, N3B 2Z1
(519) 669-2379

Adult's magical getaway. Award-winning historic 1907 schoolhouse. Near St. Jacobs, Elora, Mennonite country. Beautiful rooms. Private bathrooms. Gourmet breakfasts. Antiques, gifts, collectibles, teddy bears, air conditioning. Off-season and group specials.

Hosts: Gerrie and Vivian Smith;
  Larry and Donna Smith
Rooms: 3 (PB) $75
Full Breakfast

NOTES: Credit cards accepted: A MasterCard; B Visa; C American Express; D Discover; E Diner's Club; F Other; 2 Personal checks accepted; 3 Lunch available; 4 Dinner available; 5 Open all year; 6 Pets welcome;

Teddy Bear

Credit Cards: A, B
Notes: 2, 4, 5, 7, 9, 12

EMBRO

J & G Bed and Breakfast

115 Huron Street, P.O. Box 272, N0J 1J0
(519) 475-4796

This restored century-old home with veranda, flower gardens, antiques, ceiling fans for guests' comfort, and wood stove. Shared bath with whirlpool. Full country breakfast served. Smoke-free establishment. Just minutes south of Stratford, home of the famous Shakespearean festival. It is a pleasant drive reminiscent of Scottish Highlands. Embro is home to the Highland Games held every July 1.

Hosts: Jeannette and Gord Richards
Rooms: 2 (2 SB) $55
Full Breakfast
Credit Cards: None
Notes: 2, 5, 7, 9, 10, 11, 12, 13

ERIN

Cedarbrook Country Inn

5483 Trafalgar Road, Highway 25 N, N0B 1T0
(519) 833-1000; (800) 837-6599
FAX (519) 833-1004

Relax in this spacious air-conditioned country home and conference center overlooking rolling acres in the scenic Caledon Hills. Guest rooms with en suite baths, fireplaces, decks, 12 acres of trails. Minutes to theaters. Four golf courses, tennis courts, cycle trails, skiing, and Bruce Trail hiking; antique and boutique stores are five minutes away. Country weddings. One hour from Toronto. Spa treatments available. Full breakfast. Dinner available upon request. TV room. Smoking is not permitted. No pets.

Host: Ginny Edwards
Rooms: 8 (PB) $95-110
Full Breakfast
Credit Cards: A, B
Notes: 2, 3, 5, 7, 9, 10, 11, 12, 13

GANANOQUE

The Victoria Rose Inn

279 King Street West, K7G 2G7
(613) 382-3368

This stately mansion, with a commanding central tower, was built by the first mayor in 1872. Nine elegant guest rooms with private bath and air conditioning. Two charming new guest rooms with shared bath in annex. The honeymoon suite has a marble fireplace and Jacuzzi. Guests are welcome to enjoy the parlor, veranda, and two acres of garden. The ballroom is an ideal location for a family reunion, special party, or business meeting. The Rose Garden Cafe is open in the summer for lunch, afternoon tea, and dinner. Close to an excellent selection of restaurants, the summer playhouse, boat tours, and interesting shopping. Cross-country skiing in area.

Hosts: Liz and Ric Austin
Rooms: 11 (9 PB; 2 SB) $75-155
Full Breakfast
Credit Cards: A, B, C
Notes: 3, 4, 5, 7, 10, 11, 12, 13

GODERICH

Kathi's Guest House

Rural Route #4, N7A 3Y1
(519) 524-8587; FAX (519) 524-2969

Welcome to this farm amongst rolling hills. Close to Lake Huron, about 12 kilometers east of Goderich, near Benmiller. Enjoy the

---

7 No smoking; 8 Children welcome; 9 Social drinking allowed; 10 Tennis nearby; 11 Swimming nearby; 12 Golf nearby; 13 Skiing nearby; 14 May be booked through a travel agent; 15 Handicapped accessible.

privacy of the guest house which has two bedrooms for guests' convenience. A nice place for two couples who share friendship together or young families with children. A crib is available. A full country-style breakfast is served. The host has friendly pets. English and German spoken. Open year-round. Reservations preferred. Deposit required. Special rates for longer stays.

Hosts: Kathi Beyerlein
Rooms: 2 (PB) $60
Full Breakfast
Credit Cards: None
Notes: 5, 8, 11, 12, 13

JORDAN

The Vintner's Inn
3845 Main Street, L0R 1S0
(905) 562-5336; (800) 701-8074
www.vintnersinn.on.ca.

Elegant country inn in renovated winery building. All rooms have Jacuzzi, fireplace, telephone, and antique appointments. On the same property as an award-winning premium winery and one of Canada's finest regional restaurants, Cave Spring Cellars and On the 20, respectively. Village of Jordan has a number of artisan and antique shops. Thirty minutes to Niagara-on-the-Lake, Niagara Falls, and in the heart of Ontario's wine country.

Host: Helen Young
Rooms: 16 (PB) $199-269 Canadian
 (approx. $145-165 U.S.)
Continental Breakfast
Credit Cards: A, B, C, E
Notes: 3, 4, 5, 7, 9, 10, 12, 14

KINGSTON

Hotel Belvedere
141 King Street East, K7L 2Z9
(613) 548-1565; (800) 559-0584
FAX (613) 546-4692

A delightful collection of 20 unique rooms, each freshly decorated in period style, all with their own private bathrooms. Very convenient central location. Continental breakfast can be brought to the guests' room or served on the lovely terrace. Within walking distance of the university, downtown retail shops, Lake Ontario, and the Thousand Islands boat tours. Some non-smoking rooms are available.

Rooms: 20 (PB) $99-149
Continental Breakfast
Credit Cards: A, B, C, E, F
Notes: 2, 3, 5, 8, 9, 10, 11, 12, 14

Painted Lady Inn
181 William Street, K7L 2E1
(613) 545-0422

This stately Victorian offers seven elegant rooms, all with private baths, queen-size beds, antiques, and central air. Romance comes alive in luxury rooms with Jacuzzis and fireplaces. Join other guests for lively conversation over scrumptious gourmet breakfasts—waffles, omelets, French toast. Inn is close to restaurants, pubs, Queen's University, Fort Henry, and Thousand Islands boats. After a busy day, guests relax on a Victorian veranda in the rose garden or on the sunny balcony. Parking on-site. Four blocks to Lake Ontario.

Host: Carol Franks
Rooms: 7 (PB) $85-155 Canadian
Full Breakfast
Credit Cards: A, B, C
Notes: 2, 5, 7, 9, 10, 11, 12

KITCHENER

Aram's Roots and Wings Bed and Breakfast
11 Sunbridge Crescent, N2K 1T4
(519) 743-4557; FAX (519) 743-4166

Country living right in the city. Roots and Wings is in the north end of Kitchener on the boundary with Waterloo. Ten minutes from St. Jacobs, universities, and most activities in the Kitchener/Waterloo area. Recreational facilities include a heated pool, Jacuzzi, and walking trails. Ultra whirlpool baths in two

NOTES: Credit cards accepted: A MasterCard; B Visa; C American Express; D Discover; E Diner's Club; F Other; 2 Personal checks accepted; 3 Lunch available; 4 Dinner available; 5 Open all year; 6 Pets welcome;

bathrooms. Delicious breakfasts start guests on their day's adventures.

Host: Fay Teal-Aram
Rooms: 4 (2 PB: 2 SB) $65-80
Full Breakfast
Credit Cards: A, B
Notes: 2, 5, 6, 8, 9, 10, 11, 12, 15

LANCASTER

MacPine Farms

Box 51, K0C 1N0
(613) 347-2003; www.achilles.net/~bb
www.achilles.net/~bb/688.html

Welcome to MacPine Holstein Farm on the shores of the St. Lawrence River, south of the 401, a half-mile east of Lancaster 814 exit, 10 miles from Québec border. Enjoy this modernized century home. Shaded by large old pine trees. Five-minute walk to the cottage on the river, where guests can swim, canoe, paddleboat, relax, and watch the ocean ships go by. Attractions: golf, fishing, boating, nature trails, china outlet, and craft and antique shops. Visit Montréal, Cornwall, or Ottawa. Smoke-free home. Children are welcome.

Hosts: Guelda and Robert MacRae
Rooms: 3 (SB) $40-50
Full Breakfast
Credit Cards: None
Notes: 2, 5, 7, 8, 9, 11, 12, 13

LONDON

Clermont Place

679 Clermont Avenue, N5X 1N3
(519) 672-0767; FAX (519) 672-2449

A modern home in a parklike setting with its own heated outdoor pool. Central air conditioning, three attractive bedrooms sharing a four-piece bath. A full Canadian breakfast is served in the dining room, by the pool, or in the gardens. Four free tennis courts behind the house; two public golf courses five minutes away. Forty minutes from the Stratford Shakespeare Festival.

Close to the University of Western Ontario and University Hospital in northeast London. Cross-country skiing in area.

Hosts: Doug and Jacki McAndless
Rooms: 3 (SB) $55-60
Full Breakfast
Credit Cards: B, C
Notes: 2, 3, 4, 5, 7, 9, 10, 11, 12, 13

Idlewyld Inn

36 Grand Avenue, N6C 1K8
(519) 433-2891 (phone/FAX); (800) 267-0525

A wealthy London businessman and member of Parliament constructed this manor, which still features the original woodwork, fireplace, and stained-glass windows. A huge staircase graces the center hall. Several rooms include fireplaces or whirlpool tubs. Unique, hand-painted wallcoverings grace the conference room walls. For a romantic occasion, the hosts will be happy to arrange dining and flowers

Hosts: Dawn Lashbrook
Rooms: 27 (PB) $85-169 Canadian
Continental Breakfast
Credit Cards: A, B, C, E
Notes: 5, 8, 9, 10, 11, 12, 13, 14, 15

Quayle's Bed and Breakfast

118 Farmington Court N6K 3N9
(519) 657-2726; FAX (519) 657-2118

This modern two-story home is convenient to 401 and 402, downtown, university, hospitals, golf courses, etc. The bed and breakfast offers three bright, freshly decorated bedrooms with TV, a lovely living room for relaxing, and choice of a full hearty breakfast or cereal, fresh homemade toast, and muffins in the formal dining room. Rates are based on double occupancy, plus a third person in the party would enjoy a second bedroom for only $15 more. There is a 10 percent discount on stays of three or more days and a weekly package of seven days for the price of six.

Hosts: Mike and Lou Quayle
Rooms: 3 (3 SB) $40-50 Canadian

---

7 No smoking; 8 Children welcome; 9 Social drinking allowed; 10 Tennis nearby; 11 Swimming nearby; 12 Golf nearby; 13 Skiing nearby; 14 May be booked through a travel agent; 15 Handicapped accessible.

Full and Continental Breakfast
Credit Cards: None
Notes: 5, 7, 8, 9, 10, 11, 12, 13

The Rose House

526 Dufferin Avenue, N6B 2A2
(519) 433-9978; e-mail: mperez@wwdc.com

The Rose House is a centrally air-conditioned, 125-year-old home on a fine residential street adjacent to downtown. This area has many historically designated homes. Within 15 minutes of the University of Western Ontario, all hospitals, major malls, and recreational facilities. It is a comfortable walk to live theater, museums, art galleries, and excellent restaurants. Breakfast is a full nutritional meal served family style. No small children. No federal or provincial taxes. Free parking. Reservations recommended.

Hosts: Betty and Douglas Rose
Rooms: 3 (1 PB; 2 SB) $40-65
Full Breakfast
Credit Cards: A, B, C
Notes: 5, 7, 9, 10, 11, 12, 13

MERRICKVILLE

Millisle Bed and Breakfast

205 Mill Street, P.O. Box 341, K0G 1N0
(613) 269-3627; FAX (613) 269-4735

Forty-five minutes south of Ottawa, adjacent to the Rideau River and Locks. Three-minute walk to center of village. A restored, turreted Heritage Victorian home (1858). Bedrooms furnished with antiques. Bathrooms private, one with whirlpool for two, two with Victorian claw-foot tubs, and one with shower only. Full breakfast served in Heritage dining room. Dinner package available with nearby restaurant, in a Heritage building. Thirty minutes from U.S. border. Cross-country skiing nearby.

Hosts: Kathy and Derry Thompson
Rooms: 5 (PB) $68 Canadian
Full Breakfast
Credit Cards: A, B, C
Notes: 2, 5, 7, 9, 11, 12, 13

MILLBANK

Honeybrook Farm

Rural Route 1, N0K 1L0
(519) 595-4604

Gracious guest accommodation in the heart of Ontario theater and Mennonite country. Completely restored 1866 split granite home offers spacious guest bedrooms and bathrooms with amenities of first-class accommodation. Relax in the recreation room. Enjoy refreshments on the house. Choose breakfast from a varied menu. Gourmet dinners by prearrangement. Twenty minutes' drive to the theaters of Stratford and Drayton and the markets of Kitchener-Waterloo and St. Jacobs. Children over 12 welcome.

Hosts: Alveretta and Jack Henderson
Rooms: 2 (1 PB; 1 SB) $40-70
Full Breakfast
Credit Cards: None
Notes: 2, 3, 4, 5, 7, 9

NEW HAMBURG

The Waterlot Restaurant and Bed and Breakfast

17 Huron Street, N0B 2G0
(519) 662-2020; FAX (519) 662-2114
e-mail: waterlot@sympatico.ca

The Waterlot opened in the fall of 1974 and from the outset it has been committed to

Millisle

NOTES: Credit cards accepted: A MasterCard; B Visa; C American Express; D Discover; E Diner's Club; F Other; 2 Personal checks accepted; 3 Lunch available; 4 Dinner available; 5 Open all year; 6 Pets welcome;

The Waterlot

quality of ambiance and service. Two large and comfortably appointed rooms share a memorable marbled shower, bidet, water closet, wet vanity, and sitting area. Suite has a private bath and a living area. The Waterlot is one of Ontario's finest dining establishments. Twelve miles from world-renowned Stratford Shakespeare Festival May through November.

Host: Gordon and Leslie Elkeer
Rooms: 3 (1 PB; 2 SB) $65-85 Canadian
Continental Breakfast
Credit Cards: A, B, C, E
Notes: 2, 3, 4, 5, 7, 8, 9, 10, 11, 12, 13

NEWTON

Country Charm
Rural Route #1, Road #129, Emg. #6841, N0K 1R0
(519) 595-8789

Come and enjoy bed and breakfast in the hosts' large Mennonite country home just one kilometer south of Newton. Relax around a campfire (weather permitting) or watch the sunset near the creek. There are a sawmill and a buggy shop at the crossroads. Skideu Trail, bakery, and cheese factory are favorite spots for guests' enjoyment. Open year-round. "Share a memory with us."

Hosts: Marlene and Ezra Streicher
Rooms: 3 (1 PB; 2 SB) $45
Full Breakfast
Credit Cards: None
Notes: 2, 3, 4, 5, 8, 10, 11, 12, 13

NIAGARA FALLS

Gretna Green
5077 River Road, L2E 3G7
(905) 357-2081

This tourist home offers bright, comfortable rooms with en suite bathrooms. All guest rooms are air conditioned and have TV. Families are welcome. This is "a home away from home" where guests are treated to a full, home-cooked breakfast that includes muffins, scones, jams, and jellies. Niagara has much to offer: the falls, Skylon Tower, IMAX Theatre, the Floral Clock, the rose gardens, and museums. Bike rentals available. Personal checks accepted for deposit only. Smoking permitted in designated areas only.

Hosts: Stan and Marg Gardiner
Rooms: 4 (PB) $45-75
Full Breakfast
Credit Cards: None
Notes: 8, 9, 10, 12

Gretna Green

ORILLIA

Betty and Tony's Waterside Bed and Breakfast
677 Broadview Avenue, L3V 6P1
(800) 308-2579; FAX (705) 326-2262
e-mail: tony.bridgens@encode.com
www.bbcanada.com/9.html

A modern air-conditioned home in the Lakelands of Ontario, with lawns running down to the 300-mile-long Trent Severn waterway. Fishing, swimming, docking for

---

7 No smoking; 8 Children welcome; 9 Social drinking allowed; 10 Tennis nearby; 11 Swimming nearby; 12 Golf nearby; 13 Skiing nearby; 14 May be booked through a travel agent; 15 Handicapped accessible.

Betty and Tony's

up to 40-foot cruisers, a paddleboat, and bikes. English hosts serve breakfast on Wedgwood bone china. Charming large rooms, guest lounge, books. Nearby are Casino Rama, Stephen Leacock Museum, city parks, and beach.

Hosts: Betty Bridgens and Tony Bridgens
Rooms: 3 (1 PB; 2 SB) $60-95 Canadian
Full Breakfast
Credit Cards: A, B, E
Notes: 2, 3, 4, 5, 6, 7, 8, 9, 10, 11, 12, 13

Rest Awhile

12 Dalton Crescent North, L3V 6C7
(705) 327-7825

English and French spoken. Enjoy the comfortable stone ranch-style home. Antiques, fireplace. Stenciled walls. Large, bright bedrooms with queen-size beds. Hot breakfast in the morning. Join the hosts for tea in the Florida Room overlooking the beautiful garden and pond. City of annual Perch Festival in April/May. Close to Rama Casino. Private guest parking.

Hosts: Rita and Jerry Sirois
Rooms: 2 (1 PB; 1 SB) $45-68
Full Breakfast
Credit Cards: None
Notes: 5, 7, 8, 10, 11, 12, 13, 15

The Verandahs

4 Palm Beach Road, Rural Route 2,
  Hawkestone, L0L 1T0
(705) 487-1910 (phone/FAX)

Victorian-style home with deep verandas on three sides on large landscaped lot close to Lake Simcoe. Bright, attractive, and comfortable interior with a welcoming ambiance. Guest sitting room with fireplace, TV, books, and games. Beds are comfortable and covered with goose-down duvets. Winter season December 28 through March 31, and summer May 15 through October 15. Close to ski resorts, snowmobile trails, and ice fishing. Boat launch and beach within one-half kilometer and many attractions nearby. Inquire about accommodations for children.

Hosts: Pearl and Norm Guthrie
Rooms: 3 (1 PB; 2 SB) $60-80
Full Breakfast
Credit Cards: A, B
Notes: 2, 7, 9, 11, 12, 13

OTTAWA

Albert House Inn

478 Albert Street, K1R 5B5
(613) 236-4479; (800) 267-1982

Gracious Victorian inn built in 1875 by a noted Canadian architect. Each room is individually decorated and has private facilities, telephone, TV, and air conditioning. Guest lounge with fireplace. Famous Albert House breakfast. Parking is available, but inn is within walking distance to most attractions.

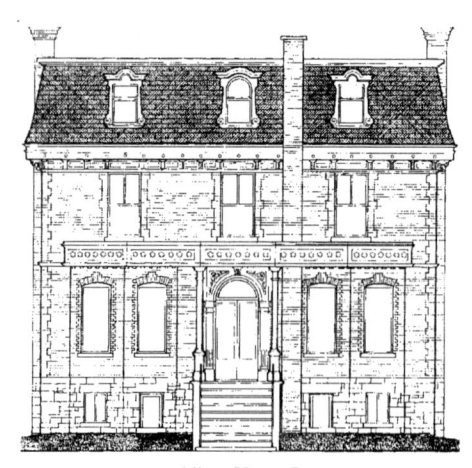

Albert House Inn

NOTES: Credit cards accepted: A MasterCard; B Visa; C American Express; D Discover; E Diner's Club; F Other; 2 Personal checks accepted; 3 Lunch available; 4 Dinner available; 5 Open all year; 6 Pets welcome;

Hosts: Cathy and John Delroy
Rooms: 17 (PB) $78-115
Full Breakfast
Credit Cards: A, B, C, E
Notes: 5, 9, 13, 14

Auberge McGEE'S Inn (Est. 1984)

185 Daly Avenue, K1N 6E8
(613) 237-6089; (800) 2MCGEES
FAX (613) 237-6201
www.coatesb.demon.co.uk/McGees

Fifteen years of award-winning hospitality. McGEE'S is a smoke-free upscale bed and breakfast inn in downtown Ottawa. Each room features a telephone equipped with computer modem hook up, enabling guests to direct-dial long distance (a savings of 30 percent) and receive messages on personal voice mail. Two Jacuzzi en suite theme rooms. Walking distance of Congress Centre, Parliament, University of Ottawa, Rideau Canal, trendy Byward Market. Ten-minute drive to ski hills. AAA-approved. Meeting rooms for 24 people. Full breakfast.

Hosts: Anne Schutte and Mary Unger
Rooms: 14 (12 PB; 2 SB) $78-170
Full Breakfast
Credit Cards: A, B, C
Notes: 5, 7, 8, 9, 11, 12, 13

Australis Guest House

35 Marlborough Avenue, K1N 8E6
(613) 235-8461 (phone/FAX)
e-mail: waters@intranet.ca
www.bbcanada.com/1463.html

This guest house is the oldest established and still operating bed and breakfast in Ottawa. On a quiet, tree-lined street one block from the Rideau River and Strathcona Park, it is a 20-minute walk to the Parliament buildings. The home boasts leaded windows, fireplaces, oak floors, and unique eight-foot stained-glass windows. The spacious rooms, including one with private bathroom, feature many collectibles from different parts of the world. The hearty, delicious breakfasts help start the day right. Winner of the Ottawa Gold Award, Star of the City for services to tourism, recommended by *Newsweek* and *Travel Scoop*. Carol Waters is co-author of *The Breakfast Companion*.

Hosts: Brian and Carol Waters
Rooms: 3 (1 PB; 2 SB) $62-78
Full Breakfast
Credit Cards: None
Notes: 5, 7, 10, 11, 12, 13

Beatrice Lyon Guest House

479 Slater Street, K1R 5C2
(613) 236-3904

This is a beautiful old-fashioned family home surrounded by gracious large trees. The bed and breakfast is within walking distance of the Parliament buildings, the Museum of Civilization, the National Archives, Byward Market, Rideau Canal, and Hull, Québec. Children are welcome, and baby-sitting can be arranged. The host is a member of the Downtown Bed and Breakfast Association. Fifteen dollars for extra person in room.

Host: Beatrice Lyon
Rooms: 3 (SB) $55
Full Breakfast
Credit Cards: A
Notes: 2, 5, 6, 7, 8, 9, 11, 12, 13

---

7 No smoking; 8 Children welcome; 9 Social drinking allowed; 10 Tennis nearby; 11 Swimming nearby; 12 Golf nearby; 13 Skiing nearby; 14 May be booked through a travel agent; 15 Handicapped accessible.

Blue Spruces
187 Glebe Avenue, K1S 2C6
(613) 236-8521

This lovely Edwardian home has been furnished with fine Victorian English and Canadian pine antiques and is in Ottawa's downtown core. Minutes from Parliament. Delicious full breakfast, including freshly ground coffee, is served each morning in the elegant dining room.

Hosts: Phyllis and John Kennedy
Rooms: 3 (PB) $85
Full Breakfast
Credit Cards: A, B, C
Notes: 2, 5, 7, 9, 10, 11, 12, 13

Bye-the-Way
310 First Avenue, K1S 2G8
(613) 232-6840

Modern, comfortable, and elegant, Bye-the-Way bed and breakfast offers all the conveniences of gracious living in downtown Ottawa. A few minutes' walking distance from the Rideau Canal, city attractions, Carleton University, and world-class museums. The host is happy to guide first-time visitors around Ottawa. Central air conditioning, smoke- and pollen-free.

Hosts: Krystyna, Rafal, and Adam
Rooms: 4 (2 PB; 2 SB) $60-80
Suite: $80
Full Breakfast
Credit Cards: A, B, F
Notes: 2, 7, 8, 9, 10, 11, 12, 13, 14

Bye-the-Way

Gasthaus Switzerland Inn
89 Daly Avenue, K1N 6E6
(613) 237-0335; (888) 663-0000
FAX (613) 594-3327; e-mail: switzinn@magi.com
www.infoweb.magi.com/~switzinn

The Gasthaus Switzerland Inn, in the heart of Canada's capital, offers guests traditional Swiss hospitality. Twenty-two well-appointed air-conditioned rooms, some with fireplace, private bath/Jacuzzi en suite, cable TV, telephone, a smoke-free environment, limited free parking, and a Swiss country breakfast buffet. Recommended by CAA, AAA, Canada Select, and Tourism of Ontario. Honeymoon/romantic getaway suite featuring king-size canopied poster bed, a double Jacuzzi, and fireplace.

Hosts: Josef and Sabina Sauter
Rooms: 22 (PB) $68-188
Full Breakfast
Credit Cards: A, B, C, E
Notes: 5, 7, 10, 11, 12, 13

Haydon House
18 The Driveway, K2P 1C6
(613) 230-2697

A completely renovated and modernized Victorian-era mansion that offers rest and comfort. It is air conditioned and has a private outdoor portico sitting area, spacious bedrooms, and modern facilities embellished with traditional Canadian pine decor. En suite, large room with double bed and two single beds, private bath. Haydon House is nestled in a tranquil residential area beside the historic and picturesque Rideau Canal and scenic parkway. All important points of interest, such as the Parliament buildings, Byward Market, museums, and National Art Gallery, are within a short and easy walk. Inquire about accommodations for pets.

Host: Mary Haydon
Rooms: 3 (1 PB; 2 SB) $60-80 Canadian
Continental Breakfast
Credit Cards: None
Notes: 2, 5, 8, 9, 10, 11, 12, 13, 14

NOTES: Credit cards accepted: A MasterCard; B Visa; C American Express; D Discover; E Diner's Club; F Other; 2 Personal checks accepted; 3 Lunch available; 4 Dinner available; 5 Open all year; 6 Pets welcome;

Paterson House (Bed and Breakfast with Health Centre)

500 Wilbrod Street, K1N 6N2
(613) 565-8996; FAX (613) 565-6546
e-mail: paterson@cyberus.ca
www.bbcanada.com/554.html

Magnificent historic Heritage mansion, beautifully restored to original elegance. Enjoy a tranquil and luxurious experience among traditional designer-decorated furnishings and objets d'art. All guest suites are individually designer-decorated in serene colors, with remote-control color TVs, telephones with data port, climate controls, and windows that open. Health Centre: for total mind and body relaxation and rejuvenation, enjoy authentic traditional Ayurvedic luxurious massage and deep herbal cleansing steam bath treatments. Recommended best restaurant: Noah's.

Host: Renée C. Bates
Rooms: 4 (PB) $135-175 Canadian
Continental Breakfast
Credit Cards: A, B, C, E
Notes: 5, 7, 10, 11, 12, 13, 14

Rideau View Inn

177 Frank Street, K2P 0X4
(613) 236-9309; (800) 658-3564
FAX (613) 237-6842
www.home.istar.ca/~rideau

Rideau View Inn is a 1907 Edwardian home on a quiet residential street near the Rideau Canal. It's just a short walk to most major tourist attractions and fine dining. A hearty breakfast is served each morning in the dining room and guests can relax in front of the fireplace in the cozy living room. There are seven well-appointed guest rooms, two with en suite baths and one with a working fireplace.

Host: George Hartsgrove
Rooms: 7 (2 PB; 5 SB) $70-85
Full Breakfast
Credit Cards: A, B, C
Notes: 5, 7, 8, 10, 13, 14

OWEN SOUND

Sunset Farms Bed and Breakfast

Rural Route 6, 398139 20th Avenue East, N4K 5N8
(519) 371-4559; e-mail: moses@bmts.com
www.bmts.com/~moses/

Well-traveled hosts own and operate Owen Sound's longest-established bed and breakfast. Forty picturesque acres just five minutes from the city's center. Ideal for day trips to Manitoulin Island, Georgian Bay touring, and bicycle trips. Bruce Trail access nearby. Gorgeous during autumn. Antique-furnished unique home. Gardens, patios, and pond for outdoor enjoyment. Artistically presented breakfasts featuring garden-fresh produce and flowers. Inquire regarding bringing children and pets.

Hosts: Bill and Cecilie Moses
Rooms: 4 (1 PB; 3 SB) $45-95
Full and Continental Breakfast
Credit Cards: None
Notes: 5, 7, 9, 10, 11, 12, 13, 14

PAISLEY

Lovat Bed and Breakfast

Rural Route 2, N0G 2N0
(519) 353-5534; FAX (519) 353-4195

Come stay at this log home built in the late 1800s. Sleeping accommodations include three bedrooms as well as a fourth bed-

Lovat

---

7 No smoking; 8 Children welcome; 9 Social drinking allowed; 10 Tennis nearby; 11 Swimming nearby; 12 Golf nearby; 13 Skiing nearby; 14 May be booked through a travel agent; 15 Handicapped accessible.

room for a family. In winter there are cross-country skiing, snowmobiling, and toboggan hills in the area. Summer is great with an outdoor barbecue. Spend the day on the beach; only 15 to 30 minutes from Lake Huron areas. Guests can travel to Tobermory and enjoy a cruise aboard the MS *Chi-Cheemaun*. Open year-round. Hot tub (new for 1998).

Hosts: Jim and Gail Dalman
Rooms: 4 (SB) $45
Full Breakfast
Credit Cards: None
Notes: 2, 3, 4, 5, 7, 8, 9, 10, 11, 12, 13

PARRY SOUND _____

Evergreen Bed and Breakfast
P.O. Box 223, P2A 2X3
(705) 389-3554

Evergreen is an elegant cedar log home surrounded by a spacious deck overlooking the parklike grounds on the shore of Lake Manitouwabing. There is a comfortable guest lounge and billiard room. Breakfast is served in the bright summer room with walk-out to the cedar decks and lawn. Swim at the safe beach, fish from the dock, or rent the canoe for a tranquil morning or afternoon on the lake.

Hosts: Shirley and Anders Wallenius
Rooms: 5 (2 PB; 3 SB) $50-75
Full Breakfast
Credit Cards: None
Notes: 2, 7, 8, 9, 10, 11, 12

Evergreen

Jantje Manor
43 Church Street, P2A 1Y6
(705) 746-5399; e-mail: jantje@zeuter.com

Welcome into an era of gracious living in the restored Victorian home. Enjoy our antiques, relax in the cosy library, front parlor or screened veranda. A full breakfast is served in the dining room. We are in the heart of Parry Sound, only a few minutes' walk from the Festival of the Sound, Rainbow Theatre, 30,000 Islands Cruise, shopping, restaurants, and Georgian Bay beaches. Snowmobile and cross-country ski trails and golf are a short drive away. Open year-round. Smoking is not permitted. No pets. Inquire about accommodations for children.

Hosts: Sharon and John Ranney
Rooms: 5 (1 PB; 4 SB) $60-95
Full Breakfast
Credit Cards: None
Notes: 2, 5, 7, 9, 10, 11, 12, 13

PERTH _____

Perth Manor Heritage Inn
23 Drummond Street West, K7H 2J6
(613) 264-0050; FAX (613) 264-0051

Romantic getaway at this 1878 mansion. Beautifully restored period rooms with antique furnishing. Bed and complimentary breakfast. Fine dining. Fully licensed solarium bar and terrace. Weddings, reaffirmations, or small banquets are the inn's specialties. Beautiful expansive garden. Downtown Perth a pleasant five-minute walk away. Major credit cards accepted. Three rooms can be made into private-bath rooms.

Hosts: Gisela and Phil Aston
Rooms: 10 (1 PB; 9 SB) $70-135
Full Breakfast
Credit Cards: A, B, C
Notes: 2, 3, 4, 5, 7, 8, 9, 10, 11, 12, 13, 14

NOTES: Credit cards accepted: A MasterCard; B Visa; C American Express; D Discover; E Diner's Club; F Other; 2 Personal checks accepted; 3 Lunch available; 4 Dinner available; 5 Open all year; 6 Pets welcome;

PETROLIA

Rebecca's Bed and Breakfast
4058 Petrolia Street, P.O. Box 1028, N0N 1R0
(519) 882-0118; (800) 530-9591

A restored historic, three-story, 100-year-old Victorian home with Italianate influences. Furnished with some antiques, including a restored player piano. Relax and visit with other guests and the hosts on the veranda or in the parlor. The tastefully decorated guest rooms are on the third floor, where guests will find the four-piece shared bath. A variety of breakfasts, changing daily, are served in the dining room. For guests' convenience baby sitting is available with adequate notice. Twenty-five minutes from Sarnia and Port Huron, Michigan. Smoking is not permitted in bedrooms.

Hosts: Rebecca and John MacLachlan
Rooms: 3 (SB) $40-45
Full Breakfast
Credit Cards: None
Notes: 2, 5, 8, 9, 10, 11, 12, 13

PORT CARLING

DunRovin
Box 304, P0B 1J0
(705) 765-7317; e-mail: dunrovin@muskoka.com
www.muskoka.com/tourism/bandb

Warmth and charm of a cottage with comforts of home. Lovely wildflower gardens. Large deck overlooking Lake Muskoka. Swim or boat in protected bay. Relax on private boathouse sun deck. Comfortable guest

DunRovin

area with library, games, hot tub in winter. Queen-size bedroom with romantic half-canopied bed with an en suite. Twin bedroom with great lake view, duvets, and private bath. Heart-healthy breakfasts served upstairs in the great room. Boat cruises, artisans, museums, boutiques are nearby.

Hosts: Wilsie and Bob Mann
Rooms: 2 (PB) $80-90
Full Breakfast
Credit Cards: None
Notes: 2, 5, 7, 9, 10, 11, 12, 13

PORT DOVER

Bed and Breakfast by the Lake
30 Elm Park, N0A 1N0
(519) 583-1010

Port Dover is a pleasant small town on the north shore of Lake Erie, a good base for exploring Long Point Bird Observatory, strolling around Port Dover Harbor's craft shops, and experiencing excellent summer theater at Lighthouse Theatre. This ranch home is bright, open, and airy, graciously furnished with antiques and art. Attractive brick patio and garden provide lovely view of Lake Erie and easy access to sandy beach.

Host: Christine Ivey and John Baker
Rooms: 3 (SB) $50-60 Canadian
Full Breakfast
Credit Cards: B
Notes: 5, 7, 11, 12, 15

ROCKPORT

Houseboat Amaryllis Bed and Breakfast
Box C-10, K0E 1V0
(613) 659-3513

Built in 1921, the 100-foot double-deck houseboat is on its own island in the Thousand Islands region. Used as a private summer residence its veranda deck, living room, dining room offer comfort and relaxation. Rooms look out on the river and forested shores, including a full breakfast

---

7 No smoking; 8 Children welcome; 9 Social drinking allowed; 10 Tennis nearby; 11 Swimming nearby; 12 Golf nearby; 13 Skiing nearby; 14 May be booked through a travel agent; 15 Handicapped accessible.

and boat transportation. The islands are five acres, with paths through woodland—stroll, fish, and swim in tranquil surroundings. Guided tours of area by sail, walking, or bicycle also offered.

Hosts: Pieter and Karin Bergen
Rooms: 4 (PB) $70-100
Full Breakfast
Credit Cards: None
Notes: 2, 7, 8, 9, 11,

THUNDER BAY

Pinebrook Bed and Breakfast

Rural Route 16 Mitchell Road, P7B 6B3
(807) 683-6114; FAX (807) 683-8641
e-mail: pinebrok@baynet.net
www.bbcanada.com/1184.html

Warm and friendly cedar chalet. Ten minutes from downtown. Welcoming. Quiet. On 43 rolling acres of meadows and pine forest along more than one-half mile of private river frontage. It is truly a place to rest and relax. Sumptuous meals. Jacuzzi. Three bathrooms. Fireplace room. Sauna by river. Canoeing. Fishing. Meadows and forest trails. Workout gym. Mountain bikes. Library and video library. Children and pets are welcome. A home away from home. Smoking permitted in designated areas only.

Hosts: Sara Jeffrey and Armin Weber
Rooms: 4 (1 PB; 3 SB) $45-70 Canadian
Full Breakfast
Credit Cards: B
Notes: 3, 4, 5, 6, 8, 9, 11, 12, 13

TORONTO

Alcina's Bed and Breakfast

16 Alcina Avenue, M6C 2E8
(416) 656-6400

Alcina's is a gracious old Victorian home. Enjoy the casual elegance of lace, stained glass, antiques, and fine old oak. Relax in this bright and tasteful setting with comfortable soft furnishings and fresh period wall finishes. Outdoors is a shady grape arbor and quiet old-fashioned English flower garden. Alcina's central location also allows easy access by subway, bus, or car to the many attractions of downtown Toronto.

Host: Tennie Coxe
Rooms: 3 (PB) $75-80
Continental Breakfast
Credit Cards: None
Notes: 5, 7, 9

Amblecote

109 Walmer Road, M5R 2X8
(416) 927-1713; FAX (416) 927-0838
e-mail: beds@torontobandb.com

A restored historical Edwardian home, built in the English cottage style. Wonderful neighborhood. Quiet street yet minutes from the subway, museums, Casa Loma, Yorkville. Plenty of restaurants, café, and shopping within walking distance. The house is furnished with antiques and Persian rugs. The guest rooms are appointed with period furniture and provide comfort and tranquilty from another era.

Rooms: 5 (2 PB; 3 SB) $65-85 Canadian
Full or Continental Breakfast
Credit Cards: A, B, C, F
Notes: 5, 7, 9

Annex House Bed and Breakfast

147 Madison Avenue, M5R 2S6
(416) 920-3922 (telephone/FAX)

Enjoy comfortable bed and breakfast facilities at Annex House, a restored turn-of-the-century Georgian home in the heart of downtown Toronto, with private parking. The tranquility and beauty of the Annex area offers a pleasant 10-minute walk to shops, sights, and restaurants. The best shopping is close by, at Yorkville, Yonge and Bloor Streets, and on Spadina Avenue. Sightseeing opportunities include Casa Loma, the Royal Ontario Museum, McLaughlin Planetarium, historic University of Toronto, and Queen's Park. Subways

---

NOTES: Credit cards accepted: A MasterCard; B Visa; C American Express; D Discover; E Diner's Club; F Other; 2 Personal checks accepted; 3 Lunch available; 4 Dinner available; 5 Open all year; 6 Pets welcome;

and buses are three minutes away, making the whole of the city instantly accessible.

Host: Carol (Ricciuto) Davey
Rooms: 3 (PB) $85
Full Breakfast
Credit Cards: None
Notes: 5, 7, 8, 9, 10

Beaconsfield Bed and Breakfast

38 Beaconsfield Avenue, M6J 3H9
(416) 535-3338 (phone/FAX)
e-mail: beacon@idirect.com

Artist/actress couple's unconventional, colorful 1882 Victorian home full of fun and sun, art and heart. In a quiet, multicultural downtown neighborhood, a short trolley ride from major theaters, CN Tower, Eaton Centre, along funky Queen Street West. Choose between imaginatively decorated rooms or a private Mexican honeymoon suite with treetop terrace. Creative breakfasts musically served in an eclectic dining room. Parking, TV, VCR, kitchen facilities, air conditioning.

Hosts: Katya and Bernie McLoughlin
Rooms: 3 (1 PB; 2 SB) $55-80 U.S.
Full and Continental Breakfast
Credit Cards: None
Notes: 5, 7, 8, 9, 10, 11

Bed and Breakfast Association of Downtown Toronto

P.O. Box 190, Station B, M5T 2W1
(416) 410-3938 (8:30 A.M.-7:00 P.M. Mon-Fri) (8:30 A.M.-12:00 P.M. Sat-Sun)
FAX (416) 368-1653
e-mail: bnbtoronto@globalserve.net
www.bnbinfo.com

Representing Toronto's largest selection of fully inspected and privately owned Victorian homes in downtown Toronto. All within 10 minutes of the major tourist attractions. Let the hosts be a guide to the international flavor of Toronto's interesting neighborhoods. Guests can choose a range of accommodations from elegant suites with fireplaces and whirlpool baths to simple, warm guest rooms for the more budget minded. For reservations, free brochure, or any other information one might need, please contact Linda Lippa. There are 50 accommodations with private and shared baths. Full and Continental breakfasts served. All rates include breakfast, taxes, and parking. Visa accepted. $45-120.

Howland at Bloor. An 1800s Georgian two-story flat in the heart of the Annex neighborhood. Walking distance to the Royal Ontario Museum, university, shopping, and great local restaurants. Only a five-minute walk to the Bloor and university subway stations. The home features original moldings, high Georgian ceilings, and much more. The host offers a guest room with TV and private baths. Full breakfast. $65-85.

Howland Street. Renovated Victorian home in the university neighborhood known as the Annex. With its great local restaurants, it is within walking distance to the Royal Ontario Museum, university, public transit to famous Yorkville for shopping, and easy access to the city center. Host offers a second-floor guest room with private bathroom and TV. Full breakfast. $60-80.

Jarvis at Bloor. Beautiful Victorian home in a great downtown neighborhood, only steps from Bloor and Yonge Streets, the shopping center of the city. Only a minute's walk to transit and theaters. Two guest rooms offered. The guest room in the main home has a private bath and the guest room in the coach house has a private bath with a single tub with jets. Breakfast is served in the main house. $65-105.

King Street West. Beautiful 1800s Victorian home overlooking the lake. On the King streetcar line, only 15 minutes from Eaton Centre, and a short walk to the Cana-

---

7 No smoking; 8 Children welcome; 9 Social drinking allowed; 10 Tennis nearby; 11 Swimming nearby; 12 Golf nearby; 13 Skiing nearby; 14 May be booked through a travel agent; 15 Handicapped accessible.

dian National Exhibition grounds. Also nearby is a walkway over the expressway to Sunnyside Park on the lake. This home is full of Old World charm, stained-glass windows, hardwood flooring, and floor-to-ceiling bookcases in the library. Hostess offers two suites for guest rooms. Private baths, queen-size beds, and kitchenettes. $55-75.

Oriole Parkway. Wonderful and spacious 1920s home in one of the more elite neighborhoods of the city. Only a 15-minute walk to the Yonge and Davisville subway or 10 minutes down to St. Clair and Avenue Roads. There is also a bus right out front. Beautifully decorated. Relax in a spacious sitting area in front of the fireplace or outside on the deck. Three guest rooms with private and shared baths. All rooms have TVs. $65-85.

Phoebe Street. Lovely new brownstone in the heart of Queen Street West Village, known for its trendier shopping and cafés. Only steps from Spadina and Queen, easy access to public transit, and a 10-minute walk from Eaton Centre and theaters. Two second-floor guest rooms, each with private bath. $50-80.

St. George. Beautiful early 1900s Edwardian home in the heart of the Annex neighborhood, only a 10-minute walk to the university, Royal Ontario Museum, Yorkville, and Casa Loma. Also only a five-minute walk to the Dupont subway stop, making easy access to the rest of the city's attractions. This home features Old World charm, antiques, nooks with leaded bay windows, and fireplaces throughout. Four guest rooms, with two common baths. $55-70.

Seaton Street. Spacious restored Victorian home in downtown, only a 10-minute walk to Eaton Centre and Pantages Theatre, and a minute's walk to public transit. This home features antiques, pine and hardwood flooring throughout, and has been totally renovated. The hosts offer a third-floor suite. It has a sitting area with fireplace, private bath with a large single tub with jets, and lots of light from large skylights. $120.

Shaw Street. This quaint home is only a five-minute walk to the Bloor subway line at Ossington station, and only 10 minutes to public transit to the city center, to the Royal Ontario Museum, University of Toronto, and Yorkville Village. This immaculate home, with hardwood flooring and antiques throughout, offers a second-floor guest room with a private bath. Continental breakfast. $50-70.

Soho at Queen. A beautiful brownstone, only steps from Spadina Avenue and Queen Street, a trendy area for shopping and wonderful eateries. Only a 10-minute walk to the Sheraton Centre and Metro Convention Centre, and to the Royal Alexandra and Princess of Wales theaters. A spacious second-floor guest room with an en suite bath is offered. Continental plus breakfast. Parking not included in rates. $60-80.

Bed and Breakfast Homes of Toronto

P.O. Box 46093, College Park, M5B 2L8
(416) 363-6362

Alcina's. (416) 656-6400; www.bbcanada.com/1104.html. This gracious, old Victorian brick house is on a shady tree-lined street in the exclusive Wychwood Park neighborhood. Close to Spadina House and ever-popular Casa Loma. Subway, bus, and streetcar are all in walking distance. Casual eateries can be found locally. Continental breakfast. Parking available. Resident cat, Cina. Seasonal rates. Smoking allowed in back yard seating area. $65-80.

NOTES: Credit cards accepted: A MasterCard; B Visa; C American Express; D Discover; E Diner's Club; F Other; 2 Personal checks accepted; 3 Lunch available; 4 Dinner available; 5 Open all year; 6 Pets welcome;

Beaconsfield. (416) 535-3338 (phone/ FAX); e-mail: beacon@idirect.com; www.bbcanada.com/771.html. Colorful 1882 Victorian Heritage home full of fun and sun, art and heart. Choose between imaginatively decorated rooms or the very private Mexican honeymoon suite with treetop terrace. Creative breakfasts. Easy highway access; driveway parking. Cable TV, VCR, air conditioning, 24-hour free tea, coffee; many extras. Theaters, restaurants, sightseeing galore. English, Spanish, Russian, some French and German spoken. $69-99.

Colwood. (416) 234-9988; FAX (416) 234-1554; www.bbcanada.com/1100.html. This stunningly renovated traditional home is in a prestigious area surrounded by parks and golf courses, yet it is convenient to the airport or downtown, both only 15 minutes away by car. Public transit is within walking distance. James Gardens and the Humber River with its bike trails, picnic areas, and walkways are nearby. Delicious full breakfast is served and complimentary tea and coffee. Air conditioning and ceiling fans. On-site parking. Smoke-free. Dog in residence. $70-80.

Feathers May and Max. (416) 534-1923 or (416) 534-2388; www.bbcanada.com/1115.html. A charming, spacious Victorian home in the popular Annex, only a five-minute walk from Bathurst subway and Bloor Street. Guests are two blocks away from one of Toronto's most delightful areas of cosmopolitan restaurants and cafés, film and live theaters, bookstores and antique shops. Nineteenth-century European and oriental furnishings, china, delicate tapestries, and an unusual collection of antique puppets lend a unique atmosphere to this interesting and beautifully restored home. Continental breakfast. Discount offered if no breakfast desired. Central air. Color TV in guest rooms. No smoking in house, please. English, Dutch, French, and German spoken. Free parking. $65-75.

Greener-Gunn. (416) 698-9061 (phone/FAX); www.bbcanada.com/1113.html. In the increasingly popular Beaches area of Toronto, east of downtown, this home offers guests friendly hospitality and a good homemade breakfast in a relaxed, casual atmosphere, served in the dining room or, weather permitting, just outside on the front deck. A two-minute walk will take guests down to Queen Street, where they can find cafés, boutiques, craft shops, small art and antique galleries, and many fine restaurants and night spots. Downtown is accessible by car in 10 to 15 minutes, or by a leisurely 20-minute trolley-car ride. Front driveway parking. Smoking on the deck only. Bathroom shared by guests. Dog in residence. Seasonal discounts. $55-65.

Kingslake Korners. (416) 491-4759; www.bbcanada.com/477.html. Comfort, relaxation, and hospitality await guests in a cheerful, quiet residential area of north Toronto in a family home setting, 20-30 minutes to downtown, depending on traffic flow. Relax in clean, spacious, and tastefully decorated guest rooms—one with private bath and the other with en suite bath, color cable TV and VCR. Children welcome; crib and highchair are available and playground and parks are nearby. Full breakfast is served in the dining room. Special diets can be accommodated. Central air. On-site parking. Smoke-free. Dog and cat in residence; no guest pets, please. $50-60.

Marlborough Place. (416) 922-2159; www.bbcanada.com/591.html. This beautifully renovated Victorian townhouse furnished with antiques is within walking distance of fashionable Yorkville and Bloor Street, the Royal Ontario Museum, the McLaughlin Planetarium, and Casa Loma. It is a five-minute stroll to the subway. A generous Continental breakfast is served. Marlborough Place offers warm hospitality and a cozy yet elegant atmos-

---

7 No smoking; 8 Children welcome; 9 Social drinking allowed; 10 Tennis nearby; 11 Swimming nearby; 12 Golf nearby; 13 Skiing nearby; 14 May be booked through a travel agent; 15 Handicapped accessible.

Bed and Breakfast Homes of Toronto (continued)

phere. On-site parking. Central air. Limited smoking. $65-90.

Martyniuk. (416) 603-2128 (phone/FAX); www.bbcanada.com/1105.html. This home, more than 100 years old, in the Kensington Market area, is quite modest in style and decor, but at prices well below average, it is an excellent choice for the budget traveler, especially for those without cars. The Martyniuk home is exactly one mile from the Eaton Centre, bus terminal, or Elgin and Pantages Theatres. European-style restaurants and Toronto Western Hospital are within walking distance. The full breakfast is served in the kitchen. English, Ukrainian, Polish, and German spoken. Very limited smoking permitted. Ten percent discount from October to March if over seven days. Rooms individually air conditioned. Parking extra $5 per day. $45-55.

Mayfair. (416) 769-1558; FAX (416) 769-9655; www.bbcanada.com/1101.html. A 1911 Edwardian home. Traditional highlights include antiques, oriental carpets, original oak paneling, leaded- and stained-glass windows. For guests' convenience their suite includes a sitting area and a four-piece en suite bathroom. Only one block from Bloor Street, the subway, and High Park. Many interesting and ethnic restaurants are only steps away. Breakfast is a special occasion. Mayfair offers a friendly atmosphere combining traditional elegance with modern comforts. Parking. Air conditioning. A smoke-free house. Easy highway access. Cable TV in guest rooms. Within five-minute walk to subway. Visa accepted. Fifteen dollars for additional guest in room. $75-85.

Morning Glory. (416) 533-6120; www.bbcanada.com/1103.html. This Edwardian home has high ceilings, maple trim, and stained-glass windows. Little Italy and Bloor Street are within walking distance and there is easy access to Chinatown, theaters, concert halls, art galleries, and most other major attractions. Public transportation is very close at hand. A generous, delicious breakfast is served. Convenient highway access; garage available for parking. Smoke-free home. Smoking area on patio. English, French, German, and Dutch spoken. $60-65.

Oriole Gardens. (416) 924-4736; www.bbcanada.com/1108.html. Enjoy a warm, friendly atmosphere in this gracious family home on an upscale, tree-lined residential street. A few minutes' walk from St. Clair subway station and Yonge Street buses, and within easy reach of Toronto's major attractions. The location offers an interesting variety of restaurants, pubs, fashion stores, bakeries, bookstores, and cinemas. Historic Casa Loma and Spadina House are approximately 15 to 20 minutes' walking distance. A full and healthy breakfast is served. On-site parking. Cat in residence. $65-75.

Sundown. (416) 657-1900; www.bbcanada.com/1102.html. A bright, spacious home on a quiet tree-lined boulevard, a block away from the colorful and lively Corso Italia with its small outdoor bistros and bustling shops. A five-minute streetcar ride takes guests right into the St. Clair W. subway. Minutes to theaters. The generous breakfast consists of hot and cold dishes and is served in the dining room. Cable TV and VCR. Parking. Central air. Smoking on the front veranda. Discounts for long stays. $69-79.

Vanderkooy. (416) 925-8765; www.bbcanada.com/1107.html. This charming older, traditional home is in an excellent

NOTES: Credit cards accepted: A MasterCard; B Visa; C American Express; D Discover; E Diner's Club; F Other; 2 Personal checks accepted; 3 Lunch available; 4 Dinner available; 5 Open all year; 6 Pets welcome;

location on a lovely tree-lined street close to Summerhill subway, a choice of good restaurants, and fine boutiques. The house is bright and sunny, with stained-glass windows, and features some original artwork. One of the bedrooms has a private three-piece bathroom and the other has a shared bath. The atmosphere of this home is relaxed and casual. A full breakfast is served on a round oak table overlooking the garden. Parking. Air conditioning. Cat in residence. No smoking. Easy access to all downtown attractions. $65-75.

Winchester Square. (416) 928-0827; www.bbcanada.com/1111.html. This recently restored late 1800s three-story brick residence is in Cabbagetown, a quiet downtown Toronto neighborhood of Victorian and Edwardian homes. Round-the-clock public transportation stops a block away, or guests can walk a few steps to the many charming shops and restaurants or enjoy the gardens and architecture of Heritage homes that make up the heart of Cabbagetown. A healthy Continental breakfast is served. The guest kitchen is conveniently equipped with a dishwasher and laundry facilities for extended stays. Visiting professionals, lecturers, and families take note: Polish is a second language. Air-conditioned suite. Smoking is allowed only on the open-air deck. Free parking. Bathroom shared by only two guest rooms and one en suite. $69-85.

Craig House
Bed and Breakfast
78 Spruce Hill Road, M4E 3G3
(416) 698-3916; FAX (416) 698-8506
www.bbcanada.com/1222.html

Guests will be welcomed to a large traditional beach home with its beautiful flower gardens from spring to fall. Craig House is in a popular neighbourhood with the air of a small town resort by the lake, a superb location close enough to downtown that guests can be there in 10 minutes by car or by a leisurely street car ride 25 of minutes on the 24-hour public transportation. The guest rooms are on a private second floor. There is a kitchen for the use of guests making light snacks, tea, or coffee. The third floor is a one-bedroom apartment that sleeps four with private bath and TV. Craig House is CAA/AAA-approved.

Host: Dorothy Maguire
Rooms: 4 (2 PB; 2 SB) $65-90
Full Breakfast
Credit Cards: None
Notes: 5, 7, 9, 10, 11, 14

Orchard View
92 Orchard View Boulevard, M4R 1C2
(416) 488-6826

Spacious 1911 home is uniquely decorated for the 1990s. Choose between the queen-sized bed with private en suite bath or the twin room with sitting area and separate entrance to the main bath. Full breakfast served. Free parking. Close to subway, shops, and restaurants.

Hosts: Donna and Ken Ketchen
Rooms: 2 (1 PB; 1 SB) $70-75
Full Breakfast
Credit Cards: None
Notes: 5, 7, 9 , 11, 12, 14

Terrace House
Bed and Breakfast
52 Austin Terrace, M5R 1Y6
(416) 535-1493; FAX (416) 535-9616
e-mail: terracehousebandb@sympatico.ca

Terrace House is in Forest Hill, a quiet residential neighborhood in downtown Toronto, with the subway a five-minute walk away. The hostess has lived in Europe, Africa, and the United States. Breakfast can include quiches, fancy omelets, fruit pancakes, French toast, fresh muffins, croissants freshly baked, etc. The host and her spouse like to exchange travel experiences with their guests in front of the fireplace in the winter. They will pro-

---

7 No smoking; 8 Children welcome; 9 Social drinking allowed; 10 Tennis nearby; 11 Swimming nearby; 12 Golf nearby; 13 Skiing nearby; 14 May be booked through a travel agent; 15 Handicapped accessible.

vide guests with detailed information about their part of the world. Children six and older welcome.

Host: Suzanne Charbonneau
Rooms: 3 (1 PB; 2 SB) $70-110 Canadian
Full Breakfast
Credit Cards: A, B
Notes: 5, 7, 8, 9, 11

Toronto Bed and Breakfast
253 College Street, Box 269, M5T 1R5
(416) 588-8800; (416) 927-0354
FAX (416) 927-0838
e-mail: beds@torontobandb.com

Toronto's oldest registry—now in its 20th year. This service represents a number of bed and breakfast homes in the downtown area. All are inspected to ensure a high standard or cleanliness, comfort, and hospitality and range from "cheap and cheerful" to more luxurious accommodation. Guests will be welcomed to this people friendly city by friendly-people. Safe public transportation nearby. Most homes in wonderful neighborhoods.

Contact: Marcia Getgood (president)
Accommodations: 40 (10 PB; 30 SB) $60-95
Full and Continental Breakfast
Credit Cards: A, B, C, F
Notes: 5, 7, 8, 9

Vanderkooy Bed and Breakfast
53 Walker Avenue, M4V 1G3
(416) 925-8765; FAX (925) 8557

Joan and the resident cat, Jazz, welcome guests to this charming home where they will enjoy comfortable guest rooms and breakfast served in an open dining room overlooking the garden. A short walk to Summerhill station on the Younge subway line allows easy access to downtown attractions, including the Harbourfront, Skydome, the Eaton Centre, and theaters. Restaurants and shopping districts are all within walking distance. Feel free to watch TV by the fire,

enjoy the waterfall and pond in the garden, or relax on the flower-filled deck in the summer. Children over 12 welcome.

Host: Joan Vanderkooy
Rooms: 3 (1 PB; 2 SB) $70-75
Full Breakfast
Credit Cards: None
Notes: 5, 7, 9,

WESTPORT

Stepping Stone Bed and Breakfast Inn
328 Centreville Road, Rural Route 2, K0G 1X0
(613) 273-3806; FAX (613) 273-3331
e-mail: stepping@rideau.net

Retreat to this peaceful, safe haven. Get back to nature. Beautiful seven-room 1840 Victorian Heritage inn on 150 acres. Relax by spring-fed pond and walk through magnificent gardens and nature trails; enjoy horses, cows, birds, skiing, golfing, and swimming. Weddings with memories for a lifetime; intimate/family dinners, mouth-watering gourmet breakfasts; receptions, seminars. Come capture winter, summer, spring, or fall in all their glory. Between Ottawa and Kingston. Cozy cabin sleeps two with private shower in main building.

Host: Madeline Saunders
Rooms: 7 (4 PB; 3 SB) $75-150 Canadian
Full Breakfast
Credit Cards: A, B, C
Notes: 2, 3, 4, 5, 7, 8, 9, 10, 11, 12, 13, 14, 15

WHEATLEY

B & B's Bed and Breakfast
216 Erie Street, P.O. Box 98, N0P 2P0
(519) 825-8008; (800) 851-3406
e-mail: brucep@mnsi net

Beautiful turn-of-the-century Victorian home features three large bedrooms with

---

NOTES: Credit cards accepted: A MasterCard; B Visa; C American Express; D Discover; E Diner's Club; F Other; 2 Personal checks accepted; 3 Lunch available; 4 Dinner available; 5 Open all year; 6 Pets welcome;

ZURICH

Brentwood on the Beach
St. Joseph Shores 1, N0M 2T0
(519) 236-7137; FAX (519) 236-7269
e-mail: beachbnb@hay.net
www.brentwoodbnb.com

Overlooking Lake Huron, spectacular sunsets, sandy beach, indoor pool, whirlpool, sauna, delicious breakfasts in the sun room, three fireside guest sitting rooms, honeymoon suites, guest kitchen, barbecue, balconies, patios. Walkways lead from one quiet garden nook to the next. Nearby theatres—including Stratford Shakespeare Festival. Blend culture with nature. Hiking, cycling, golf, tennis, fishing, shopping. Relax in an oasis of calm. Stroll the beach, curl up with a book. Year-round getaway. Two and one-half hours west of Toronto, two hours north of Detroit. Delicious breakfasts served each morning.

Hosts: Joan and Peter Karstens
Rooms: 10 (PB) $95-225
Credit Cards: A, B
Notes: 5, 7, 9, 10, 11, 12, 13

B & B's Bed and Breakfast

private bathrooms. Enjoy a full breakfast including homemade breads and preserves in the bright and spacious kitchen. Less than 20 minutes from excellent bird migration sites such as Point Pelee National Park. Enjoy a swim in the in-ground pool and relax. Easy to get to, hard to leave. Open year-round.

Hosts: Bea and Bruce Patterson
Rooms: 3 (PB) $75-88
Full Breakfast
Credit Cards: A, B
Notes: 2, 3, 5, 7, 8, 9, 11, 12

---

7 No smoking; 8 Children welcome; 9 Social drinking allowed; 10 Tennis nearby; 11 Swimming nearby; 12 Golf nearby; 13 Skiing nearby; 14 May be booked through a travel agent; 15 Handicapped accessible.